Total Body Detoxification

The Way to Healthy Aging

Robert E. Moroney, MA, DA

Swing-Hi Press

Total Body Detoxification: The Way to Healthy Aging

Published by Swing-Hi Press

For more information:
www.amajordifference.com

Cover design by Nita Ybarra

Book design by:
Arbor Books, Inc.
www.arborbooks.com

Printed in the United States of America

Total Body Detoxification: The Way to Healthy Aging
Robert E. Moroney, MA, DA

1. Title 2. Author 3. Health

Library of Congress Control Number: 2010932653

ISBN 13: 978-0-9724335-1-8

Disclaimer

I was unofficially diagnosed with lung cancer twenty-nine years ago—the natural outcome of a turbulent lifestyle filled with cigarette, alcohol, and drug consumption. Several years earlier, I had been told by Marty, an oncologist friend, that all his clients died, so I knew where not to seek treatment. Not knowing what I was doing, I researched every alternative modality that came to my attention, earning a master's degree, a doctorate, and several certifications along the way. I not only survived the cancer; I went on to play competitive basketball and enjoy a career in the healing arts.

I do not advise anyone to engage in this type of healing journey alone as I did. Cancer treatments have improved immeasurably over the past thirty years, and many cancer treatment facilities now include nutritional, psychological, and spiritual counseling as part of their program. Don't be afraid to ask questions; don't be afraid to research what different programs have to offer. If you are diagnosed with cancer, your life is at stake.

Total Body Detoxification Defined

I define total body detoxification as an ongoing process of removing toxic material accumulations from the physical body, toxic emotions from the emotional body, and toxic attitudes and beliefs from the mental body with the ultimate purpose being the attainment of a more unified relationship with our spiritual source. I believe that disease emanates from toxic emotions and attitudes that hold us in separation from our spiritual source as well as the world around us. And I believe that each individual life experience contains within it an opportunity to dissolve the rants and illusions of the personality-ego system and fully reunite with Spirit.

First, total body detoxification is a journey back to our spiritual source that begins when we seriously undertake to remove toxins in the form of chemical residues and heavy metals from the physical body. One cannot hope to deal with toxic attitudes and emotions while the physical body is overburdened with pollutants that induce mental fog and impair nervous system function; conversely one cannot detoxify the physical body deeply enough without a willingness to recognize and release toxic emotions and attitudes.

Table of Contents

Appendices

Introduction

I am a walking miracle.

In 1982, at the age of forty-three, I was smoking more than a pack of cigarettes and twenty marijuana joints a day, snorting an ounce of cocaine a week, and topping that off with several bottles of fine wine. Then I was diagnosed with lung cancer by a medical doctor when I checked into a drug rehab program. Her diagnosis was not verified with a biopsy, so it wasn't a medically or legally valid one. I didn't care one way or the other, as I knew I was in trouble—name of the disease notwithstanding.

Several years earlier I had played poker with Marty, a well-known oncologist (a tumor specialist), who told me that all his patients died. So when I was diagnosed, I knew where *not* to go for treatment. Instead I sought alternative practitioners in varying disciplines who taught me different ways to remove toxins from my body.

I took herbs, fasted, and did colonics. I sat in a sauna. I had my liver and gallbladder flushed. I even visited a practitioner of acupuncture—a centuries-old Chinese healing procedure that uses thin needles to open energy pathways in the body. After three treatments I was able to stop smoking marijuana.

My cravings for alcohol and cigarettes persisted, however, forcing me to look elsewhere for relief. My search led to a book with a long one-word title: *Psychoneuroimmunology*, edited by Robert Ader.[I-1] It refers to the study of the interaction of behavioral, neural, and endocrine factors and the functioning of the immune system. The book cited many studies that linked disease to personality and emotional traits. Reading it convinced me that, since alcoholism is regarded as a disease, my cravings had to be motivated by a mishmash of emotions and attitudes that would take years to sort through.

Within a few weeks of reading the book, I decided to participate in a meditation class. The format of and imagery used in the sessions awakened long-suppressed anger and fear within me, causing an almost constant discomfort that brought me to the point of quitting on several occasions. Bottled-up emotions are repressed pain that, if left unattended, create disease in the physical body. Releasing them after years of repression is like opening the steam-release valve on a pressure cooker—except that the pain has worked its way into the tissues and organs.

Bringing these repressed pains back to conscious awareness hurts physically. If we came into life with an owner's manual, we would know to release them immediately.

These powerful emotions hurt like hell, and I knew it would take years to rid my body of them. I had to come to an understanding that I had the power to make new choices about how I would deal with the events and circumstances of my life. Within three months of starting with the meditation group, my cravings for cigarettes and alcohol stopped, but I knew I still had a long way to go. I continued the alternative protocols, experimenting with ionized footbaths, infrared saunas, and their awesome power to stimulate detoxification. I continued these practices long after my cancer symptoms disappeared, because my body felt better, and I had more energy. (According to standard medical practice, cancer never totally disappears from the body even though the physical signs and symptoms have disappeared.)

My recovery taught me something profoundly simple about disease and healing: the lower the levels of toxins in the body, the better the body feels and performs. The immune system is stronger as well.

Unfortunately despite my success over the next twenty years and because of enormous stress brought on by an expensive lawsuit, I stopped detoxifying for two years. I went back to drinking, and as a result my liver crashed; nonviral hepatitis was the official medical diagnosis. My energy level and appetite plummeted, my body swelled by twenty pounds, and my skin turned a yellowish brown. I had to rebuild my damaged liver and remove the large amount of toxins it could no longer process.

It took three years of disciplined eating and cleansing to restore healthy function completely, but within seven weeks of my hepatitis diagnosis, I was feeling well enough to return to the office and the gym—not too shabby for a sixty-five-year-old man with a lifetime of abusive habits. Eating nutritious foods and consuming supplements along with my renewed detoxification efforts enabled my body to function under the extreme stress of a liver crash.

To combat the cancer and overcome the addictions, I abandoned my career as a professional poker player—which had required long, stressful hours in smoke-filled environments—to concentrate on cleaning and rebuilding my body. I returned to graduate school and earned a master's and a doctorate in two healing disciplines.

In January 1986, I started a nutrition and peak-performance practice that quickly morphed into a lifestyle- and emotional-counseling practice. At that time I did not have a clue about the role that emotions played in creating diseases and addictions. But my powerful desire to rid myself of those addictions led me to look at my emotions and the beliefs, attitudes, and perspectives that they had nurtured.

Throughout this book I frequently refer to my healing journey through cancer and drug and alcohol addictions by insetting the text between two grey lines, as shown here. These sections separate my personal experience from the clinical portion of the text. I had originally intended to write a clinical how-to book; however, just as I was forced to confront my emotions to heal myself, I found that describing high-powered, technology-based detoxification techniques and supplement support protocols did not begin to touch the real meaning and purpose of total body detoxification.

We humans are much more than a chemical reaction to our environment. We all have many roles in life—as children, adults, parents, siblings, breadwinners, spouses, teachers, homeowners, and so forth—and each of these roles impacts the way we think, feel, and react to our physical reality.

Treating body chemistry, as the symptom, separate from the totality of who we are does not address the causes of addiction and disease, and therefore never heals us. If we do not make dietary changes, let go of anger and fear, and change our childhood and childish ideas about who we are and the way we interact with others, we will not get very far with *any* detoxification protocol. Building a healthy body that is relatively immune from disease requires an elimination of bad habits, such as smoking, heavy consumption of alcohol, indiscriminate food intake, and negative attitudes. Building a healthy body requires an optimistic and loving attitude, nutrient-rich food, exercise, and focus.

Much has been made about the beneficial antiaging effects of bioidentical hormone replacement therapy (chemicals with a cell structure that are identical to the hormones produced by the body). However, you cannot put a Corvette engine (increased hormone levels) in a sedan body (weak and clogged organs). Hormones increase the body's energy-production capacity, but the organs that must process and dispose of the increased toxic residues—which come from the increased energy production stimulated by these hormones—can become stressed from this extra burden placed on them.

Among other beneficial effects, total body detoxification will improve hormone utilization by clearing petrochemical residues from cell receptor sites normally reserved for hormones. Since there are fewer toxins floating in the bloodstream as a result of detoxification, hormones will travel more efficiently to the cell receptor sites.

I intend this book to be a basic, self-health-care manual that outlines what a high-level health maintenance program should look like and why. The practices described in these chapters are intended to do the following:

- enable you to greatly reduce the incidence of diabetes, heart disease, cancer, and Alzheimer's disease in your life
- vitalize and energize your aging experience
- greatly reduce your reliance on allopathic medications
- greatly enhance your mental function
- open your body to release old traumas, and thereby
  - ▲ create a stronger, more flexible body and most importantly
  - ▲ give new meaning and purpose in the latter part of your life

Total Body Detoxification, as I have titled this book, is a healing vehicle requiring commitment, effort, and energy. Over the course of my healing journey I have come to think of my body as a circuit board powered by the magnetic pull of accumulated emotional and traumatic responses from a lifetime of experiences. The greater the intensity of anger, fear, sadness, grief, guilt, shame, anxiety, frustration, hatred, and worry carried in the body-mind system, the greater the amount of toxins held in its tissues, organs, and blood. Reduction of toxic emotion and trauma residues in the body-mind system through visualization, meditation, yoga nidra, and chi kung is an absolute *must* for anyone who has lived a difficult life. I will go into more detail about these disciplines in a later book.

How This Book Is Organized

In part I of this book, I present complete protocols for novices to initiate a total body detoxification program and for experienced detoxers to deepen and intensify their detoxification activity. I go further into my story to establish the mental-emotional connections to health and the first three basic laws of total body detoxification. I also introduce the chakra system and nutrition considerations.

In part II, which deals with disease and healing, I talk about specific detoxification protocols for the colon, lymphatic system, liver and gallbladder, kidneys, and the heart-arterial system.

Part III deals with food considerations, food and herbal supplements, antioxidants and other vital nutrients, and water as it relates to health and detoxification. I initiate a discussion of the energetic systems that govern the body's overall function. I also introduce the integrated practice techniques of Dr. Ted Winchester, a guide for modern practitioners to emulate. Subsequent chapters cover the spiritual connection, the electrical-chemical relationship in body function, and contraindications. The final chapter explains my ongoing health-sustaining program, and the afterword contains a preview of my next book, which deals with consciousness-building issues and techniques.

Part I

The Tenets of Total Body Detoxification

Chapter One

Initiating a Total Body Detoxification Program

By my forty-third birthday, my hair was thinning and graying; I was tired all the time; I had pain in my shoulders, knees, and fingers; I had no energy to exercise; and I was losing my ability to focus at the poker table. A friend and fellow poker player who had experienced similar symptoms was excited and impressed by the valuable information he had received from Dr. Gordon Tessler, a nutrition consultant, so I booked an appointment to see what the fuss was about.

After testing samples of my blood, hair, and urine, Gordon sat me down and enumerated my problems: I was borderline diabetic. My adrenals were exhausted, which was the main reason for my fatigue. I was not digesting and eliminating food properly, and as a result my colon was clogged. I was deficient in calcium and magnesium, and my body was overloaded with cadmium, mercury, and aluminum—toxic heavy metals that were destroying my brain and nervous system and weakening my immune system.

"I haven't tested for it," Gordon went on, "but based on your alcohol and sugar intake, I'm positive you have yeast and microorganism overgrowth. In a word your body is breaking down in several different ways, and you are looking at developing a chronic degenerative disease in the not-too-distant future."

Six months later I was unofficially diagnosed with lung cancer, so Gordon's prognosis was right on the money.

Undoubtedly you purchased this book, because you are seeking a solution to some physical, mental, or emotional dilemma, just as I sought help when my health began to slip. You've come to the right place. Over the past twenty-nine years, I have rebuilt my body and brain to the point where I can work and perform like a much younger person. I have studied and employed many healing modalities and exercise disciplines to rebuild my body and slow my aging. If you have ever done an Internet search for information on health and aging, you were shown millions of websites—too many to be of any value. In your quest for information, you may have talked to many learned specialists from several disciplines, and because their knowledge is so specialized, you came away feeling confused and overburdened, unsure of where to begin or how to integrate what you were learning into an effective course of action. This book will introduce you to most of the information you need to begin an effective, lifelong program that will sustain your vitality and minimize the probability of your succumbing to a chronic degenerative disease. Since my primary goal at this stage of my life is to remain vital and productive up to my last breath, I devote part of each day to researching and testing new developments in aging health, and I will share them with you on my website, the Association for Conscious Evolution at www.Association-ForConsciousEvolution.com (www.acei.com).

The Association for Conscious Evolution is a nonprofit association supported by revenues from the sale of this book and membership dues from its members. It does not charge the equipment and supplement companies it recommends nor does it get any kickbacks or commissions for their sales to its members. Instead the association asks these companies to give a product or service discount to its members. In this way you can be sure that there are no conflicts of interest. I have personally used and tested every product mentioned in this book.

As you can see from my experience, disease is the outcome of a buildup of toxins accompanied by organ and gland malfunction caused by years—decades, in my case—of poor dietary intake and lifestyle habits. Unfortunately we were not given an owner's manual when we were born. Whether I would have used mine is another matter, but this book can be your owner's manual: a lifetime guide whose teachings will enable you to maximize the opportunities of becoming older and to minimize the pitfalls that befall those who do not know how to take care of themselves.

Pain, fatigue, and loss of mental capacity are the three most common complaints of aging humans in so-called civilized countries. When I started my private practice specializing in nutrition and peak-performance counseling twenty-five years ago, I rarely saw someone under forty with these symptoms. These days, practitioners are just as likely to work with troubled teenagers or with young adults exhibiting the same difficult symptoms.

As a species we may be living longer, but our youth are showing signs of degeneration much earlier than their parents and grandparents did. This is not surprising when you think about it. It starts so early on. Babies are exposed to substantial doses of toxic vaccinations at the beginning of their lives. Add to that a diet of denatured and highly processed food, chlorinated water, and petroleum-laced air, and you have the makings of a highly stressed immune system before these babies are out of diapers. The result of this toxic onslaught is a growing army of children with ADHD, autism, and emotional impairments—humans whose bodies cannot adapt to their environments.

However, many of the alternative health practitioners I've spoken with over the years have reported marvelous reversals of these conditions when they combined dietary modification, chiropractic adjustments, and detoxification protocols. Chiropractic adjustments realign and strengthen the body so it can produce more energy. Eliminating processed and allergy-forming foods and adding fresh vegetables and fruits will greatly reduce many symptoms, particularly fatigue and headaches. So will detoxification modalities. The greater the amount of toxins held in the body, the greater the likelihood of allergies and diseases. For example arthritis is the result of calcium buildup in the joints as well as allergic reactions to foods; heart and kidney diseases primarily involve the buildup of plaque in the arteries; and fatigue and headaches are oftentimes the result of bowel toxins backing up into the bloodstream.

Getting Started

Earlier I mentioned Gordon's diagnosis of me, which included several predisease or disease-support conditions. If you are not as mentally acute or as physically energetic as you once were, you are probably harboring one or more of these disease-support conditions, and I believe that most people with degenerative diseases—cancer, heart disease, diabetes—have all or most of them long before they are medically diagnosed. Each disease-support condition by itself is capable of causing some form of chronic degenerative disease, because each disease-support condition disrupts normal body function to the extent that serious physical or mental breakdown will eventually occur.

When I went to Gordon, my body was in disarray, overrun by microorganisms, totally exhausted and incapable of defending itself. His diagnosis enabled me to rebuild my adrenals, make dietary modifications, and begin the process of reducing yeast, microorganisms, and heavy metals—a task that took three years to accomplish.

This is the road that I aim to set you upon. Let us start by taking a look at the disease-support conditions in detail.

Adrenal Fatigue

This is the most common affliction of modern society. Virtually everyone over forty has adrenal fatigue to some degree. The adrenals are the prime regulators of energy production, and when they have been weakened by stress and bad diet, no real recovery will occur until they are regenerated.

Metabolic Syndrome

Taber's Medical Dictionary defines this condition as the presence of four interrelated atherosclerotic factors: insulin resistance, hyperlipidemia (overabundance of fat clogging the lymph system), hypertension, and obesity. The main event here is insulin resistance, wherein cells lose their ability to take in insulin—an essential step in the utilization of blood sugar from carbohydrate metabolism.

This condition evolves from the overconsumption of carbohydrates, especially from refined flours and sugars. As cells become resistant to insulin, the condition can extend to complex carbohydrates as well. In its early stages, insulin resistance expresses itself as a slow weight gain of three to four pounds annually. Ten years later a person may be forty pounds heavier with an elevated lipid profile and a fasting blood-sugar reading between 120 and 130. In other words you are borderline diabetic. Normal fasting blood sugar levels should be around eighty-five.

Leaky Bowel Syndrome

This is fecal matter leaking back into the blood through a weakened bowel wall. Causes include a prolapsed colon from overeating and lack of exercise, a low-fiber diet, excess carbohydrate consumption, constipation, and stress.

Yeast Overgrowth

Products to treat vaginal yeast are frequently advertised on television, but yeast can accumulate throughout the body as well. Consumption of birth control pills, prescription drugs, and too many refined carbohydrates are the primary physical causes, but emotions play a role as well.

Microorganisms

These include but are not limited to tapeworms, pinworms, flukes, and many forms of undesirable bacteria too numerous to mention here. Again poor diet, stress, and emotional factors create an environment in which these critters will flourish.

Heavy-Metal Poisoning

The most common heavy metals are mercury from vaccinations and dental amalgams; cadmium from cigarette smoke; and lead, arsenic, nickel, aluminum, and beryllium from industrial products. Keep in mind that all metals, including calcium, can be toxic if they are not properly assimilated.

Digestive Disorders

As we age the amounts of hydrochloric acid and pancreatic enzymes secreted by the stomach and pancreas diminish, thus slowing, and in some cases seriously impairing, digestion. Incomplete digestion means that nutrients will not be completely absorbed and assimilated by the body. This creates additional toxic burdens.

An Important Recommendation

Even though this is a how-to book, I strongly advise that you seek the services of a health professional to run tests, take a health history, and survey your symptoms to determine what your specific problems and needs are.

The process of detoxification requires the body to expend energy, and before you embark on this task, you should consult a health professional to determine if your adrenal strength, mineral balances, and hydration are sufficient to start an intense detoxification program. If your energy level is low, as mine was, your health professional may recommend that you take food supplements for a month or so before you begin an intense detoxification program.

Throughout this book I talk about products from several manufacturers, some of which offer free health advisory programs run by highly qualified practitioners. Feel free to look into any of the products or programs that suit your needs.

Finding an Alternative Health Practitioner

If you are new to the process of total body detoxification, consult with a reputable authority—a naturopathic doctor, a nutritionist, a chiropractor with postgraduate training in nutrition, or a trained nutrition specialist.

The Life Extension Foundation (Life Extension) is a major distributor of several hundred food supplements and chemical-isolate specialty products that add up to the largest product line in the United States. (Chemical-isolate specialty products include any product that has been separated from its plant or animal constituents, like the various categories of vitamin B expressed in milligrams on the label.) Life Extension offers free in-house health consultations based on results from the discounted blood tests that are a part of its program. This is an invaluable service and an inexpensive way for many people to start a comprehensive health program. Based in Fort Lauderdale, Florida, Life Extension markets its wares through *Life Extension Magazine*, a high-quality monthly featuring peer-reviewed, in-depth, nutrition-based research on topical health problems. The magazine offers blood test panels that readers can purchase at a discount from a private lab along with a follow-up consultation, if you so choose. All consultants of Life Extension are licensed doctors who are well qualified to give guidance on how to best deal with basic health challenges.

The scope of your consultation with the doctor will obviously be limited by time and distance constraints but will probably include supplement and lifestyle suggestions along with referrals to the products best suited to help you deal with your specific health challenges. Unfortunately *Life Extension Magazine* does not talk about or feature a specific line of detoxification products. Maybe one day they will. Their contact information can be found in the endnotes of this book.[1-1]

A Major Difference (AMD) offers a more comprehensive, discounted health-evaluation service that involves blood and hair tests along with a health and diet history. You will be given a comprehensive multipage report (see example report in appendix V). This program is under the direct supervision of Dr. Ted Winchester, a practicing chiropractor with over twenty-five years of experience in detoxification and nutrition-based healing protocols.

If you are looking to find a practitioner with whom you can work face to face, the most effective and efficient way to proceed, I suggest you check the websites of Standard Process, Inc.,[1-2] Nutri-West, Inc.,[1-3] Apex Energetics, Inc.,[1-4] A Major Difference, Inc.,[1-5] and the Association for Conscious Evolution.[1-6]

Most alternative practitioners, especially chiropractors, learn about nutrition and detoxification by attending manufacturer-sponsored seminars intended to help them integrate the company's products into their practices. Conducted by doctors with many years of clinical experience, these seminars are of exceptional quality—far superior to my graduate-school classes. Their sponsors offer diverse lines of high-quality supplements designed to facilitate a detoxification process. Go to their websites and punch in your zip code to find a practitioner near you. There are thousands of qualified practitioners throughout the United States, so you should have no trouble finding one.

> ***Note to readers:*** To maximize your health benefit from a total body detoxification program, view your practitioner as a teacher or a coach rather than as a doctor. Allopathic practitioners use terms such as *cure* and *disease management* to describe their treatment protocols, which consist primarily of prescription drugs. Alternative practitioners teach diet and lifestyle changes to build immune and endocrine function. They also teach how to sustain a high quality of life. Learn what they have to teach you. Take notes, keep a diary, and learn about your body and its needs. Maintaining a high-level of wellness should be your primary objective as you age. The economic value of an additional twenty to thirty years that are disease-free as you age is beyond measure. Vibrant health means the difference

between leading a productive, meaningful life longer than the one you would have if you did nothing or the one you would have if you did the bare minimum of eating good food and exercising regularly. Don't get me wrong: a little is much better than nothing. My personal aging experience helps prove that food supplements, prudent dietary habits, total body detoxification, and exercise can effectively deter aging and disease.

Working with Your Practitioner

The availability of consultants makes your first step an easy one. Here's what you should expect once you begin your new journey.

1. Your practitioner will begin by creating detailed medical, medication, and dietary histories for you. Be specific and detailed when stating your medical history, as you do not want withdrawal reactions to interfere with your progress. Tests on samples of your blood, urine, and hair will provide the practitioner with a detailed view of your present health status. From this he or she will design a personalized food supplement protocol to start you back on the road to vibrant health. If you are on several allopathic medications, you may not be a candidate for intense detoxification as this will impact the levels of the medications in your blood, and the food supplements that support detoxification may conflict with the medications you are taking.

   Most alternative practitioners will try to work cooperatively with allopathic doctors, but some state boards may not allow for this type of combined medical care.
2. Be prepared to make significant dietary changes. Most Americans eat to excess and consume foods—such as sugars, starches, and fats—that activate allergic responses, destabilize blood sugar, support yeast and microorganism growth, and stimulate mucous and fat accumulation throughout the body. What you put into your body can heal or harm you. Your alternative practitioner will assist you through the necessary and important dietary changes.

Note to parents of autistic, ADHD, and emotionally disturbed children: These conditions listed above are seriously aggravated by allergy-promoting foods and sugars. Removal of these foods has been known to greatly improve these conditions.

3. Most disease begins in the gut, where proteins, starches, fats, and sugars are broken down and assimilated. Enzyme excretions must be sufficient to break the food down into its nutritional constituents. Transit time through the bowel is critical: too fast means diarrhea and too slow means constipation, which causes toxins to accumulate on the bowel walls. These accumulations eventually seep through the bowel wall where they are taken through the bloodstream and carried to all parts of the body. Your practitioner should introduce you to digestive aids and pre- and probiotics on your first or second visit. Beyond forty years of age, most of us lose the ability to digest food efficiently, and our colons become clogged with all manner of debris and microorganisms. These supplements will improve digestion and recolonize the colon with healthy bacteria that can improve nutrient assimilation.
4. I have recommended colonics to all my clients, because few people experience adequate elimination. Healthy elimination means two to three fully formed bowel movements each day. Most of my clients were content if they had one bowel movement every other day. Over time, colons become blocked with mucous buildup or simply collapse from inadequate exercise and poor posture, resulting in the classic protruding gut that is common in many men over fifty.

   Virtually all large cities have professional colon therapists, but you can also purchase a Colema Board on the Internet and do colonics at home. A Colema Board slants downward, allowing you to administer enemas that will travel through the entire colon, similar to colonics, though not as powerful. You will love the feeling of a clean, empty colon and the improved elimination it facilitates.
5. Your practitioner should evaluate your thyroid and adrenal functions. Most Americans have low thyroid function and exhausted adrenals, and you cannot effectively detox if this is the case. Under normal conditions it should take a month to rebuild adrenal function. It can take longer if you are on allopathic medications.
6. Your practitioner will require that you take, at a bare minimum, large amounts of minerals, omega-3 fatty acids, and antioxidant supplements during your detoxification process. Detoxification accelerates the production of free radicals—in a process known as oxidation, wherein an oxygen atom loses an electron,

creating a free radical; free radicals have the capability to run (literally) through the body, damaging every cell they bump into.

Oxidation is a normal occurrence—a by-product of digestion that increases in intensity because of systemic inefficiencies resulting from the aging process. The body produces the antioxidant enzyme catalase and superoxide dismutase (SOD) to neutralize these free radicals, but alas the body does not produce enough to offset the inefficiencies of aging. Free-radical buildup underlies all aging diseases and is easily neutralized by consuming a variety of antioxidants. I will say more on this topic in chapter twelve; for now keep in mind that heavy antioxidant supplementation is a must for anyone over forty to maintain health and slow aging.

Detoxification increases anabolic and catabolic activity throughout the body: anabolic refers to the buildup of physical structures like cells, tissues, organs, and bones; catabolic refers to the tearing down of physical structures. Accelerating these activities requires additional quantities of minerals and fatty acids—essential components in every cell in the body.

In addition to the above recommendations, your practitioner will probably require you to take herbal and food supplements to support liver, gallbladder, kidney, urinary tract, colon, lymph, and blood detoxification as needed. These are the main organs and pathways for the elimination of toxins, and some or all of these organs and pathways become weakened by age or a lifetime of bad habits. Not supporting these organs and pathways will only place them under greater stress, perhaps causing them to fail outright.

I devote several chapters later in this book to the detoxification of specific organs and pathways.

7. Ionizing footbaths are the final step in the total body detoxification process. This is a relatively new technology that has caught on around the world and has generated amazing results for millions of people. It should be a part of every practitioner's detoxification protocol.

   Prior to the development of ionization technology, fasting and severe dietary restriction were the most common ways to deeply detoxify the body. However, few people possess the adrenal capacity to endure a long-enough fast—between ten and thirty days—to detoxify adequately. Persons with blood-sugar imbalances and weak adrenals should not consider fasting or severe dietary restrictions under any circumstances.

I tried fasting and severe diet restriction several times but never got past the third day. By nature I am a fast metabolizer, meaning that food passes through me quickly, and my blood-sugar levels require constant replenishment to keep me going. Additionally my drug and alcohol addictions had weakened my adrenals and destabilized my blood sugar. Looking back I don't think I benefited much from those fasts, because I was too uncomfortable.

Ionizing footbaths, on the other hand, facilitate detoxification of every organ and joint in the body more effectively than any fasting ritual and without the discomfort and risks. Let's take a closer look at the process.

How Ionization Therapy Works

Two long-standing scientific principles govern the operation of ionizing footbaths: electrolysis of water and osmosis.

Electrolysis of water is the process of running a low current through water to separate each molecule into its H^+ and OH^- ionic components. *Ionic* means electrically charged. H_2O is electrically neutral, because its positively charged H atoms and negatively charged O atoms offset each other. Pull them apart and they become ions. *Osmosis* is a physical law governing the movement of a fluid or other substance through a semipermeable membrane from a lower to a higher ionic concentration. In other words the process of splitting the water molecule into its ionic components sets up an energetic pull that draws toxins out of the pores of whatever skin surface is in contact with the water.

At least that's how it works based on a number of testimonial reports compiled by several doctors who attest to significant increases of toxic metals and chemicals in the water that were not there prior to contact with live tissue.[1-5]

This conclusion is speculation on my part—absent from an FDA-approved, peer-reviewed study that could take years to complete. With that said treat this statement as theory not fact.

I first experienced an ionizing footbath in February 2000. A friend introduced me to a primitive footbath manufactured in Australia with cheap electrical components. The small, black power supply weighed over six pounds and shorted out easily. After a thirty-five-minute session I removed my feet from the water and found that I could bend my right ankle without pain for the first time in fifteen years. About two months, ten footbaths, and many chi kung exercises later, my ankle regained full range of motion.

How did that device do what no other therapy could do with my ankle? Since I can produce no definitive proof, I can only speculate that the pain and lack of motion were the result of scar tissue and calcium buildup from old athletic injuries.

The ionization process dissolved the calcium, which has a plus-two charge (Ca^{++}), and loosened the scar tissue so it could be massaged and manipulated out of the joint.

Solid toxins, such as unassimilated calcium deposited in joints (arthritis), heavy metals, and chemical residues carry positive charges. Top-of-the-line ionization devices can be programmed to produce a majority of negative and positive ions alternately. Positively charged toxins are neutralized when the device is in the negative mode, and negatively charged toxins—blood gases—are neutralized in the positive mode. The ion production in the bathwater sets up an osmotic pressure that gently pulls the neutralized toxins out of the body.

Again this is theory not fact, but the reduction in pain and inflammation experienced by hundreds of thousands of people worldwide thanks to this method indicates that something beneficial is happening. Unfortunately no manufacturer of footbath devices has the financial resources to conduct the extensive testing required by the Food and Drug Administration (FDA) to make a medical claim. The IonCleanse, conceptualized by and manufactured by A Major Difference, is the only ionization device that has received FDA clearance as a nonmedical device, meaning that it is the only one to pass all government-required electrical safety and quality checks. Otherwise for prospective purchasers of ionization devices, it is buyer beware. If a manufacturer or distributor cannot produce a comprehensive safety evaluation, I would not purchase its device. Improperly shielded devices will interfere with and unbalance electrical flows in the meridians and chakras that pervade and surround the body. Many state medical boards ban footbaths that have not been cleared by the FDA. So if you intend to administer footbaths to others for a fee, make sure your device has been cleared.

In my opinion ionization technology is the greatest health-building advancement since the development of whole-food supplements. Prior to its emergence, effective detoxification protocols like fasting and long sweats were uncomfortable and tended to discourage all but the most devoted from engaging in a detoxification program.

Concluding Comments

Research in alternative medicine has grown substantially since I went into private practice in 1986. As pharmaceutical companies do for their drugs that treat symptoms, supplement manufacturers employ a host of researchers to develop herbal, food, homeopathic, and amino acid formulations to support and rebuild weak organs and flagging body functions.

Alternative practitioners have access to food supplements and nutraceuticals (supplements that serve some medical function) to rejuvenate cells, bones, skin, organs, and glands; homeopathic remedies for alleviating emotional traumas; and herbal formulations for treating metabolic malfunctions and imbalances.

Allopathic medicine, driven by pharmaceutical interests, has a poor track record when it comes to dealing with chronic diseases and does not recognize any of the disease-support conditions I described earlier in this chapter. Pharmaceuticals are designed to neutralize symptoms, not to strengthen the body or treat toxic buildup that will lead to disease.

All alternative medical systems—Chinese medicine, Native American medicine, homeopathic medicine, and ayurvedic medicine—are based on removing toxins and correcting inappropriate life habits. If you are ready, as I was, to look deep within yourself and make the needed changes that your search will illuminate, you will experience the same healing miracle I did. My healing journey has convinced me that no disease or condition is impossible to overcome.

Chapter Two

Weight Loss and Weight Management

Is obesity a disease or the product of several bad habits? I don't think anyone likes carrying around thirty, forty, or a hundred extra pounds, but millions of people, in spite of their best efforts to lose those pounds, gain them back over and over again. Based on these observations, I believe obesity is the product of several bad habits, and the failure to keep weight off once it's been lost is the disease. There are many contributing conditions to obesity:

1. poor dietary choices
2. little to no regular exercise
3. high internal stress
4. thyroid imbalance
5. sluggish or exhausted adrenals
6. insulin sensitivity, metabolic syndrome, or diabetes
7. liver impairment
8. allergies
9. sluggish metabolism
10. emotional trauma

There may be other factors contributing to obesity, but these are the most common. The problem facing anyone wanting to lose weight is where to begin, and the best place to begin is by formulating an intention rather than a goal. Yes, you want to lose weight, but you also want to keep it off permanently. That is where intention comes in. By intending to develop your own personal health-improvement practice—one that involves dietary modification, exercise, detoxification, and stress management—you will evolve a daily practice that will enable you to maintain your own optimum weight over time.

Overweight comedians like to joke that they know how to lose weight, that they've lost hundreds of pounds over the course of their lives. In their trial-and-error process they failed to cultivate a sustainable habit, so that when the weight loss goal is achieved, they returned to their previous lifestyle and eating habits.

The techniques and protocols in this book are offered as lifetime practices for sustaining health, and dealing with obesity is no different than my seeking healthy longevity. Many physical factors may contribute to obesity, but they can be corrected or neutralized over time. Glands can be strengthened, the liver can be detoxed and nutritionally supported, and allergies can be neutralized. But unless you actively manage the food, exercise, stress, and detox parts of the program for the rest of your life, you will always be looking for another weight-loss program.

In the following section, I will describe the program I recommend for everyone desiring to achieve vibrant health or get off the wheel of perpetual weight gain. For all intents and purposes, the programs are the same.

My Suggested Lifetime Weight-Management Program for Everyone

1. Start with the intention of developing a lifetime health and wellness program that will enable you to maintain your optimum weight.
2. Find a practitioner not only with the knowledge to guide you through the food selection, exercise, and detoxification protocols but also with the availability to support you when you run into mental and emotional obstacles, like feeling deprived when you can't have the dessert you so crave. If you eat right, exercise daily, and detoxify regularly, you will not have an obesity problem. Your unconscious emotional process and some inappropriate ideas you have about yourself are probably holding you to habits that do not serve you. They will surface as you restore your body to health, and you will need to deal with them.
3. Educate yourself about the role of food and the different types of foods that can hurt or help you. Become an educated participant. The more you know and understand, the easier it will be for you to maintain your program and be motivated to do so.
4. Make the achievement of vibrant health your number-one goal in life. Let every one of your other life goals—career, money, family, business—flow from the attainment of your number-one goal. It's difficult to have a successful career or business if you are not healthy, and your family will be much happier and less burdened if you *are* healthy.

What to Do When You Break Your Program Guidelines

The key to maintaining optimum weight over the long term is the speed at which you get back into your health-maintenance program after you binge or stop your health-building routines. Emotional stress is a part of everyone's life, and a well-thought-out weight-management program should provide you with the resources and support you need to cope successfully with the challenges in your life. You will experience emotional upset; you will experience setbacks. They are a part of everyone's life experience, and how you, or anyone else, deal with them determines the success or failure of any endeavor. The only real failure in this process is quitting.

Over the past twenty-nine years I have regressed many times in my challenge to get cigarettes, alcohol, marijuana, and sugar completely out of my life. I don't always know why I get a craving for something I don't want. Sometimes it passes quickly, and other times it lingers for days until I imbibe. Once I imbibe, the craving dissipates, and my life moves on.

Sometimes I can relate the craving to a specific issue; other times I cannot. I have come to accept that these cravings are a guide into my more deeply held issues and that one day they will disappear entirely. In the meantime I awaken the next morning and get myself back on the program. It's working; the cravings are coming further apart from one another, and their intensity keeps diminishing.

Sugar is my biggest problem. To combat the sugar cravings, I do a candida cleanse every four months, adding caprylic acid, oil of oregano, and restricting carbohydrate intake like starches and sugars from my diet and I do a series of four footbaths to alter my body's pH. Marijuana is my second-biggest ongoing challenge that is exacerbated when I don't get a good night's sleep. I have not smoked cigarettes in twenty-six years, but it took six years to completely wean myself off them. As for alcohol I have one or two drinks a year to quell a tension or anxiety that I can't alleviate through exercise or meditation.

To put my present predicament in proper perspective, I have been a sugarholic ever since I was a child. I started smoking cigarettes at age thirteen, drinking alcohol at fifteen, smoking marijuana at twenty-seven, and snorting cocaine at thirty-five. I was consuming so much alcohol that at age twenty-one a doctor warned me that I was a candidate for cirrhosis. Smoking marijuana neutralized the alcohol problem, but by age thirty-five I was smoking upwards of fifteen joints a day. Based on this previous rate of consumption, I've made great progress and will continue to make further progress.

The point I wish to make here is that recovery from a chronic degenerative disease, including obesity or a drug or food addiction, is a lifetime journey to be taken one day at a time. I cannot say it enough times: this journey has been the most rewarding endeavor I've ever undertaken.

Of all my addictions—sugar, cigarettes, alcohol, marijuana, and cocaine—I consider sugar to be the most dangerous because of its enormous impact on health. Consider that one-third of all children born in the United States will get diabetes at some time in their lives. Manufacturers add sugars primarily in the form of high-fructose corn syrup to virtually all processed foods, and most people feed these convenience foods to their children. Movements are afoot to remove corn syrup from foods, but the power of the corn lobby and the addictive nature of the substance ensure that permanent removal from food will take many years, if ever. The best way to effect permanent removal is total boycott: *don't buy the junk.*

In terms of lethal impact: cocaine, alcohol, and cigarettes will kill you. Cocaine will destroy your health in a few months; alcohol and cigarettes will take considerably longer, but they will contribute to health problems throughout your life. Marijuana will lower blood-sugar levels (which create sugar cravings), interfere with testosterone utilization, and cause lung damage if smoked. I know many long-term, low-use—less than one joint per day—pot smokers who have lived normal, productive lives without physical or mental impairment. Heavy use will cause serious lung and bronchial damage.

Chapter Three

My Healing Journey and the First Three Laws of Total Body Detoxification

I was diagnosed with lung cancer in September 1982, at age forty-three, when I checked into a drug rehab. The doctor who conducted the physical exam made the tentative diagnosis from X-rays, listening to my breathing and analyzing my medical history.

"You came here because you knew you were in trouble, and your chest X-ray shows black shadows across both lungs." She spoke quickly, waving a metal pointer over a blackened area of the X-ray where one would expect to find lung tissue.

"Black is not good?" I asked offhandedly, mentally grabbing my gut. *You idiot! You really screwed up now*, echoed through my head. Those seven words summed up my life to that point. In that microsecond I knew and accepted that I had done this to myself. Everything I had done—the alcohol, cigarettes, pot, and cocaine—had led directly to that moment.

"I'm not a pulmonologist, but I've done an internship in that specialty," the doctor continued, as I jolted myself back to attention. "I've seen this pattern before, and I can tell you with some degree of certainty that you have lung cancer." Without pausing she quickly added, "But I can't be absolutely certain unless we do a biopsy. As of now I surmise that you've lost about ten percent of your breathing capacity, and it's imperative that you stop smoking immediately."

Her gaze met mine, and I looked directly into her eyes for several seconds while I tried to gather myself. I was a dead man. She knew it and I knew it. Why couldn't she state the obvious? I was going to die soon. End of story. Why drag it out with biopsies, chemo, and radiation that would only make the trip more painful?

Of course I had known I was in trouble when I had checked into the rehab. I had been smoking a pack of cigarettes a day for thirty years and fifteen to twenty joints of marijuana a day for ten years, with liberal amounts of cocaine and alcohol thrown in for good measure. I had decided to check into the rehab when I discovered that I could not breathe after jogging fifty yards. My lungs could not expand to take in the extra air I needed for that effort.

"Would you like to schedule a biopsy?" she asked.

"No, thanks. I know your diagnosis is correct, so I don't want a biopsy."

"But you will need one for insurance coverage, and it will confirm the diagnosis. The damage looks extensive, and without treatment you could die within six months."

"I know you mean well, doctor, and I also know that chemo and radiation don't work."

"Perhaps you're right, but you have to do something. What are you planning otherwise?"

"I don't know, but I know what I'm not going to do."

Given my conversation with Marty, I was not about to undergo treatments like radiation or chemotherapy that would further incapacitate me—especially treatments that wouldn't cure me.

I completed the rehab program, which reduced my cravings for cigarettes and pot but not to the point where I was able to completely do without them. The program, designed by L. Ron Hubbard, the founder of Scientology, a genius ahead of his time, consisted of a daily four-hour sauna accompanied by large amounts of vitamin, mineral, and fatty acid supplements that cleansed and strengthened my body.

I attended four Alcoholics Anonymous (AA) meetings after completing rehab, but I found the AA environment unsupportive of my belief in the use of nutrition and food supplements in overcoming addiction. I maintain the highest regard for AA as a bridge for recovering addicts to begin the journey back to permanent sobriety. However, I refused to accept the belief that once an addict, always an addict, because that belief relegated me to a life of victimhood.

Maybe some people could fight all their cravings, but I was not one of them. And I saw the result of such a fight. I saw too many "dry drunks" at AA: four cups of coffee with three or four spoons of sugar in each cup, chain smoking cigarettes to get through a one-hour meeting. I could see from their shaking bodies and angry demeanors that they were just one eye blink away from their next drink. Unlike many of these recovering addicts I saw at AA, who were totally depleted emotionally and physically and easily set off by the smallest slight, my sauna companions became calmer and gradually regained the ability to focus. They came away from the program with healthy-looking skin and a glow in their eyes. Clearly the supplements and detoxification helped to rebuild their weakened bodies.

I liked the way I felt physically after completing the Scientology program, but why I continued to crave drugs still remained a mystery to me for several years. I believed that if I could identify and change the causes of my addictions, I would move beyond them. I feel that I have done that.

Prior to entering rehab, I had been working with a nutritionist and colon therapist, and so I understood that diet, food supplements, and detoxification played key roles in building health. My diminished cravings at the end of the program, coupled with an ability to jog two miles unhindered, showed me that the process had been effective and that I was moving in a positive direction. I vowed to continue rebuilding while I searched for a way to fully neutralize my cravings.

Toward this end I sought the help of a well-known Colorado herbalist, Hannah Kroeger, who saw people out of her ramshackle store in Boulder. She was a tiny woman in her late sixties; she dressed like a nun and spoke in a heavy German accent—she looked like a character out of Hansel and Gretel. I told her my story while she circled my body, waving a pendulum and occasionally muttering to herself. Completing her examination in less than two minutes, she faced me and said in her thick accent, "Yes, you haff lung cancer, but for you there is time."

She then recommended seven or eight herbal formulations and told me to see her again in sixty days. I was happy that someone expected me to be around that long, even though the source of the positive news did not seem credible at the time.

As I drove back to Denver on Route 36, I lit a joint and pondered what she had said: for me there was time. Beating lung cancer seemed impossible, and I still had to contend with pot and cigarette addictions as well. I wasn't sure how I would do it. I had tried giving up marijuana on two occasions.

On the first occasion, I became angry at my wife for no reason and left the house for a week; I calmed down and returned only after I started back on pot. On the second attempt, my liver pain became unbearable after two days of abstinence. When I went back on pot, the pain ceased.

What this led me to believe was that I was physically and emotionally addicted to two substances—marijuana and nicotine—that assaulted my lungs every time I indulged in them, so my chances of surviving the cancer were less than slim. I was a dead man walking. Lung cancer killed 100 percent of the time, and I was systematically antagonizing my lungs with continuous inputs of carcinogens, and I had no immediate way of stopping.

The thought of my imminent demise momentarily jolted me into an altered state, and I was directed by an invisible force to park along the shoulder of the highway, next to a green pasture where fifty or sixty cattle were feeding. It was a pastoral vista; the Rocky Mountain foothills provided a scenic backdrop, but I barely saw it. Inside my head a streaming video of my life showed me the people I had hurt when I was younger and the actions I had taken to gain advantage over others in my quest to survive. (I did not know anything at that time about chakras—the electrically charged energy wheels emanating from the spine. But from my present view, I would say that the movie was playing in my sixth chakra, where the pituitary gland is located. I will discuss chakras in the next chapter.)

As a professional poker player, I had separated people from their assets with no concern at all that I was contributing to their pain. I thought only of myself—never considering the consequences of my actions on the lives of others. So what if my success hurt a few people? "They had it coming," as one of my organized-crime mentors would often say to justify his intimidating collection methods. "People got to pay for play. I don't force them to do anything, but they got to pay."

And I played life the way it had presented itself to me. How could I have done anything differently? I'd had to stand up to a mother who beat and berated me constantly. By age ten I could tolerate pain and punishment, and I used that to challenge whatever obstacles were in my way—up to and including the God whom my parents and the Bible talked so much about. Who the hell was this insane deity? If there were a God who created the human race, I didn't want anything to do with Him. Anyone capable of creating this reality had to be one cruel son of a bitch.

My thoughts returned to my present dilemma. Sure I had been a bad guy and probably deserved to die. That was all right with me. Living had never been a positive experience, and I had never asked for this life in the first place; it was not going to get better as I aged, and now seemed like a good time to give it up. But I had choices about how that could happen. I could choose the way I wanted to go out. I could afford to buy some heavy drugs and party right to the cemetery. That would be the easiest way to go. *Yes, but what happens if you don't die right away? You may run out of money and leave your family destitute. Is that what you want for them?* The voice, coming from somewhere deep within me, was soft, gentle, and nonjudgmental.

No, I did not want that, I answered as I beheld an image of my wife and baby son living in poverty. I brought the kid into the world. I owe him something. Okay, what about simply blowing my brains out? Quick and easy. A hundred bucks for the gun and a bullet.

Is that the legacy you want to leave your son? Committing suicide when he's less than two years old? How do you think he would live with the knowledge that his dad committed suicide shortly after he had come into the world? No, I did not want that either. The voice was starting to annoy me; its questions poked me like a pitchfork, forcing me to look at the painful reality I had to confront.

So what was left? Lung cancer plus several addictions meant certain death, which I did not fear, but I was apprehensive about the debilitation that would take place before the lights went out. Legal painkillers would alleviate some of the pain, and maybe I would just OD quietly.

Then it came to me—not a solution to my problem, but a way of coping with it. The only thing I knew how to do was fight. I had been doing that my whole life, and it looked like I would be doing it until the day I died.

I didn't have a clue where to begin, but I promised myself that I would put forth my best efforts for no other reason than to stick it to God, if in fact He really existed. I wanted to be able to look the son of a bitch in the eye and tell Him what I thought about the tortured world He had created.

But in order to do that, I would have to be impeccable in my efforts to heal myself. If I were to ever meet up with Him, I wanted to be able to look Him in the eye and condemn Him for His cruelty. He had created this mess, and I wanted to spit it back in His face.

In quick order I resolved that I would fight the cancer and the addictions with all my might. I would be willing to change anything about myself that needed changing. And I would be willing to teach others how to do the same thing if I succeeded.

I would do these things with one proviso: that I would find life to be a worthwhile experience. I did not want a continuation of the painful existence I had been enduring. Why would anyone choose a life of constant suffering?

I did not know nor did I understand why God would deliberately create a cauldron of pain in which four or five billion lunatics whaled away on one another. Everyone I knew suffered in some way. Just like my insane mother who had hurt me with her words and blows, the God who created this world was not someone who acted out of love, and I wanted a piece of Him. I didn't care how almighty He was.

Creating My Process

My first step was committing to do whatever was necessary to fight the cancer with all the effort I could muster. That, it turns out, was crucial; as researchers have since discovered, the will to fight plays a significant role in reversing cancer.

For my second step, I was willing to change anything about myself that needed changing. That was easy to say, but in reality it involved a long and extremely challenging process of dismantling a structure of beliefs, attitudes, and perspectives about myself that were anchored in anger, hatred, bitterness, and fear. As I discovered a few years into my healing practice, that is what being human is all about: freeing ourselves from the domination and control of the ego—a self-fabricated structure anchored in angry and fearful emotions that distort reality and create conflict, pain, and destruction for the person who harbors them.

My twenty-nine-year (and counting) journey out of anger, hatred, and addiction has brought me into acceptance and alignment with my spiritual source, a place of peace and tranquility that is who I really am. My healing journey that began with the cancer diagnosis has taken on a life of its own as, little by little, all of the addictions, judgments, angers, and fears that once ruled my life continue to be eroded in my daily meditations.

There are still challenges as I seek to imbed this new consciousness into my every waking act and thought. As I look back on the arduous journey, I am grateful I took it, because I now find life to be an exciting and rewarding experience. Without this shift I would have died long ago, an unhappy and embittered failure.

What Does This Have to Do with Detoxification?

On a simple, one-dimensional level, *detoxification* is defined as the removal of toxins from the body by some process or method. However, nothing is ever as simple as it seems. In my healing journey it took seven years to detoxify, rid my body of cancer, and get myself to a point where I could play competitive basketball again. However, it has taken twenty-nine years and counting to get rid of the angers, hatreds, and fears that provided the structure for the cancer to grow.

The detoxification rituals I utilized over the years to overcome lung cancer, hepatitis, and osteoarthritis caused me to become more aware of my multidimensional nature and the awesome power I possess to reinvent and heal myself. And it all began with the herbs Hannah Kroeger gave me. They initiated a powerful detoxification reaction that kept me bedridden for five days with a constant 105-degree fever—my body's way of burning off toxins, an indication that it was strong enough to sustain a detoxification process. This was part of Hannah's prognosis that I still had time.

Since then I have initiated many clients into detoxification programs, and I have noticed that those who are physically and energetically weak cannot detoxify. Their bodies simply are not strong enough to expend the energy required to release toxins. That discovery has enabled me to formulate my first law of detoxification:

> ***It takes physical energy and a powerful commitment to detoxify the body. If either is missing or in short supply, the body will not detoxify to the level required for healing.***

I have seen this law expressed many times over the years, even in young people. However, it is not always an easy journey.

I have seen people fail to dump toxins into the water even when they used ionization technology, which adds energy to the detoxification process. Where possible I would question them about their feelings, and 100 percent of the time I found that they were either emotionally rigid and unforgiving or in denial of their feelings. This process of discovery enabled me to formulate the second law of detoxification:

> ***You cannot detoxify beyond what you are willing to release emotionally.***

These two laws govern all detoxification procedures, regardless of the methodology or the detoxification protocol employed.

I was one of those rigid, unforgiving people when I began my healing journey. During the first three years of my recovery, I stopped using marijuana and cocaine; I filtered sugar and junk foods out of my diet; I consumed massive doses of vitamins and herbal supplements; and I sweated, fasted, and did weekly colonic and bodywork sessions to soften hard, brittle muscles that reflected my mental and emotional attitudes.

Still my long-standing mantra remained: life is hard, and I must make myself harder and tougher than my opponents in order to survive. I did not know how to bend, compromise, or negotiate, and my body mirrored those attitudes perfectly. I distinctly recall how I felt after my first colonic. As I walked out of the therapist's office, I was bent over in pain, arms wrapped around my lower abdomen, which felt like it had been internally mowed by an electric eggbeater. The therapist had explained that, because of poor digestion and a bad diet, my colon had become petrified by a dense mucous coating, which would take many colonics to dissolve.

Three years into the journey I joined a meditation group called the Light Work, the purpose of which was to help people focus on and work through life issues. By that time I was feeling anger, rage, and fear more acutely than ever. I had never felt those emotions when using marijuana, and now that I was off it, they hit me full force. I still used cigarettes and alcohol in small doses, but the absence of cocaine and marijuana—especially marijuana—made it virtually impossible to deny or suppress my emotions.

The structured meditation and visualizations of the Light Work were designed to relax the body and mind by disconnecting them from their routine thought streams.

During one of my first meditations, I attempted to sit quietly and let my thoughts drift through me without being attached to them. But my mind screamed at me, rattling off hundreds of emotionally charged words and noises that made no sense—exactly the way my mother had sounded throughout my childhood and adolescence. I made up my mind to let my thoughts rant and not buy into them, and within a few minutes, the ranting stopped, having been deprived of the energy I routinely gave it.

Unbelievable! I thought. In a detached way, I was observing the mind noise that had been running my life up to that moment. The phrasing and emotional content of the words and noises were familiar to me. Yet when I stepped back and listened dispassionately, these words and noises made no sense—they were just a bunch of run-on, chopped-up, emotionally charged sentences, conveying a sense of continuous urgency and rage. They were the essence of my mother—the queen of suffering revisited. Oh my God! She was playing inside my head. I had become her.

The Light Work practice brought more revelations. I recalled getting drunk for the first time at age fifteen—it had taken just one can of beer. The alcohol induced a peaceful silence throughout my brain and body, as it blotted out my mother's screeching voice. I welcomed this silence and promised myself that I would consume as much alcohol as I could to remain in that place.

Ah! A new insight. The fifteen-year-old had found a solution to his pain that would relegate the adult to a life of drug and alcohol addiction. The drugs suppressed the noise, but they did not remove it. The meditation exercises immediately enabled me to access the noise, but it was too overwhelming for me to maintain the meditative state. My nervous system had been too traumatized to process the information that the meditations were bringing into consciousness. Another method would be needed to help me process my internal pain.

The great yoga instructors teach that in meditation one should sit quietly and view the thoughts that surface into consciousness and then passively let them go. These thoughts are part of humanity's grand illusion, to be observed and dispassionately released. That's great for a twenty-five-year-old kid in an ashram in India, but what about someone who had to pay rent, feed a wife and son, and support a half-dozen addictions? The noises raging inside me were way too powerful simply to pass through me.

I felt and understood the magnitude of influence the noise had on my nervous system, behavior, and physical body. And in the meditations, I could feel the noise grabbing onto my nervous system and altering its electrical charge in a manner that tightened muscles and constricted organs, thus distorting their functions. Day after day, month after month, year after year, the noise played its deadly messages through my body-mind system, forming it into a biomagnetic ecosystem that continually attracted trauma and conflict—a self-reinforcing energy loop that intensified as I aged.

The only way this noise could be neutralized was through my own conscious intervention. In other words I would have to take full responsibility for that noise and the emotional states and events it attracted to me. No more blaming parents, police, teachers, or any other outside influence for my failures. I had to force myself to accept that my painful, diseased, and depressed life was my exclusive creation. If I ever wanted to be free, I would have to patiently dismantle a highly destructive mental-emotional structure that had been with me all my life.

How did this structural dismemberment turn out for me? Well, here I am, twenty-five years later at age seventy-one, disease-free and with all body parts working. I am a successful businessman, enjoying the best years of my life and preparing to fulfill the last part of my commitment to show others they can free themselves from the negative influences governing their lives.

My journey was difficult and challenging—to put it mildly—primarily because I had no road map to help me understand and guide me through my inner jungle. I was fortunate to have several great teachers along the way, but none could give me the overview I'm describing in these pages.

The most difficult part of the journey involved recognizing and letting go of the many false beliefs through which I justified violence and lawlessness to make my way in the world. Among these beliefs were "the world is totally corrupt; therefore I am justified in doing whatever I deem necessary to survive" and "the world is a dog-eat-dog place, and I choose to be one of the dogs who eats." As I slowly accepted that I was the creator of my life dramas, I knew I had to change those survival beliefs.

But what would I substitute? At first I had no clue, but going back to the old way was not an option. I would take this journey on blind faith, but I was tired of suffering. "No matter what" became my mantra.

As I entered the later years of the journey, I began to see and appreciate the benefits of trusting my spiritual source and letting go of the accumulated angers and fears of a lifetime. The more negativity I expelled from my body-mind, the more I experienced an internal state of unconditional love and gratitude for my existence. My life used to be a living hell; now it is a constant joy, interspersed with challenges. I used to be diseased, depressed, and addicted; now I am healthy, happy, and relatively free of cravings (unless I ignore or deny my emotional issues).

My friend and practitioner-teacher, Dr. Ted Winchester, calls these cravings "idiot guides." He defines them as symptoms emanating from issues we automatically deny or hide from our conscious awareness. The process goes on and on, and each time

I release another issue, my inner noise lessens. And then I experience longer periods of unconditional love, gratitude, and inner peace as a result.

My healing journey began with the removal of toxins and impacted wastes, as their overwhelming presence fed my drug cravings and impaired my nervous system to the point that it was incapable of handling the pent-up emotional charges that I had systematically suppressed and stored over a lifetime. Accumulations of heavy metals—including lead, arsenic, aluminum, mercury, cadmium, and nickel—can severely impair nervous-system function. Petrochemical residues impede hormone utilization, which disrupts all body systems, and toxic bowel accumulations leak back into the bloodstream, doing further damage to the nervous system and organs.

Over sixteen years of clinical practice I have watched my clients' energy levels rise, their moods brighten, their ability to focus and concentrate greatly improve, and their willingness to look at and process difficult issues grow. In time I came to view the body as a toxin magnet with the amount, type, and location of toxic accumulation varying with the emotional issues and traumatic experiences of each individual.

The body-mind unit resembles a circuit board that modifies and transports electrical energy through an obstacle course of electronic components. However, this body-mind unit traps toxins according to where the electrical charge flow is restricted and blocked: microorganisms in the liver and colon; heavy metals in the fatty tissue and nervous-system sheath; unassimilated calcium in the joints; petrochemical residues over every cell and organ surface; crystallized sugars and cross-linked proteins in the kidneys and liver; mucous in the liver and intestines; and fat in the gut, thighs, buttocks, and liver.

Detoxification begins at the physical level, but to make any real progress, emotional and traumatic issues must be addressed to break up the energy blocks that attract and accumulate toxins. Total body detoxification is gaining in popularity today, because more people are getting sick earlier in their lives. Poor dietary habits, poisoned and denatured food, and exposure to petrochemicals, heavy metals, vaccinations, and chemical pollutants have created a population of mutant humans. This is a harsh term, but it describes the growing number of young people suffering from allergies, ADHD, autism, behavioral abnormalities, eating disorders, and addictions.[3-1]

Researchers from a number of disciplines have noticed that the greater the toxic content of the body, the lower its resistance to disease and stress, and this is not only for humans but for amphibians and land mammals as well. We have recently become aware of the serious threat of global warming and its consequences for our planet, but the threat to human survival from hormone disruptors—petrochemical residues that occupy cell receptor sites normally occupied by naturally created hormones—is even greater. Human birth defects have increased more than 1,600 percent since 1980, breast cancer has increased 250 percent since 1980, and standard sperm counts have decreased by 59 percent since 1940, all because of the presence of hormone disruptors in our environment. (I suggest you look up the work of Dr. Theo Colborn, of the National Institutes of Health, for more information on this distressing subject).[3-2]

I wanted to introduce you as early as possible to the mental, emotional, and spiritual implications of total body detoxification, and I will cover these topics in greater detail in the closing chapters. As I said earlier, I cannot separate my physical condition—my experiences of disease, addiction, and well-being—from my mental attitudes and emotional states. In my present healthy, nonaddicted state, I have more energy, I think clearly, and I am happy, joyful, and productive. I don't always maintain emotional mindfulness, but when I do, my life works better and I am at peace. This brings me to my third law of detoxification:

> ***Total body detoxification is an essential component of any consciousness-raising and healing effort.***

It is my fundamental belief that the physical body, our emotional content, and our attitudes and perceptions form a single entity that is inseparable from Spirit and is subject to the physical laws of the universe. The greater the emotional and traumatic events experienced by the individual, the greater the amount of toxins held in the physical body. Conversely the greater the toxic load held in the physical body, the harder it becomes for the individual to connect to emotions. Heavy emotional charges act like magnets, in that they attract and hold toxins. These toxins, held in shellac-like layers over cells and tissues, amplify the influence of these emotional charges in our daily lives. This deadly loop intensifies with age.

My brother, Brian, shared his experiences of our parents during their declining years. His one-sentence summary, "they became more of what they always were," elegantly described the solidification of the unresolved fears, anxieties, angers, and frustrations in their bodies and personalities. Their beliefs, attitudes, and perspectives of themselves as impoverished, helpless people had become hardwired into their brains and nervous systems, eventually rendering them incapable of movement and coherent thought.

Their lives did not provide the opportunity for conscious transformation as mine did provide. I would like to believe I had grown weary of violence, conflict, and confrontation in previous lifetimes, and when presented with the opportunity in this lifetime to rid myself of those tendencies, I decided to rid myself of every last angry thought-form.

When confronted by the prospect of an early, painful death, my willingness to change anything about myself that needed changing was sincere and purposeful. I wanted to stop suffering badly enough to completely dismantle the Bob Moroney I had been without reservation or qualification. I am still carrying out that task. Perhaps my parents will use the suffering of this lifetime as fuel for transformation in their next lifetime. I'd like to believe the system works that way.

Chapter Four

The Chakra System

Chakra, from the ancient Sanskrit language, means "wheel." The seven chakras running up the midline of the body form its basic energy support structure. These energy wheels or power centers are recognized directly or indirectly in the Hebrew, Hindu, Taoist, and Buddhist traditions. The chakras are mentioned in several spiritual texts, including *Bhagavad Gita*,[4-1] *The Upanishads*,[4-2] and *The Yoga Sutras of Patanjali*.[4-3] In later chapters I will describe how chakra testing is used in alternative healing environments to root out hidden issues that disrupt the body—an undeniable demonstration of the body-mind-spirit connection.

This book attempts to show the direct relationship between toxins held in the physical body and the mental-emotional issues that attract and hold them. If the laws of detoxification apply to all humans, it logically follows that in order to heal our minds and bodies we must change the mental and emotional attitudes that consciously and unconsciously govern and motivate our lives.

Twentieth-century physicists have shown that all matter is formed from the same energy source. As we are made from the God-energy of the universe, as supported by a number of religious and spiritual teachings, we then have the godlike power to recreate ourselves in a way that allows us to live a loving and healthy life.

The main intention of this book is to show the interrelationship of the mind (beliefs, attitudes, and perspectives), emotions (feelings), and total body detoxification. Thoughts attached to emotional charges, called *mental-emotional dynamics*, create energy blocks throughout the body, and these energy blocks attract and hold toxins. Pain and inflammation are primary indications of toxin buildup. The body does not distinguish between physical trauma and emotional trauma; it stores both somewhere in the body. Football players know they will suffer permanent damage from injuries incurred by playing the game. People whose minds dwell on hateful, fearful, and anxious images wreak similar traumatic injuries upon themselves without any physical contact.

From my study of Chinese medicine and from my own experiences, it appears that the hate-filled person creates toxins through the liver, while the fearful and anxious person will tend to block the exit of toxins from the body through the kidneys and the colon. Anger and fear-based emotions have, in effect, different metabolic pathways that negatively impact different organ systems and ultimately result in different types of diseases. Total body detoxification starts the removal of physical toxins from the body. This detoxification creates an opening for identifying and changing unpleasant thoughts and inappropriate emotions.

Figure 1 shows the location of the seven chakras that control and regulate all aspects of the human body.

Figure 1: Seven chakras

I've known about the chakra system for more than twenty-five years, but until recently I was clueless about its purpose and function, which Caroline Myss describes in her book *Why People Don't Heal and How They Can*:[4-4]

> *[T]he physical body has seven levels of internal power. Each level of power is not only aligned to a physical system within the body, but also relates to external and internal issues that are a part of our lives...*

> *The teachings and scriptures from the Buddhist, Hindu, Christian, and Hebrew spiritual traditions all make reference to the seven sacred levels of power that contain and manage the life-force that flows through the body... The seven levels of our energy body record the most miniscule details of our lives* and how we distribute our life-force. [Emphasis mine]

"Life-force" refers to the quantity and quality of energy flowing through the body. In electrical parlance, "quantity" refers to the amount of energy or voltage, while "quality" refers to the frequency of the energy—the number of beats or repetitions per second. The higher the frequency, the higher the function of the person, organ, or system impacted by the energy; the lower the frequency, the lower the function level.

Myss, a renowned medical intuitive and teacher of energy-healing techniques, portrays chakras as "energetic" computer disks that collect information:

> *I describe for people the nature of their physical diseases, as well as the energetic dysfunctions that are present within their bodies. I read the energy field that permeates and surrounds the body, picking up information about dramatic childhood experiences, behavior patterns, even superstitious beliefs, all of which have a bearing on the person's physical health. Based on the information I perceive intuitively in their energy fields, including the chakras, I can make recommendations for treating their conditions on both a physical and spiritual level... As you learn the language of the chakras, you will come to recognize the emotional, psychological, and spiritual stress factors that affect your health and correspond to your physical symptoms.*

Because of my clinical training and orientation (I do not see or read energy fields or auras), I think of chakras as programmed computer chips sitting on a circuit board, the physical body. A circuit board consists of pieces of material upon which printed or integrated circuits are installed. These printed circuits direct and regulate the current's flow through the board to the appliance in a manner determined by the board's designer.

Myss states that "the physical body has its origins in spirit," a view similar to mine, which states that "we are spirit-manifested in matter." The programming of the chakras begins in Spirit, as the soul shapes the lessons, challenges, and karma it wants to work through in a particular lifetime.

That programming is reinforced by fetal experiences in the womb as the emotions, traumas, and attitudes of the parents are imprinted into the fetus's energy field. That early programming shapes and directs the energy (current) flow through the chakras into the physical body, thereby establishing a platform for developing human beings to process, interpret, and respond to the life experiences they attract to themselves. This current flow shapes the attitudes, perceptions, and emotional reactions of developing humans; forms a biomagnetic path that attracts their lives' experiences; and determines the types of illnesses, addictions, and allergies they will experience.

To paraphrase the previous paragraph, each of us is a creature of habit. Have you ever stopped to consider why you keep falling for the wrong girl or guy? Why you have trouble finding the right job or career? Why you keep getting into debt no matter how many promises you make to yourself to cut expenses? We all have our stories, our tales of woe—and do we like to tell them.

When I was in private practice as a nutritionist and peak-performance counselor (a peak-performance counselor designs mental, emotional, and physical programs that enable individuals to raise their energy and improve life performance), an attractive forty-five-year-old woman named Annie came to me with a complaint that she had just found out that her new boyfriend was using crack cocaine. She had been married twice before to men who turned out to be alcoholics, and now her new beau, a tenured professor at a state university, was addicted to a far more severe drug.

In my first session with all my clients, I go over the ground rules governing my approach to their healing: "You create your reality. If something happens to you that you don't like or makes you unhappy, it's because of something within you that causes you to attract it. If you are willing to take full responsibility for your life, I can help you identify those hidden dynamics and neutralize them. Are you willing to accept that level of responsibility?"

Annie immediately agreed, so I took a brief medical history, reviewed some key events in her life, and scheduled our next appointment. At that second meeting, I stood with my arm around her shoulders in front of a full-length mirror and asked her to repeat after me: "I deserve a loving, supportive relationship with a man."

She scrunched up her shoulders and looked away from the mirror. "I can't say that," she said. She turned away from me and sat in her chair. "I can't say that," she said again, as she picked up her handbag and prepared to write a check for her visit.

"Hey, where are you going?" I asked. "We still have plenty of time."

"No, no, no. I don't want to go there right now. I just want to leave."

"Okay, Annie, but try to come back soon. We got to the pain inside you that has been causing you to attract the wrong men, and with a little effort, we can get it out so that you won't be attracting the wrong guy anymore." But she wanted no part of this work, and I never saw her again.

Another client, Carol, a successful career woman in her mid-fifties and whose husband of thirty years had recently died, came to me because she was having trouble adjusting to single life. Her marriage produced two children, but the relationship between her and her husband had been distant and difficult.

We had been working together for several months when she reported bumping into an old boyfriend at the bank where she worked. It wasn't a happy reunion; she described herself as feeling like a little girl curled up in the corner, ashamed of her now-overweight body. She was a tall woman, so the forty or fifty extra pounds were not unsightly enough to warrant her reaction. Her body-image issue had not come up before, but now that it surfaced, I suggested that we work on it and, perhaps in the process, put her on a diet and exercise program that would take off some of the weight. As I talked I noticed that she raised her stocking feet up on the half sofa and wrapped her arms around them in an unconscious attempt to get into the position she had described a moment before.

"I'm not so sure I want to do this," she said, as she gently rocked herself.

"This would be a great opportunity to work through some important issues and lose some weight in the process. The diet part will be easy; don't be concerned about that."

"I'm not concerned about the diet. These feelings are too painful. I don't want to work on them now."

I never saw her again either.

How did those women know how to react the way they had to those issues? Where did the emotional pain, which their body postures clearly portrayed, come from? What secret message was Annie broadcasting that caused her to attract addicted men, and what mechanisms were operating that permitted her to become involved with them? On some level she was sending out a message from her body-mind that attracted emotionally unavailable men, and on some other level, she remained blind to the multitude of signs that these men were broadcasting, especially after being previously married to two alcoholics. How had she not seen the crack addict coming?

According to Myss and other experts on chakra energetics, "not deserving a loving relationship" is a second chakra issue: relationship with self. The pains and traumas of accumulated, failed relationships could spill over to the first chakra, which governs tribal relationships, and also to the third chakra, which governs relationships with others.

Annie's belief attracted emotionally unavailable men who offered her unfulfilling relationships that ended painfully. Like all of us, she tried to suppress those pains. Since she did not have an owner's manual telling her how the body-mind system functioned, she wound up storing them as biomagnetic charges in the chakra system, where they (1) reinforced her belief about not being a deserving person and (2) intensified the attraction to future unfulfilling relationships. The charges will increase in intensity over time, eventually forcing Annie to completely withdraw from men or confront her issue. The repeated pain of failed relationships brought Annie to the realization that she needed some kind of help, and her two sessions with me put her in touch with the inappropriate belief about herself which attracted those relationships. When she finally decides to confront this issue, in addition to altering her inappropriate belief, she must also neutralize all those biomagnetic charges that would continue to hold her in her old patterns. Deciding to change a belief is a necessary first step, but the pain and trauma caused by events that the belief attracted must also be neutralized for real change to manifest itself.

Though the story was different for Carol, the issues were similar. She was disgusted with her body, a second-chakra issue, but remained in an unhappy marriage for thirty years, a third-chakra issue. Had she stayed in the marriage for the sake of the children or because her negative body image convinced her that this was the best she could expect? Thirty years in an unrewarding marriage was a high price to pay for a negative body image, but apparently it was not high enough for her (or Annie) to confront the pain she has been carrying for several decades.

My suggestion that she work on her body image with diet and exercise would have been an excellent and gentle way for her to begin her journey out of self-disgust. As she gained strength and endurance from the exercise and as she shed the first ten pounds of fat, she would gain mental and emotional strength from those successful efforts. She would have then begun to confront the mental-emotional components of her self-disgust. But for reasons unbeknownst to both of us, she chose not to work with that issue. Regardless of her conscious choice, the issue will continue to work on her.

Many people repress or deny their pain in the mistaken belief that feeling it or expressing it will make it worse. Instead they try to bury it in their subconscious, where it continues to silently play out in brain and nervous system pulsations.

What do these stories and traumatically charged chakras have to do with taking toxins out of the body? *Biomagnetic* means life attracting, and these women, along with every other human being on this planet, are carrying emotional charges coupled with beliefs about themselves that will cause them to attract more of the same traumas into their lives. They will continue to attract pain into their body-mind systems, and that pain will overstimulate the nervous system, which in turn will stimulate or shut off electric signals to muscles, glands, and organs.

Over time these stimulations will alter body shape, destabilize blood-sugar levels and metabolism, trap and block the flow of bodily fluids, and weaken every organ's ability to do its job. A weakened, anxiety-filled body does not produce the energy to effect a deep detoxification in the same manner as a calm, relaxed one. As Annie and Carol carry their internalized pain into middle and old age, their bodies will become tighter and more inclined to hold rather than to release toxins. And where toxins accumulate, disease occurs.

A Happy Ending—Overcoming Lupus

Marian, a homemaker and mother, age thirty-eight, came to me as a referral from Dr. Stuart Tessler, whose light therapy I discuss later in this chapter. Marian was suffering from lupus, a painful joint condition diagnosed by blood titer counts. (A *titer* is a test that determines the count of certain bodily substances, indicating the presence of a disease or condition.) I did an intake and the usual blood, hair, and urine tests. Her test scores indicated a basically healthy person, so cleansing and emotional work could begin within a week or two.

Based on my past experiences with anger- and fear-riddled clients, I told her there was a good chance she could reduce her lupus pain by confronting and releasing her pent-up emotions. I told her that the work would be painful and that she would need all the support she could get. She explained that her husband would be away for another month on an engineering job and that she would wait to have his support available.

True to her word, she returned six weeks later, and we began the process of getting her in touch with her hidden emotions through the use of a simple breathing technique that relaxes the body and increases access to the subconscious, where stuck emotions are held. Stuart's light therapy protocol had already de-stressed her nervous system of much of the tensions stored there over a lifetime of tension, so getting in touch with painful emotions would be a relatively simple task. But I was not prepared for the angry phone call I received from her two days later.

"What kind of terrible human being are you?" she asked.

"What happened, Marian?"

"You know what happened. I feel so much pain; I can't stand it!"

"That's a good thing. Keep doing the exercises, and the pain will pass. You are doing a great job."

"No, no, no. No more pain. I want this to end, and I'm going to call Stuart. You should not be allowed to do this."

Three hours later Stuart called to say that he had heard from Marian. He asked her what I had told her to expect from the therapy, and she repeated that I had said there was a good chance she could significantly reduce her pain if she got in touch with her pent-up emotions. Stuart's retort and Marian's response to that retort cut directly to the core of self-healing.

"Marian, lupus is forever. Bob said your suffering could possibly end in three months if you do the work."

"Lupus is better than this" was her terse response.

If we were handed an owner's manual at birth, that manual would emphatically state, "Don't repress or deny any painful emotion if you wish to avoid disease."

Marian had made up her mind at an early age that she would not feel the pain of outside criticism, just as I had decided that I was willing to take on physical punishment to get my way. All humans do this in their own unique way. The greater the quantity of trauma and abuse in one's life, the sooner a disease will manifest. Reversing that process, allowing the pain to be expressed and resolved, oftentimes restores the organism to health. However, in Marian's (and my) case, that process was painful, and our initial reactions to allowing ourselves to feel the pain were to revert to form: repression, which only made the releasing process more uncomfortable.

The central theme of this book—the proposition that pent-up or denied emotions attract and hold toxins, which in turn cause diseases—is demonstrated in Marian's dilemma of preferring to suffer from that painful disease rather than feeling her stored emotions.

Most humans store pain: the pain of physical competition; the pain of childhood and adolescent stresses; the pain of family and marital stresses; the pain of succeeding and failing, of winning and losing, of gain and loss. We develop our own unique physical holding patterns: tight neck and shoulders, tucked-in tailbone, concave chest, potbelly, and thick thighs among them.

We develop our own unique emotional holding pattern as well: worry attaching itself to the stomach, anger to the liver, fear to the kidneys, joy to the heart, and grief to the lungs. By the time we reach adulthood, most of us have become so accustomed to holding in and denying emotion that we are well into disease-creating patterns that are painful to intrude upon.

Forty-eight hours after she had called Stuart, Marian was back in my office with an apology for her discourteous behavior.

"No apology needed," I assured her. "You got the point and came back. That's all that matters. I've been told by clients on a number of occasions how they hate me for putting them in touch with their suppressed pain. Those who persevered got relief, and those who did not never came back." I then asked what had triggered her fear attack.

"Just lying still and breathing the way you taught me."

"Good. Continue the exercise, and release what's coming up. Listen to what it's saying, and continue to release the fear through the breathing. Do this by the numbers—exactly as I say. The more diligently you perform the exercise, the faster your pain will diminish. There's only so much energy the body can release at one time, and that depends on how concentrated and compacted the energy has become. Since you manifested a seriously debilitating disease, you probably have a lot of compacted stuff."

Marian was out of pain within six weeks, and her blood tests, taken six months later, showed that no lupus titers were present. Technically she was "cured," but I told her that the lupus was her designated driver—a constant, painful reminder that she was glossing over some emotions that required attention. The pain would always reappear when she attempted to hide or deny her fears and anxieties. Her lupus process would always be playing in her subconscious until she eventually disconnected it from her nervous system. Yoga, tai chi, chi kung, and meditation are excellent ongoing assists in repatterning the nervous system.

When I last spoke to her ten years later, she was pain-free and enjoying a career in business.

Light Therapy

Annie and Carol were referrals from Dr. Stuart Tessler, an optometrist by profession and a pioneer in the use of light to reduce stress in the nervous system. Of all the healing modalities I have experienced, his was the most effective over the short term for reducing stress levels and the physical symptoms of stress. Each woman complained of a number of apparently unrelated symptoms: headaches, PMS for Annie, inability to focus and concentrate, acid reflux, chronic fatigue, confusion, and memory loss for Carol. From Myss we learned that chakras are power centers that govern physical systems in the body, and charges from traumas flow into and through the nervous system, directly affecting organ and gland function—hence their physical symptoms.

Stuart calls his approach *Flight or Fight Therapy*, because it alters the ongoing messages that play through the brain and nervous system, holding the body in a constant state of stress and anxiety. By administering a simple test that measures the size of a client's visual field (how wide an area they are capable of seeing while maintaining a steady focus on a single point) and blind spot (the sightless part of every human's visual field), Stuart can determine the amount and intensity of stress held in the nervous system. A diminished visual field and enlarged blind spot reflect an attempt on the part of the individual to deal with a particular painful reality by blocking it out—restricting the visual field in an attempt to see less of life's pain.

Stuart further discovered, by testing the strength or weakness of certain indicator muscles, that he could weaken the patient's body by stimulating the eye with different colors. He referred to the muscle weakness as an allergic response, resulting from exposure to an antagonistic color, which he indicated represented the body's response to the accumulated impact of traumas on the nervous system. These accumulations create an aversion to one or more colors or frequency bandwidths. Stuart then uses this information as the starting point of his therapy. He chooses the most antagonistic color (the one that makes the body the weakest) and has his client stare at it through a funnel for twenty minutes at a time, once or twice a day, over twenty to forty sessions.

This process activates the nervous system to throw off the suppressed emotion attached to the trauma, thus enabling the client to release it. Once the client completes the first round of sessions with the most antagonistic color, Stuart retests, he selects a second antagonistic color, and the client begins the visualization process again. This continues until the client has no more antagonistic reactions. As the traumas subside, the once-collapsed visual field expands to triple or quadruple its original, compressed size, and the symptoms relating to the stored traumas subside as well.

People do not want to feel their stored emotional traumas, which is why they collapse their visual fields in the first place. The collapsed visual field mimics the physical compression of the nervous system as it attempts to withdraw from the repeated pain of life experiences. The light therapy stimulates the release of these emotions by bringing them back into conscious awareness; it is from there that they can be released from the body.

Many of Stuart's clients don't complete the therapy because they won't allow themselves to feel that stored pain even though they were told that their symptoms and problems were related to those pains. Annie and Carol completed the light therapy before coming to me, meaning they were able to release the traumas stored in the nervous system that created their symptoms, but they balked when confronted by their key life issues that helped to attract the traumas. Consequently they will continue to maintain the same outlook on life that created the symptoms in the first place.

Stuart's therapy shows a link between emotional trauma held in the nervous system and physical symptoms. A few days before her last visit with me, Carol reported by phone that her original symptoms had returned. In session she revealed meeting an old boyfriend, which triggered her negative self-image reaction and which in turn caused her to initiate an automatic defense response that again collapsed her visual fields and brought back her old symptoms. All of us have this automatic defense response hardwired into our neural pathways—a programmed response to adversity that began in the womb as the fetus's nervous system responded to the environment of its parents.

Pain—be it physical, mental, or emotional—causes the brain and endocrine system to produce a number of neurochemicals and hormones to increase the body's ability to cope with stress. These neurochemicals and hormones are ideal mechanisms for dealing with infrequent threats such as predators. Life in civilized society presents a host of different challenges—financial issues, relationship issues, marital issues, job security issues—each potentially capable of stimulating the fight-or-flight response several times a day.

Each stimulation creates an adaptation response, which in turn causes a toxic cascade of neurochemicals and hormones that, over time, negatively impact all body functions. Worse, this adaptation response quickly morphs into an automatic defense response in which all body systems and parts respond continuously outside the person's awareness. This is exactly the way Carol's body responded. Psychologists use the terms *suppression* and *denial* to describe this phenomenon, but *automatic defense response* is a more accurate and a less judgmental depiction of that behavior.

The next step in the process is taking up an addictive or obsessive-compulsive behavior: alcohol, drugs, cigarettes, or a behavioral response, such as becoming a workaholic. Think of the narrowing of the visual field as a narrowing of behavioral choices—the smaller the field, the more imbedded and predictable the response to stress and adversity.

With their programmed responses, what is the likelihood that Annie and Carol will attract loving, nurturing relationships in the future? Zero. What is the likelihood that they will attract a negative relationship or no relationship at all with these responses? Certainty. Each woman has fully programmed herself to repeat the past until she consciously decides to interrupt the program and dismantle it.

My experiences with Annie and Carol and Stuart's therapy enabled me to form my fourth law of detoxification:

> ***Suppressing emotional pain and trauma creates energetic blocks in the body that attract and hold toxins. These energetic blocks trap body wastes and fluids, thereby restricting the flow of toxins out of the body. These toxins will be released only when the blocks are dissolved, and the only way to dissolve the blocks is to get in touch with and release the emotional pain they hold.***

The Alphabiotic Alignment

The Alphabiotic Alignment is another extraordinary tool for neutralizing stress patterns. Originally developed in the 1930s by Dr. Virgil Chrane, a West Texas chiropractor, this tool, consisting primarily of a manipulation to decompress the spine, has gained favorable notice over the past twenty years because of the efforts of his son, Dr. Virgil Chrane, Jr., who has taught this technique to hundreds of chiropractors and laypeople through the school he founded, Alphabiotics International, in Dallas, Texas.

Stress shortens ligaments, tightens muscles, compresses spinal vertebrae, and torques the body into assorted shapes—think of hunched-up shoulders, tucked-in tailbones, and twisted spines (scoliosis)—which cause the body to lose strength and functionality.

Cranial nerves that attach the brain to all internal organs must pass through vertebrae to get to their destinations. Compressed and misaligned vertebrae distort and weaken the signals (instructions) generated by the brain that govern the functioning of these organs. Over time these malfunctioning organs break down, first causing acute symptoms such as variations in blood pressure and blood-sugar levels, and later, full-fledged diseases such as diabetes, cancer, and heart disease.

One of the guiding principles of this book is the observation that all chronic degenerative diseases emanate from a buildup of toxins or cause toxic buildup. Stress causes body distortions that lead to spinal distortions that then lead to organ dysfunction. Dysfunctional organs create metabolic errors, which lead to poor breakdown and utilization of nutrients, which in turn lead to toxin buildup, which eventually becomes disease. Metabolic errors include but are not limited to insufficient hydrochloric acid secretion in the stomach, thus impeding protein digestion and assimilation. Another common metabolic error is the under- or over-secretion of insulin, which creates blood-sugar imbalances that could lead to diabetes. From a basic clinical perspective, minimizing the physical impact of stress is a crucial part of the healing process, and the Alphabiotic Alignment accomplishes that task faster and less expensively than any other technique I have experienced.

As I state throughout this book, detoxification (and healing) requires energy, the willingness to change attitudes, and the willingness to get in touch with and release pent-up emotions. The alignment generates an instant signal disrupt—a partial or complete cessation of stress messages coursing through the nervous system. This disruption creates an opportunity for the muscles to let go of the tension they have been holding, which then allows the body structure to realign itself back toward a healthier, stronger posture for a few hours or days, depending on the intensity of the issues and emotions stimulating the stress response. This new posture creates an internal listening space in which the stressed-out individual can access the mental-emotional content of the stresses at the subconscious level—the key element in the healing and consciousness-raising process.

Stress is a response to outside stimuli based on a mental-emotional predisposition that is deeply embedded in the nervous system, most likely since birth. In other words *stress* is a preconditioned response based on beliefs, attitudes, perceptions, and one's emotional attachment to them. By the time we have reached adulthood, these messages and emotions have become so deeply embedded in our subconscious that we don't know they exist. Signal disruption is the single most vital skill that the aspirant must develop in order to perform the arduous process of self-examination—the only way to permanently alter nervous-system and brain programs that are a primary source of our diseases and addictions.

I refer to this activity as "keeping the pipe open." My body typically reacts to stress by tensing all its muscles as if it were bracing to receive a punch—a reflex I programmed into myself in response to childhood beatings. Over time this muscle tensing became my fight-or-flight response to all stressors. In this defensive posture, the pipe is closed. There is no subconscious communication—only an aggressive, defensive response to a perceived threat. Until I can back off physically, mentally, and emotionally from this response, no growth, no healing, no alteration in consciousness is possible. Having continuous access to Alphabiotic Alignments will greatly accelerate the consciousness-raising process and reduce the pain and symptomology caused by the stress.

Addictions

According to Myss, the body is formed from energetic patterns laid down in the chakra system. These patterns combine with information contained in the genetic material of both parents to initiate the programming of the fetus's nervous system. As the fetus develops, its nervous system begins to react to inputs from the emotional and physical environment of the parents. By the time the fetus is ready to start life on its own, its nervous system has created neural networks and synaptic firing patterns that release neurochemicals and hormones to cope with the environment it will share with its parents.

Contained in the genetic material of the parents is the genetic material of their ancestors for several generations. Built into all of this genetic material is an automatic flight-or-fight response to life-threatening situations, the all-important survival mechanism without which our species would have perished centuries ago. Knowing when to run from a dangerous predator and generating the physical means to do so is an important survival trait. But when the mind broadens the flight-or-fight response to include the non-life-threatening inputs of modern civilization into its survival matrix, it begins to construct larger neural networks to handle the increase in flight-or-fight traffic. As these networks grow in space and intensity within the brain, they form the dominant response to any antagonistic stimulus, replete with damaging neurochemicals and hormonal secretions—the automatic defense response I mentioned earlier.

Over time the body-mind loses its ability to distinguish between serious threats and simple problems. Any difficulty becomes an opportunity for the automatic defense response to kick in, causing a cascade of emotions and chemicals that spread their tentacles throughout the nervous system, disrupting metabolic functions; tightening muscles, ligaments, and tendons; blocking the orderly flow of fluids; and trapping toxins in fats, tumors, and joints. As this automatic defense response deepens, the body-mind begins to explore ways of lessening the pain.

In my case I found by age fifteen that alcohol silenced my mother's perpetually screeching voice inside my head, and desiring that silence to be permanent, I promised myself that I would never be without it. I later replaced that addiction with marijuana—a far less debilitating drug that did a superior job without the hangover.

Addiction is defined as "the state of being enslaved to a habit or practice that is psychologically or physically habit-forming, as narcotics, to such an extent that its cessation causes severe trauma."[4-5] I do not distinguish between behavioral and chemical addictions as the law does.

Have you ever seen someone with obsessive-compulsive disorder (OCD) try to break a habit? What about the workaholic who has no time for family? These are adaptation responses to pent-up stresses and traumas, just like my alcohol and marijuana addictions were adaptation responses. The list of possible adaptation responses is endless: work, power, money, food, sex, shopping, exercise, cutting, all compulsive behaviors, cigarettes, alcohol, and drugs (both legal and illegal). While some addictions are legal and socially acceptable, all addictions are inappropriate adaptations that increase the body's production of harmful chemicals and do nothing to solve the organism's basic problem: a nervous system overloaded with stress and trauma patterns.

Chapter Summary

In this chapter I have attempted, in a simplified way, to link the functioning of the physical body to its occupant's spiritual purpose and life experiences. The fetus emerges from the womb with a fully formed response pattern to its parents' physical and emotional circumstances imbedded in its nervous system. This response pattern has already created programmed neurochemical responses to its parental environment that will influence the way it will think, behave, react, and feel as a fully developed human being.

Since environments and emotional responses don't change quickly, the newly born human can expect to lay down similar neural networks as its life experience unfolds. By the time it reaches adolescence, these neural networks and their biochemical by-products have been hardwired into a body that has already begun to shape itself to reflect its emotional adaptation to life. From this point onward, the organism will mechanically respond to its life experiences in a manner dictated by these neural programs until such time as it consciously decides to change itself.

Consider the profound impact this natal and childhood programming has on human behavior, especially in our high-stress modern world. We grow into adulthood with fully developed response mechanisms based on our interactions with parents, teachers, and playmates, who have been similarly programmed. Layered on top of these socializing agendas are programs for coping with unprecedented amounts of petrochemical and heavy-metal toxins, programs for coping with war and conflict, programs for coping with depressions and recessions, and programs for coping with high-volume electronic pollution. All of these programs increase the amount of stress and toxic chemicals housed in the nervous system and the body.

Chapter Five

What Does This Mean for You?

Not only have we been powerfully programmed by our highly stressed-out parents who have spent their entire lives inhaling petrochemical and electronic pollutants, we have also added our own more intense toxic exposures to the toxins we have inherited.

Humankind began burning hydrocarbons for energy about 170 years ago, and now these pollutants threaten our survival as a species. Compared to our ancestors of two hundred years ago, we are mutants. We live longer because we've eliminated infectious disease, decreased infant mortality rates, and improved disease care, but we are not healthier. We now have the highest rates of ADHD and ADD, autism, allergies, mental disorders, cancer, diabetes, Alzheimer's disease, and heart disease in our species' history. Many of these conditions did not exist two hundred years ago. We stay around longer, but we get sicker younger.

Chances are that you have been battling some physical, mental, or emotional problem since early childhood. Your body has been bombarded by mercury-laced vaccinations. These, in combination with a chronic lifetime exposure to electronic and petrochemical toxins and what you inherited from your parents and earlier ancestors, have permanently compromised your immune system. Unlike your parents, who appeared healthy for most of their lives, you have been bothered by nagging symptoms and sensitivities for most of yours. To paraphrase Bill Maher of *Politically Incorrect* fame: many conditions that used to be rare have now been mainstreamed: asthma, autism, acid reflux, arthritis, allergies, adult acne, attention deficit disorder—and that's just the *A*s.

I was born in 1939, a few years before poisoning our environment became big business. My parents, born in the early 1900s in rural Ireland, had almost zero exposure to petrochemicals, pesticides, and electricity, so I came out of the womb with my genes and immune system intact. Forty years later, however, I passed my toxic exposures on to my son, and he has environmental sensitivities my wife and I don't have. All toxic exposures are held in our DNA, blood, and tissues and are passed on to the gestating fetus. Newborn babies have tested positive for the same toxic chemicals and drugs their parents ingested, even though they had no direct environmental exposures to those toxins.

Most of the doctors I speak with on a regular basis report that their patients are getting sicker at a younger age and with a wider range of symptoms than the previous generation had. What price will *your* children pay for your environmental abuses? Based on the lack of government response to the buildup of pollutants, your children will have to cope with an even more hostile environment.

In adversity there is opportunity. As you have probably already discovered, you have little room for error in choosing your foods, liquids, and lifestyle. Eat in a Chinese restaurant that uses MSG, and your body bloats. The seasons change, and you start sneezing. Get a whiff of car exhaust, and you start coughing. Use the wrong detergent or cleaning agent, and your skin breaks out in a rash. That's the adversity.

The opportunity is that you must take steps to strengthen your immune system if you wish to remain healthy and functional. If you are fortunate, your symptoms can inspire you to take steps to neutralize them by exercising regularly and adopting a healthy diet. You soon notice that you are feeling better and thinking more clearly. You may even want to take your process further and read a book, such as this one, that teaches you how to remove toxins from your body. Then you can initiate an intensive detoxification program, and within a few months, you discover my fifth law of detoxification:

> ***The greater the amount of toxins stored in your body, the more sensitive you are to environmental onslaughts and the less capable you become at coping with stressful situations. Conversely, the lower the toxic levels in your body, the less reactive and better able you are to cope.***

Total body detoxification is a health-building, disease-sparing procedure that has become a necessity for maintaining healthy mental, physical, and emotional function. I suggest that you look into ways to develop an inner communication that will enable you to identify and release your suppressed emotions to optimize your efforts at releasing toxins from your body. Many new disciplines for energetically releasing stored emotions have been developed over the past twenty years, and I plan to write a second book dealing directly with inappropriate and limiting beliefs, attitudes, and emotions and ways to safely release them.

Shamans, Native American medicine men, Buddhist monks, Taoist practitioners, and yogis have spoken and written about an alternative inner reality that is free of the burdens that we carry in our ordinary waking reality. Traditionally an aspirant achieved this alternative reality after years of dedicated yogic, meditative, and purification practices under the guidance of a guru or a teacher.

Today we can apply our understanding of science and technology to the teachings of these yogis with a plan to learn how they impact the mind and body. It turns out that all of these practices change the neural wiring that holds old programs in place.[5-1] Surprise, Surprise! This vital information has been available to humankind for several thousand years, and now it is resurfacing in a format that modern humans (and modern medicine) can understand.

Can we as a species take a great step forward? We have pinned ourselves against an implacable wall from which we can only move forward or perish. Global warming threatens earth's ability to sustain life, and toxic by-products from petrochemicals impair the ability of all species to procreate. Toxins from thousands of manufactured products invade every cell in our bodies, causing allergic reactions that weaken our immune and nervous systems. We have killed, raped, plundered, and poisoned throughout our history. We have attempted to bend natural law to conform to our lusts for power and wealth, and now we have come to the end of our tether. What we do from here on out, as individuals and as a species, will seriously impact our quality of life and earth's ability to sustain itself. Our adversity has created an incredible opportunity for those willing to seize it.

Chapter Six

Triaging, Toxins, and Biochemistry

In emergency medicine, *triaging* is defined as the categorizing and administering to injured victims according to the seriousness of their injuries. This rations treatments when resources are insufficient to treat all victims immediately and maximizes chances for survival of the victims. Dr. Bruce Ames, a leading researcher in the development of strategies to reverse the diseases of aging, has developed a theory on the triaging of nutrients in the body. In order to provide the organism and species with the best chance to survive, short term reproductive needs and health maintenance get first call on nutrients; all other functions get what is left. In a recent interview printed in *Life Extension Magazine*, Ames stated that the body requires forty essential micronutrients to adequately perform the functions required to maintain health. According to Ames:

> *If you are even modestly deficient in one of the essential micronutrients, your body has to "ration" them in terms of priority. Under this scenario, the body will always direct nutrients toward short-term health and reproductive capability and away from regulation and repair of cellular DNA and proteins that increase longevity. This means that while your body may be providing nutritional support in an effort to sustain system-wide physiological function and reproduction, at the cellular level, the process of decay and death is accelerating.*[6-1]

In light of this discovery and given the increasingly higher intake of factory-farmed, genetically modified, irradiated, pesticide-laden, and antibiotic-laden foods by an uninformed public, it is easy to understand why the population of the United States has become fatter and sicker than any other cultural group. Ames also wrote:

> *Micronutrient intake below recommended concentrations, but not severe enough to cause overt clinical symptoms, is widespread not only in poor countries but also in the United States (especially in the poor, children, adolescents, the obese, and the elderly), in part because of the high consumption of calorie-rich, micronutrient-poor, unbalanced diets.*[6-2]

The American Diabetes Association estimates that one in three children born in the United States will become diabetic in adulthood. (Diabetes was so unknown in 1900 that my researchers could not find any statistics relating to the occurrence and mortality rates. Apparently the disease did not occur frequently enough to land on anyone's radar screen).

The significance of Ames' findings for our younger generations is that they are incurring more physical, mental and emotional disturbances at younger ages that require greater amounts of medical and psychological support. This is good for the pharmaceutical industry but a huge drag on societal resources. For individuals entering the middle and later stages of their lives, this means more frequent physical and mental breakdowns, requiring extensive medication to relieve. While children may be limited by peer and economic pressures to consuming school lunches and Big Macs; informed adults can make significant dietary adjustments to insure that they are consuming nutrient dense foods and food supplements that support longevity promoting processes in the body. Personally I have found that the older I get, the more nutritional support I require, especially digestive and detoxification supports, because my organs of digestion and detoxification are not as efficient as they were thirty years ago.

Throughout the remainder of this book you will be reading about the role of vitamins, minerals, fatty acids, enzymes, amino acids, phytonutrients, antioxidants, and food supplements in supporting organs and detoxification processes.

Methylation

From the previous section, we learned that the body prioritizes nutrient utilization according to survival and reproductive needs, and it uses an internal body process known as methylation to accomplish this. Methylation is a chemical conversion procedure that takes place thousands of times each second. In this procedure micronutrients from foods are combined with methyl groups (a methyl group consists of one carbon atom and three hydrogen atoms) to convert nutrients into chemicals that the body can utilize to support and sustain all its functions. Methyl groups are made in a metabolic pathway from dietary nutrients. To get an idea of what happens when food enters metabolic pathways, visualize a Cuisinart where, by changing speeds and attachments, you can cut, blend, slice, dice, chop, and mix foods to obtain a desired product output. In a somewhat similar fashion, the body sorts through proteins, carbohydrates, and fats; identifies the micronutrients; and rearranges them into chemicals that fit into whatever body need is ranked first on the triage board. Nutrients like folic acid, B vitamins, and

SAMe are key components of the methyl-making pathway and therefore are instrumental in the body being able to methylate properly.

The subject of methylation is far too complex to cover in this book and would require the writer and reader to hold an advanced degree in organic chemistry in order to communicate and understand the precise pathways governing these chemical transformations. Nutritional inadequacies affect the methylation cycle in the body, which leads to chronic illness, serious health conditions, as well as advanced aging. The following examples taken from "The Many Faces of Methylation Defects," a seminar given by Dr. William Billica,[6-3] will convey a few of the vital body functions affected by methylation processes:

1. Inadequate methylation has been proven to be involved in fibromyalgia, hormone disorders, cancer, neurodegenerative disorders of all types, dementia, and premature ageing.
2. Inadequate and excessive methylation processes are involved in the formation of diabetes, metal detox, hormone balances, neurologic inflammation, chronic infections, autism, Alzheimer's disease and dementia, and autoimmune disorders.
3. One-third of all cancer mutations have been formed at methylation cluster sites.
4. Inadequate methylation can alter activation of viral sequences inserted into our genes.
5. Fetal development disorders emanate from compromised methylation pathways.
6. Compromised methylation pathways cause inadequate homocysteine detoxification, thereby increasing the risk of stroke and heart disease.
7. Heavy metals impair all the methylation enzyme sites, different metals for different sites.
8. Blocked methylation pathways increase allergic responses of all types.

Methylation figures prominently in gene mutations. Epigenetics is the study of heritable changes in gene expression without a physical change in DNA structure—something that can occur with impaired methylation of DNA (See chapter fifteen for further insight into the science of epigenetics.) Since the late 1990s, Dr. Amy Yasko has been at the forefront of gene mutation diagnostics and the development of nutritional protocols to compensate for imbalances in the resultant methylation and related pathways. Most large blood-draw laboratories throughout the United States now offer tests for several genetic mutations. Yasko maintains that gene mutations provide a disposition toward a disease, but environmental toxins, stress, and exposure to infectious agents play a role in the manifestation and severity of that disease. In one case study, she detailed an autistic girl with severe genetic mutations who exhibited only a mild form of the condition, noting that the child was never fully vaccinated and fed an organic diet.

Yasko's website[6-4] offers a full genetic panel and self-help for understanding results and implementing an appropriate nutritional program.

Environmental toxicity is a factor in the mutation of gene expression and alteration of methylation pathways. Humankind began using petrochemicals 170 years ago at a time when it could not understand the devastating influence those chemicals would have on health and the environment. In the decades that followed and well after the systemic dangers of petrochemical pollution had been well established, manufacturers were producing thousands of derivative chemicals, each capable of wiping out native populations and the lands that supported them.

In the next few years, we will begin to chronicle the physical devastation wrought upon the human race by our failure to ignore escalating rates of chronic degenerative diseases and ecological disasters and their possible connection to petrochemical use. As the meaning of the word *methylation* begins to creep into community awareness through books, periodicals, and the Internet,[6-5] the human race will develop new biomarkers from which to assess the real cost of fossil fuel energy when escalating disease rates, genetic deterioration, and human performance are factored into the equation.

We modern humans are confronting two major threats to our survival, both of which can (and will) annihilate us, unless we reduce petrochemical use, eat better food, and detoxify, detoxify, detoxify. The methylation problems mentioned earlier are either caused by or cause toxic buildup somewhere in the body. With 60 percent of Americans presenting inadequate methylation pathways in recently designed clinical tests, it is easy to conclude that our species-wide exposure to petrochemical and heavy-metal toxins has caused significant variations in modern-day genetic blueprints from those of our ancestors. While we may appear to be bigger, faster, and stronger than previous generations, our physical and mental health profiles attest to our getting sicker younger, with greater numbers of our young people experiencing mental and emotional breakdowns.

Nutritional Guidelines

Computer programmers are fond of quoting an axiom that goes back to the time when computers were first invented: "garbage in, garbage out." If you input faulty information, you will get faulty information back. The same axiom applies to the human body. No amount of exercise and detoxification will offset the damage created by a prolonged intake of addictive substances and toxic foods. Whether you have been encouraged to do so by a professional health practitioner or you have decided on your own to embark on a total body detoxification program, you should have some understanding of the relationship between food and the body with a plan to change the eating habits that are harmful to your body.

Hippocrates, a famous physician who lived in ancient Greece, was reported to have said, "Let your food be your medicine." He was not talking about the garbage offered in fast-food restaurants and commercial supermarkets that contain chemicals, trans fats, and toxic residues from pesticides. All foods are not created equal, and most that are sold in supermarkets and fast-food chains throughout the country are decidedly harmful, especially the stuff that comes in packages. If it does not look the way God made it, perhaps you shouldn't eat it.

A wholesome diet is essential for optimum health and detoxification. Even modest deficiencies of some nutrients limit the body's ability to repair and rejuvenate. Lack of nutrition, GMOs, and estrogens from food block methylation pathways. With impaired methylation the body's energy-producing system is comprised, and it does not detoxify; therefore its immune system and the regulation of hormones and neurotransmitters is compromised. Detoxification does not work if you continue on a diet of bad food. Everything you take out of your body will be back in again the next day, and the older you get, the worse the problem becomes. As you age your body becomes less adept at processing food and ridding itself of toxic chemicals. Eating wholesome food and eliminating addictive habits are essential first steps in following and completing a productive total body detoxification program.

The following are general guidelines that will hold you in good stead. If you have health challenges, I suggest that you work with a qualified health practitioner. Wholesome foods and proper supplementation can do wonders in boosting the body's energy level and reducing symptoms, and a health practitioner—specially trained medical doctors, chiropractors, naturopaths, and nutritionists—can perform the necessary lab tests to determine your specific needs. I say, "Specially trained," because medical doctors and chiropractors have to learn these skills after they graduate. Unfortunately they are not part of medical or chiropractic school regimens.

General Nutrition Guidelines

One through seven are the don'ts. When you successfully incorporate them into your daily life, your health will improve considerably, and many of your allergy-based symptoms will diminish or vanish entirely.

1. Eliminate refined flour and sugar from your diet as much as possible, especially if you have weight or blood-sugar problems. Included in this category are all breads and pastas made from refined flour, sodas, candies, cakes, pies, ice cream, syrups, potatoes, and refined rice (white rice has the outer husk, where the real nutrients are, sanded off). These foods cause blood sugar to rise rapidly, forcing the pancreas to produce excess insulin. This eventually creates cellular insulin resistance, a precursor to metabolic disorder and type 2 diabetes. More importantly, these foods are the primary cause of weight gain.[6-6] In my opinion refined and processed flours and sugars are as lethal to body health and performance as any drug. See my discussion later on metabolic syndrome.
2. Eliminate all foods containing trans fats. These include foods cooked or processed in vegetable oil (except olive oil which does not contain any trans fats).
3. Eliminate foods containing excitotoxins (additives such as aspartame, hydrolyzed protein, MSG, and artificial sweeteners), which over time will seriously impair nervous-system function. Stevia and xylitol are excellent sweeteners that do not stimulate insulin reactions.
4. Keep caffeine and alcohol intake down as much as you can. Caffeine stresses the adrenal glands, and alcohol raises blood-sugar levels in addition to its inebriating effects. One or two cups of coffee and one or two glasses of wine a day won't hurt most people—at least not until they get into their fifties and sixties. Green tea is an excellent caffeine substitute for coffee, but even though I have access to high-quality teas, I admit that I much prefer a cup of coffee.
5. Do not drink pasteurized cow's milk, and keep your intake of other dairy products to a minimum. Most humans are allergic to dairy products, and they leave high amounts of mucous residues in the body, especially in the small intestine and colon. Several long-lived cultures consume dairy products in a fermented state, like yogurt and kefir, which means they have been predigested by their own enzymes. That allows them to be easily assimilated by the human digestive system.
6. Limit your intake of grains and starches. Wheat and soy are common allergens, and grains are high-calorie foods not recommended for those with slow metabolisms and weight problems.
7. Most drugs—whether prescription, over-the-counter, or street—create serious metabolic disturbances, hence the side effects

listed in the *Physicians' Desk Reference*. Some medications are necessary to sustain life, but you should seek out alternatives that are less disturbing to body processes when you can. If you are on life-sustaining medications or medications that cannot be replaced with benign alternatives, don't despair. Follow these guidelines as best you can. A diet of wholesome food will always benefit the body, and junk food will always hurt it.

Joseph Brady, an instructor and gerontology researcher at the Colorado University School of Health Sciences, told me several years ago that the average healthy sixty-five-year-old is on five medications; if unhealthy, eleven. Many of those medications moderate some mental-health aspect that could be ameliorated in some other fashion, for instance by exercise, meditation, yoga, relaxation, yoga nidra, or diet modification.

For those who want to take their game a step further, here are some dos:

1. Try as best as your budget and location permit to eat organically raised foods. They are more expensive than commercially grown foods, but their nutritive content is much higher, and especially in the case of animal products, the toxic content is less.
2. Food supplements are nutrient-dense products that supplement daily dietary intake. Many of our foods are nutritionally depleted, especially commercially grown fruits and vegetables, because of overfarming and pesticide use. Additionally we are subject to unprecedented physical and mental stresses from our lifestyles and environments, and these require a higher nutrient intake to mitigate.
3. Keep stress at a minimum. I can't emphasize this enough. I lived a high-stress life up until age sixty-five. Looking back I developed metabolic syndrome at age sixty, and my health completely caved in five years later when my liver crashed.

Although I stopped playing professional poker and taking street drugs at age forty-three, I continued to push myself and test my mental and physical limits up to my liver collapse. I thought I had minimized my alcohol consumption, but as I look back, I realize that I had been drinking more than twenty ounces of alcohol a week over three or four evenings—not enough to separate me from my senses but more than my liver could tolerate after fifty years of abuse.

I started a new business in 2000, and by 2004 I was up to my eyeballs in a major lawsuit with a nasty competitor. Although I exercised and ate correctly most of the time, my alcohol intake increased, and my liver function became severely impaired. My body felt weak and lethargic, and my skin turned a yellow brown. The powerful energy machine that had withstood lifelong abuse finally said, "No more." Fortunately I had the expertise and technology to recover, but my energy level is nowhere near what it was in 2000.

As a result of that crash, I was forced to live within a limited energy output, which in turn forced me to discontinue alcohol and develop meditation and contemplation practices to neutralize the stresses in my life. A stressful life results in an accumulation of compensation patterns throughout the body and mind. A tucked-in tailbone and dowager's hump are examples of compensation patterns in the physical body; high blood pressure, shaky leg syndrome, and panic attacks are examples of compensation patterns in the mind expressed as physical symptoms. These patterns build and intensify as we age—their messages playing subconsciously even when we sleep. I believe that these accumulated patterns form the basis for the increasing rate of mental-emotional breakdowns among the elderly and their increasing use of mental-health medications.

The two biggest mistakes I made in my fifties were continuing to play demanding competitive sports (until I broke my wrist in a collision on the basketball court) and not allowing for the natural decline of my body's metabolic processes that take place as we age.

My first mistake created a permanent knee weakness and serious pain along my left arm, from the wrist to the middle of the scapula. The second mistake caused my liver to crash and my cells to develop insulin resistance. Living with mistake number one means I can't run for long distances or perform certain lifting exercises. Living with mistake number two means I cannot consume alcohol and cannot eat any refined carbohydrates without putting on weight.

Overall, these restrictions are not a bad deal, considering the lifelong abuse that created them. They force me to make a conscious choice every day: do I want joint pain and a fat gut, or do I want to live in peace and harmony with my body? Pain is pain, and a fat gut decreases mobility and may breed cancer and diabetes. I find the healthy way to be the easiest way. Everyone must come to that same decision point. The macho-man, tough-guy approach only added to my aging burden.

Part II

Disease and Healing

Chapter Seven

Disease Begins in the Colon

Dr. Bernard Jensen made the pronouncement that disease begins in the colon a mere twenty-seven years ago in his groundbreaking book *Tissue Cleansing through Bowel Management*.[7-1] The chart on page 62 of the digestive system (figure 2) shows the complex pathway food takes from ingestion in the mouth to its final destination through the anus. From the mouth, food goes to the stomach, where hydrochloric acid and pepsin break proteins into their amino-acid constituents. Food then goes to the duodenum, where the bolus (food ball) is mixed with several pancreatic enzymes to break down carbohydrates, fats, and proteins. Then this food travels through twenty feet of small intestine, where it is absorbed and assimilated into the bloodstream and liver. It then takes its final journey through five feet of large intestine at the end of which waste and partially digested remnants are eliminated through the anus.

What took humankind so long to figure out that the functioning of the organ responsible for removing the bulk of the body's toxic waste solids had a prime influence on overall health and vitality? And what took them so long to figure out that inefficient toxic waste removal might be a primary cause of a number of painful and debilitating diseases?

Duh! If food is not chewed sufficiently, it will not be completely broken down. If the stomach does not produce enough hydrochloric acid (a common occurrence), proteins will not be broken down into amino acids and therefore won't be utilized by the body. If the pancreas does not produce sufficient amounts of amylase, protease, and lipase—enzymes that help to digest carbohydrates, proteins, and fats respectively—these foods will not be broken down and assimilated.

Putrefying proteins and fermenting carbohydrates can leave as many as thirty-six toxic chemicals in their wake as they churn through the small and large intestines. To neutralize the impact of these chemicals, the large intestine produces a thick, yellow mucous that encases the toxins and literally glues them to the colon wall, thus narrowing the space available for fecal matter to pass through. Toxic material from a clogged colon can seep through a leaky bowel wall and can cause havoc anywhere blood travels in the body. Bowel tissue deteriorates and thins when the organ becomes clogged with fecal matter or in the presence of harmful bacteria. No organ or body system

Digestive System

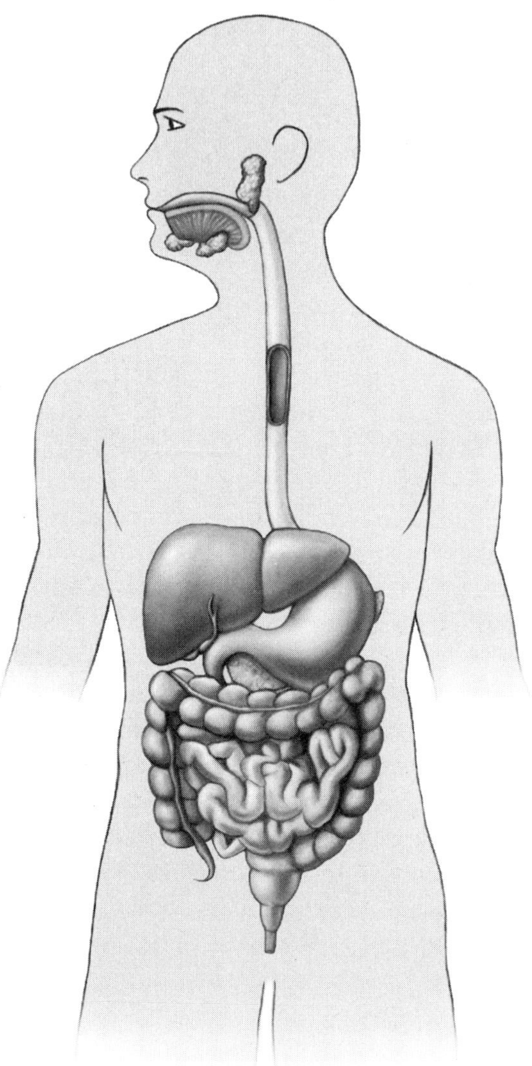

Figure 2

is exempt from the ravages of these leaking toxins. Erratic and infrequent bowel movements exacerbate all the processes previously mentioned and create opportunities for microorganism and yeast proliferation.

Figure 3 shows material expelled from an impacted colon as the result of an intense cleanse.

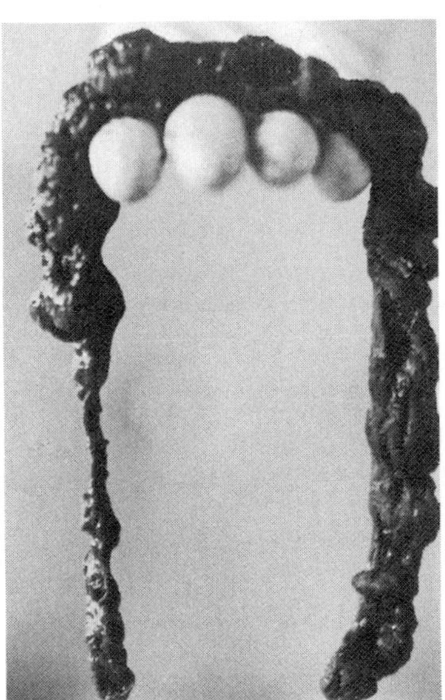

Figure 3: Material expelled from impacted colon

I have not examined these fecal masses personally, so I can only repeat what I have read about their origin and consistency. "A tar-like mass with the consistency of an automobile tire" was the most common description. Partially digested food gets stuck in the mucous that is lining the entire large intestine. The food decays and degrades, creating toxins and also sustenance for harmful bacteria to consume. The colon produces another mucous layer to protect itself from being infected by the toxins housed in the first layer, and this process repeats itself over and over, distending the bowel until it can no longer function. Figures 4 and 5 show photos of a normal colon and a badly distended colon respectively.

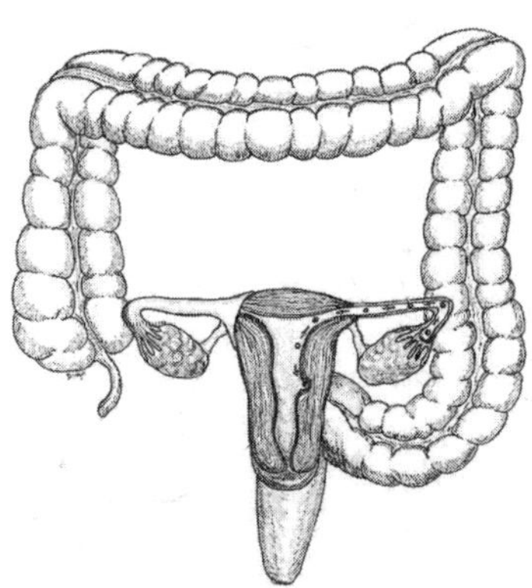

Figure 4: Normal Colon

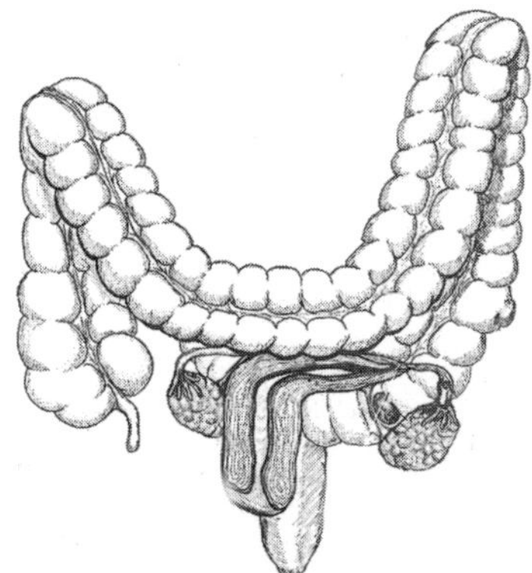

Figure 5: Distended Colon

When the colon attains this latter shape, disease cannot be far behind.

To put bowel health into proper perspective, I took an informal survey on a New York City street corner. I counted the number of men over forty with protruding abdomens. (Toxic men typically grow guts, while women spread the toxicity to thighs, butt, and gut.) Then I compared that percentage with a similar survey taken at a King Soopers supermarket in Denver. New York City registered twenty-one "protruders" out of 100, versus forty out of 100 in the Denver supermarket.

According to my unofficial survey, approximately 30 percent of men over forty have a protruding gut—an indication that their bowels may be distended or impacted. Add to that the number of adults who don't experience regular daily bowel movements—virtually every client I saw in my practice—and we can make a case that most adults suffer some form of bowel malfunction. Interestingly New Yorkers walk to many of their destinations, while Denverites ride everywhere. Could routine daily exercise play a role in bowel health? I am betting yes.

I expanded my Denver survey to include clientele walking into Whole Foods, an organic-food supermarket, and found that the Whole Foods clientele had a profile similar to that of the New York walkers, with nineteen out of 100 obviously overweight. In this comparison the reasons for the discrepancy between King Soopers and Whole Foods shoppers appears obvious: organic foods cost more and therefore attract a more affluent and probably better-educated clientele who spend more money and expend more energy on their health and well-being.

Life is not fair in that educated people with some discretionary income do have advantages over their uneducated counterparts, but colon care, good eating habits, and exercise routines can be taught to the population at large. The savings to a society in danger of being crushed by mounting health-care costs would be astronomical, but no one seems to care.

One Size Does Not Fit All

Rather than recommend a specific colon-care program, I thought I would describe my own colon-reclamation experiences, the first one took place soon after my lung-cancer diagnosis at age forty-three in 1982.

I had been to a nutritionist and was adjusting to his dietary restrictions and food-supplement regimen when he suggested that I do a series of colonics to clean out what he guessed was a highly impacted bowel. As I mentioned earlier, he believed from my test results that I had microorganisms and yeast in the bowel; my adrenals were exhausted; I had metabolic syndrome; I had slightly elevated blood sugar; I had high levels of aluminum, cadmium, and mercury; and I had an inability to digest food properly. Each of these issues was being addressed by my food choices, supplements, and eating schedule, but the colon cleanse would be necessary if I wanted to make real progress in rebuilding my health.

After I completed my first colonic, I felt like someone had stuck an eggbeater up my butt and turned it on full power. I had so much abdominal discomfort that I could not walk upright when I left the therapist's office. Looking back I realized that my colon had hardened over the years with accumulated layers of mucous and putrefied fecal matter. The water from the colonic device literally forced a pathway through the hardened wall of the large intestine, like stretching an atrophied muscle that hasn't moved for years. The effort left a painful residue in my lower abdomen that took a day or two to get over. (Modern colonic devices do not resort to this kind of force, which could and probably did increase fecal-matter leakage through the bowel wall into the bloodstream.) Undaunted I returned for many more colonics, once a week for the next year and once a month for six years after that. The bowel wall softened, and my discomfort vanished in the next few sessions.

I added hydrochloric acid (HCL) and food-enzyme supplements to improve digestion, and I added kefir, which is a fermented milk product, and probiotics to build and maintain healthy intestinal flora. Food-enzyme supplements increase the body's ability to digest fats, carbohydrates, and proteins, and kefir in its fermented form has been predigested by beneficial bacteria for easy assimilation. The HCL supplement never felt good, so I quickly discontinued it. A few weeks later, I discovered Swedish bitters, an HCL herbal stimulant, and that has worked well for me.

In addition to prodigious amounts of vitamins, minerals, and antioxidants, I took herbs to detoxify the liver, gallbladder, blood, kidneys, lungs, and urinary tract. I read all the available material on total body detoxification (there wasn't much), and my personal experience confirmed what authors, such as Jensen, were writing about the bowel—that it is the main event in a detoxification process. How can one clean the organs, lymph, and blood effectively if the colon can't eliminate toxins efficiently? Toxins will simply recycle through the blood to other areas of the body if their main way out is blocked.

It took me seven years to recover sufficiently to resume playing basketball. I knew within six months of starting my recovery that I was going to survive the cancer. My energy had increased, my mind began to function better, and my mood became upbeat and positive. The physical detoxification paved the way for the far more arduous and demanding emotional detoxification that followed.

I abandoned my physical detoxification efforts in the 1990s, although I continued to take large amounts of food supplements. It was time to build a practice and raise my son, so I did what most people do: I relegated my health concerns to a lower priority and made the mistake of thinking that food supplements and diet by themselves would take care of me.

In 2000, I was introduced to a primitive ionizing footbath from Australia, and that rejuvenated my interest in detoxification. By then I had developed a full-blown case of osteoarthritis in all the joints used during my basketball-playing days, but frequent treatments in the footbath eliminated the pain and restored my mobility. Then in December 2004, my liver crashed from a combination of business stress and heavy alcohol intake. It was time to return to basics.

I had been working with the ionizing footbath since early 2000 and liked the results, especially the fact that it ameliorated joint pain. But as good as the technology was, it was no match for the stress and alcohol consumption that had been dominating my life since I started my business. I immediately eliminated alcohol intake and set about rebuilding my liver with supporting and detoxifying herbs—milk thistle for the liver, red clover and stillingia for the blood, black walnut for the colon—but it wasn't until I went back to colonics at the end of 2007 that my energy and mental clarity fully returned. In my concern about the liver, I had forgotten about the important role the colon played in maintaining health and vitality. With the liver unable to process nutrition properly, my colon and lower abdomen became bloated with all manner of toxic waste that was obviously contributing to an ongoing mental and physical fatigue.

In October 2007, I had a series of eight colonics in the office of a colonic therapist, each of which took seventy-five minutes to complete. From my perch on the therapist's table, I had a clear view of the material flowing out of me. For the first five sessions, all I saw was thick, yellow mucous, some of it encasing black, slithery objects that the therapist identified as parasites. I finally got to a black layer of fecal matter in the middle of session six, and that was quickly followed by another flow of yellow mucous. Session seven brought up another layer of black substance, which was followed by more mucous. Session eight brought up yet another layer of black, but this was followed by clear water. My bowel was finally clear to its wall.

The therapist ended each session with an injection of pre- and probiotic solution to recolonize the bowel with beneficial bacteria. I added a black-walnut and wormwood tincture to my nutrition regimen as soon as the parasites were discovered, and they disappeared from view by the third colonic.

Other Colon-Care Techniques

Most people don't have easy access to a colon therapist, especially in small- to medium-sized towns, and colonics can be expensive for those with no discretionary income. The cheapest and second-best way to accomplish what I did would be to purchase a Colema Board, which will allow you to lie at a downward slant, permitting your self-administered enema to travel through the transverse and descending colons. You may add herbal and fiber supplements to your enema or your diet to accelerate the cleanse. Colema Boards and herb therapies can be found on the Internet. Type "colon therapy" or "Colema Board" and search. I've used Colema Boards with some success, but I have not used any herbal therapy that claims to dissolve impacted fecal matter.

Colon-Care Controversies

I reviewed all the criticisms of colon therapy on the Quackwatch website (www.quackwatch.com) and found the quality of the criticism completely lacking in substance. Dr. Stephen Barrett, the founder of Quackwatch, offers the unsubstantiated testimony of an older woman who died from liver failure eight months after perforating her colon during a colonic. That doesn't make sense. Couldn't the doctors patch the perforation or remove that section of the bowel? How did they know the colonic was the cause of the perforation, and what does the perforation have to do with the liver failing eight months later? Barrett or his references didn't say.

He also talks about several colon therapists being prosecuted by the Texas attorney general for either practicing without the proper credentials or making false or misleading claims. There are many well-meaning, poorly trained people who are practicing modalities that they do not fully understand and who make unwise and misleading statements about the healing effects of that modality.

Regulatory authorities such as the Food and Drug Administration (FDA), the Federal Trade Commission (FTC), and the Texas Department of Health tend to overregulate alternative modalities for several reasons, none of which are pertinent to this discussion. But in fairness to those agencies, they usually issue warnings or cease-and-desist orders before prosecuting unless they have received reports of injuries. For colon therapists to be prosecuted, they must have ignored one or more warnings. These prosecutions, however, have no bearing on the viability of colonics as a health-building modality as they involved cure rather than injury claims.

Barrett is clearly opposed to any alternative therapy. He operates under the assumption that only medical doctors know how to treat physical ailments, when in reality, medical science has no remedy for most if not all of chronic degenerative diseases or problems such as fibromyalgia—a catchall word for systemic, nonarthritic pain.

From an alternative or natural medical approach to health and healing, drugs poison the body and are to be avoided as much as possible unless the present symptom is life-threatening. Doctors who practice the allopathic approach prescribe drugs for just about every symptom to the extent that drug-induced dementia has become a major problem for hospital emergency rooms and society in general.[7-2, 7-3]

To my knowledge allopathic medicine has no procedures for the noninvasive removal of toxins from the body. Based on my experience and twenty years of medically based research, all diseases are either caused by toxins accumulating in the body, or they accelerate the accumulation of toxins. Most heart disease is caused by calcified plaque that blocks arteries. *Cancer* is defined by tumor buildup (encapsulated toxins). *Diabetes* is defined as high blood sugar caused by faulty insulin utilization, resulting in glycation (crystallization of blood sugar, like the top of a crème brûlée dessert) throughout the body. Alzheimer's disease is defined by the buildup of amyloid plaque in the brain. Those four conditions account for approximately 88 percent of deaths in the United States, and allopathic medicine has no cure for the underlying causes of these problems.

Despite this dismal track record, allopathic medicine, through its influence with the FDA and state medical boards, has had the political clout, the money, and the media access to block or delay effective alternative treatments for years, even decades. When I first started in private practice in Denver in 1986, seven medical doctors and osteopaths were offering chelation therapy—a relatively inexpensive alternative method of dissolving arterial plaque by IV injection of EDTA, an amino acid originally approved by the FDA to treat lead poisoning. By 1995, all seven were out of business, their medical licenses having been revoked by the Colorado Medical Board for offering unauthorized medical procedures.

Alternative medicine is an umbrella term covering many different modalities, including chiropractic, naturopathy, nutrition counseling, acupuncture, herbology, massage therapy, and many other forms of body manipulation. This diversity is its strength as well as its weakness, because these modalities have lacked cohesion and organization—each individually has been an easy target for criticism and retribution by government agencies and medical organizations.

The average naturopathic doctor earns less than $60,000 a year, and colonic therapists make less. How can they defend against an attack by Quackwatch or a state medical board? How can small vitamin companies and device manufacturers afford to expend the massive amounts required to make the kinds of claims the pharmaceutical companies can make on television? The deck is stacked against alternative medicine. Education, word-of-mouth, and self-research are the only ways individual health seekers have to learn how alternative modalities can help them.

Are there risks associated with colon therapy? Yes, if the therapist does not keep his or her station sterilized or if the speculum gets jammed into the colon wall—which is difficult to accomplish as most speculums are not long enough to reach beyond the anus and rectum into the intestine. If a colonic station is not properly sterilized or a speculum gets jammed into the colon, it's the fault of an incompetent therapist or a deranged client, not the modality. If colonics were truly dangerous, as Barrett would like you to believe, why doesn't he list the thousands of complaints that would have resulted from a dangerous modality? Maybe because there aren't any.

Health seekers should investigate and research modalities and practitioners as thoroughly as possible and learn how to evaluate criticism. What is the bias of the critic? Does the modality take away business or credibility from the established allopathic medical community? Is the criticism supported by reliable facts? In the case against colonics, the answer is no.

Chiropractors were castigated and condemned by the medical establishment for decades until five chiropractors sued the American Medical Association (*Wilk v. American Medical Association* 895F 2d 352) and won a landmark verdict that finally put an end to the AMA's conspiracy and false accusations. Through sheer force of numbers and the accumulation of wealth in state chiropractic organizations, the chiropractors were able to hire the expensive legal talent they needed to hold the AMA accountable for its actions.

Other businesses, such as Life Extension, have fought the FDA in court on several occasions to win back basic constitutional freedoms that the FDA had been denying. If you are new to the alternative-healing world in the United States, you should be aware of the decades-long attempts at sabotaging and outlawing alternative modalities and the disinformation that is still being disseminated about them.

All the information in this book is based first on my personal experience of the modality and second on how well the science or logic behind it holds together. Chinese medicine, with its focus on acupuncture, evolved 2,500 years ago out of a philosophy that "if it works do it and figure out why later."

That's exactly the philosophy I have used in my twenty-five years of experience with alternative-healing modalities and their practitioners. I have experienced homeopathy, ayurveda, Chinese and herbal medicine, massage, Rolfing, the Trager approach, and Feldenkrais body routines as well as various forms of chiropractic and emotional-release therapies. I have used any number of vitamin, herbal, and food-supplement formulas from a variety of manufacturers. I found that every modality had something going for it, even though that something may not have been what I needed at the moment.

Some practitioners are more competent than others, while others are more caring—and caring counts. Over the years I have developed a complex set of standards for screening and evaluating each modality and its practitioner as follows:

1. ***Did I get the result I expected or was told to expect?***
   Some modalities, such as chiropractic, should yield immediate results. It should not take ten adjustments to relieve the pain of a pinched nerve. The pain should be relieved with the first or second adjustment, but it may take five or six more visits and the application of other modalities, especially yoga and stress-reducing routines, to keep the pinched nerve from reoccurring.

2. ***Who referred me to the modality or practitioner? What were their symptoms and results, and what is my opinion of their ability to judge a result?***
   My twenty-five-year journey through addiction, lung cancer, and liver collapse qualifies me as an expert in overcoming those conditions, but I have no experience in dealing with spinal fractures or balancing female hormonal problems. What I have to say about coping with cancer and addiction may be invaluable to some and useless to others who are unwilling to deal with emotional issues.

It's an individual thing. Please walk away if I start telling you how to treat female hormone problems, as I can only repeat what I've read on the subject, which may not be correct. I never use the word *cure*, as that implies a finality that does not exist in the real world. *Healing*, a more appropriate word than *cure*, depends on an intensity of effort, a positive attitude, and a willingness to make lifestyle changes. In other words consider the source of the referral in your evaluation.

3. ***Can I understand and accept the science or logic behind the therapy?***
Acupuncture, like chiropractic, should produce an immediate reduction in symptoms at a bare minimum, even if the presenting problem does not completely go away. Once I accepted that the body is electrical, I had no trouble accepting the concept of blocked or disturbed energy flow. My symptomatic relief allowed my mind to open to an understanding of this ancient concept, even though I did not understand it when the practitioner first explained it to me.

This concept of understanding after the fact is an important one for you to grasp. The Trager practitioner talks about nervous-system repatterning, the acupuncturist talks about energy flow, and the homoeopathist talks about cellular memory. As a layperson, how can you expect to understand these concepts even if the practitioner explains them well? Once you have had the experience of symptom relief, you will find it much easier to understand the concept of an old habit held in the nervous system or the memory of an old trauma held in the cells of your body as being the cause of your problem. A theory or concept takes on real meaning when it is concretely demonstrated. Until then it just sounds nice.

4. ***Can I relate to or develop a rapport with the therapist?***
Who is this person I'm trusting a part of my life or body to? Is he or she interested in my well-being or in a hurry to get me out the door? Do I get a good feeling or a negative feeling about him or her? Am I being talked to or at?

My biggest criticisms of Western medicine are its one-size-fits-all approach to healing and its emotional disconnect from the patient. Prescriptions take the place of a detailed analysis of an individual's lifestyle and emotional processes, and medical doctors tend to address the patient from a position of authority, not from a position of care or love. Over the course of my personal dealings with allopathic practitioners, I have chosen caring practitioners rather than highly trained technicians because of their ability to relate to me with compassion, given that the compassionate practitioner had the requisite skills to do the job. Seek that quality in all the practitioners you work with, and you will be well served.

5. ***Is the therapist or doctor making cure claims?***
Healing a symptom or disease is a complex process, because most disease symptoms involve mental and emotional traumas that create lesions and scar tissue throughout the body. I can state that you should feel better from colonics and other detoxification protocols, because they result in fewer toxins in your body. However, I cannot tell you that your joint pain or bloated abdomen will go away because I don't know why these conditions exist within you. I can only recommend that you try a protocol and see what relief it brings or what it stirs up.

I have had several hundred colonics without injury or problem, and believe they have saved my life by improving my body's ability to get rid of toxins. I don't know any commonly available alternative modality that is dangerous, but some practitioners can misrepresent or overstate the benefits of their modality.

In my experience over the years, I have found that state medical boards and state attorney generals are quick to crack down on alternative therapies for the slightest infractions. You can be sure that if an alternative therapy or therapist is injuring people, the state will be on it quickly. Medical-prescription errors kill more than one hundred thousand patients a year, yet no one seems concerned about sanctioning allopathic practitioners.

Dietary Recommendations for Proper Colon Care

Eat as much fiber-rich food as possible. I'm not a big fan of grains and beans, as they are difficult to digest. Wheat is a common allergen and soy should be avoided in its unfermented state. Fruits and vegetables, especially in their raw states, are excellent sources of fiber that you should consume several times a day. You might also add a fiber supplement, especially if you have bowel problems. Fiber takes up excess moisture in the colon and helps to form stools for easier elimination.

Since my digestive system is weak, I supplement it with a probiotic twice a day and a teaspoon of Swedish bitters and food enzymes with every meal, convenience permitting. A probiotic is a supplement or food containing various microorganisms to help the colon maintain a healthy balance of beneficial bacteria to promote healthy assimilation of nutrients and flow of fecal matter. Probiotics can be taken as an encapsulated supplement or in fermented milk products such as yogurt and kefir. Swedish bitters are a combination of herbs designed to stimulate HCL in the stomach to facilitate protein digestion. HCL is commonly sold in health food stores, but I'd rather let my body manufacture its own HCL, so that when I'm unable to use supplements when I'm traveling, my body will continue to produce HCL on its own.

Pancreatic enzymes are essential to the digestion of protein, carbohydrates, and fats as they gravitate from the stomach to the duodenum. Raw-food advocates say that foods in their raw state contain the enzymes required to digest them and that heating food kills its enzyme content, thus putting stress on the pancreas to produce more digestive enzymes. That sounds great in theory, and they are probably right, but I have found a completely raw food diet to be unhealthy and unsatisfying the three times I tried it. I and others who have shared my experience with the raw diet felt constantly fatigued, and we lost weight we did not need to lose. I blend fruit and sprout shakes with various powdered forms of protein, vegetables, and fiber, but I like my steaks and fish cooked. I estimate that my daily raw food intake comprises 40 percent of my overall intake, and that seems to work fine for me.

Mentally and emotionally based stress causes over- or underproduction of HCL and pepsin; poor diet and bad eating habits cause overproduction of pancreatic enzymes. These imbalances eventually lead to organ exhaustion and permanent weakening of the organs involved in the production of digestive fluids. Antibiotics and other allopathic prescription medications destroy the beneficial bacteria that form the intestinal flora, further weakening the body's ability to break down and assimilate nutrition.

As you can see from the above paragraphs, digestion and assimilation of nutrition is a complex process requiring the cooperation of several organs. Most people don't notice digestive problems in their youth, as the energy of youth is strong enough to overcome stress and a poor diet for a while. The effects of bad habits start to show in adolescence with the appearance of acne and weight gain.

By the time most people reach their midthirties, their hips, thighs, and abdomens have extended to the point that they seriously distort body shape and impede locomotion. And the results of all of these bad habits accumulate in the colon in the form of putrefying and fermenting waste, the breeding ground for most human diseases. No one is immune from this process, as stress is a part of life. An ongoing colon-care program is the only way I know to offset the impact of day-to-day stresses on the body's main organ of elimination.

Worms, Parasites, and Microorganisms

Putrefying and fermenting foods provide an ideal environment for worms, parasites, and microorganisms, both beneficial and destructive. The beneficial microorganisms break down partially digested substances, while the destructive ones eat away microflora and infect tissues. If you are just starting a colon-care program, your therapist will quickly be able to tell if you are housing these non-rent-paying guests (most people are). These parasites, like tapeworms and flukes, feed off undigested material and excrete powerful toxins that can leach through porous intestinal walls and wreak havoc anywhere in the body. Fatigue and exhaustion are but two of the symptoms emanating from microorganism infestation, which can be easily eliminated by adding a black-walnut tincture to your colon-care program and eliminating intake of refined carbohydrates. Far-infrared light and water-ionization protocols will provide a great assist in microorganism removal.

Chapter Summary

Keep in mind the following key points about the colon and colonics:

1. The colon is the body's main organ for the elimination of toxic waste.
2. The improper and inefficient breakdown of food during the digestive process will result in the buildup of partially digested waste products in the colon that may not be totally expelled from the body.
3. This buildup of toxic waste will cause the colon to secrete mucous to protect itself from the toxins created by putrefaction and fermentation. This mucous buildup will then trap future partially digested foods that will, in turn, cause the production of additional mucous layers until the colon is completely blocked.
4. The toxins produced from putrefaction and fermentation eventually seep through the intestinal walls into the bloodstream from where they can lodge anywhere in the body. Wherever their resting place in the body is, disease results and fat will accumulate.
5. Periodic colonics (the act of running lukewarm water through the entire length of the large intestine) is the quickest and most reliable way of maintaining a highly functional colon.

6. Other colon-cleansing methods include herbal cleanses and enemas, self-administered while lying partially inverted on a Colema Board.
7. When properly administered, colonics are safe, and it is difficult to administer a colonic improperly.
8. In my opinion, websites such as Quackwatch are set up to dispense misinformation about various forms of alternative therapies. Carefully and logically evaluate such website's criticisms—most of which do not stand up under scrutiny.
9. I do not know of any unsafe alternative therapies, but there are differences in practitioner abilities and motivations. Don't use a practitioner or modality with which you are uncomfortable or one that you don't understand.
10. An ongoing colon-care program includes the taking of food enzymes and bitters to aid digestion, and probiotic substances to maintain intestinal flora.
11. Most people new to colon care will harbor some form of parasite infestation. Black-walnut tincture, colonics, and ionization therapies will eliminate them, and a sugar-free diet with digestive aids will prevent their return.

Chapter Eight

The Lymphatic System

Think *sewer* and *sewage* when you hear *lymphatic* and *lymph* and you will have an accurate picture of what the lymphatic system does. To give you an appreciation of the lymph system's size and scope, it holds three times as much water as the body holds blood. It covers the entire body, front and back, with reflex points from the brain to just below the groin, as evidenced by maps of neurolymphatic reflex points (NRPs) in figures 6A and 6B. NRPs are electrical points along the length and breadth of the lymph system that can be stimulated to recharge and unblock stagnant lymph nodes. Lymph

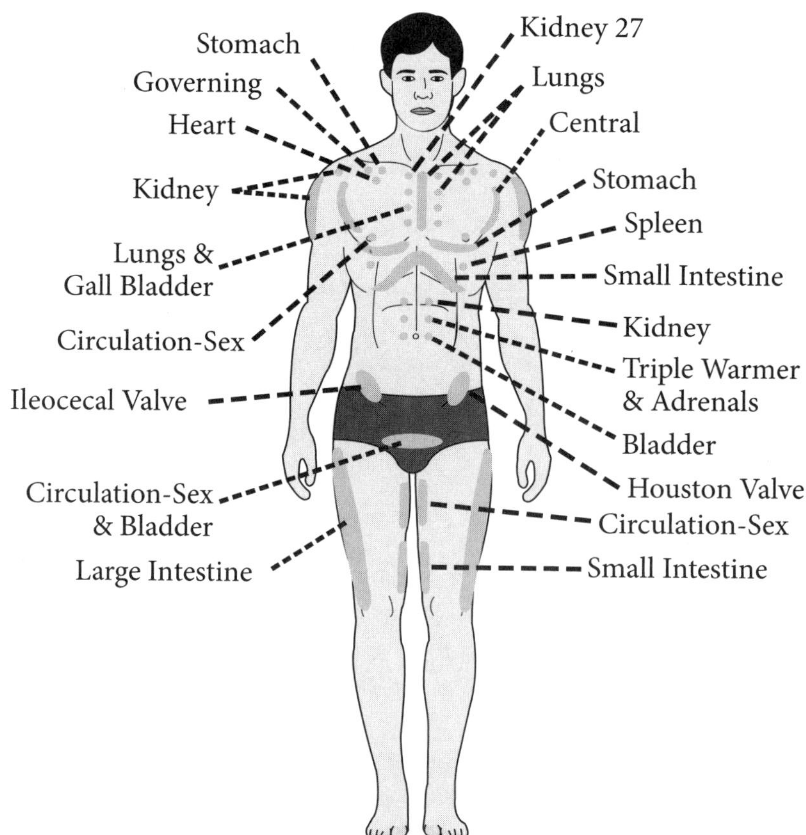

Figure 6A: Neurolymphatic reflex points, front

nodes stagnate when fat and other debris cannot get through the opening of a node, similar to garbage backing up in a sewer.

The lymph system (carries the body's debris, the excrement from every cell, through the blood to the kidneys and colon. It filters out bacteria, microorganisms, dead cells, and other unidentified flying objects (UFOs) that clog lymph nodes. As in the colon, stagnant toxins in the lymph system will cause the body to encapsulate them in fat and mucous, and mucous will attract new toxins, which create more fat and mucous. I speculate that this process of toxic and mucous buildup throughout the body is the primary cause of aging.

Once you understand that toxic accumulations are the primary cause of aging in the body, it should logically follow that the most effective way to slow aging would be to keep the internal organs as free of toxins as possible.

A clogged lymph system will quickly overwhelm and weaken the immune system. Because of my experiences with friends who died from

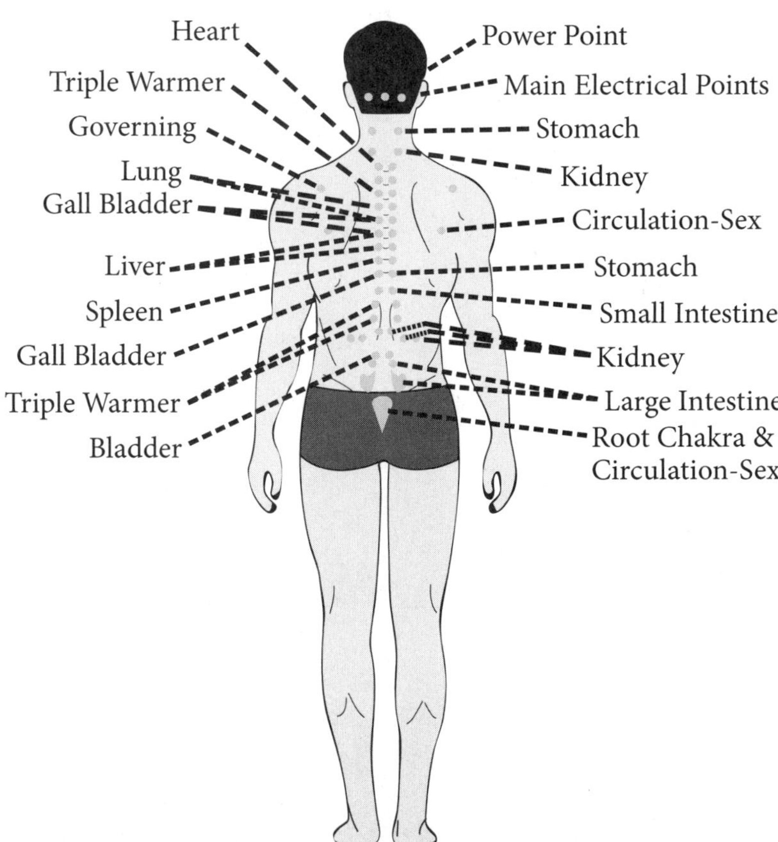

Figure 6B: Neurolymphatic reflex points, back

cancer, I believe that the opposite is also true: a weak immune system will eventually weaken the lymph system.

As we age, our bodies tend to accumulate water by way of inflammation and bloating, indicating a weakened or blocked lymph system. Even with good eating and exercise habits, all body systems lose efficiency over time. (My lymph system has slowed significantly, and I stimulate it with a low-level

Lymphatic System

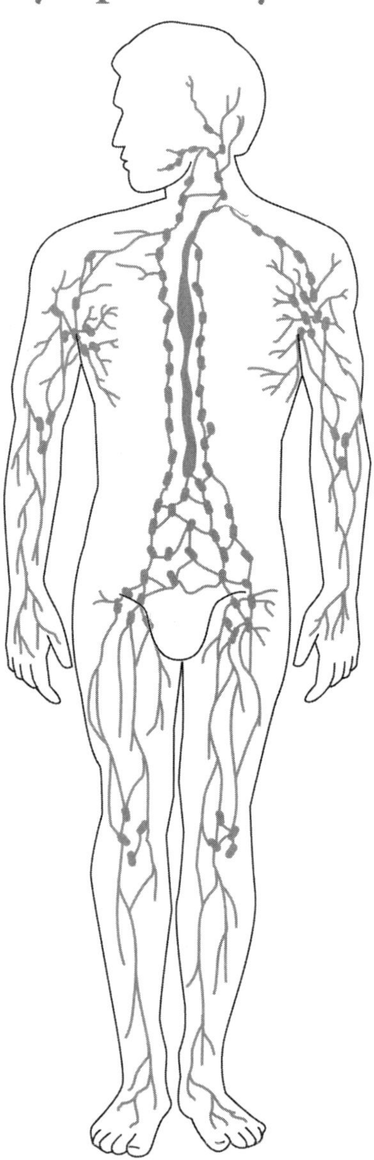

Figure 7

cold laser every time I do a footbath. See the discussion of ionization therapy in chapter one.) So, as with the colon, we must learn to clean the lymphatic system and keep its contents flowing.

Lymph Drainage (Cleansing)

Lymph-drainage techniques are often featured alongside colon therapy in many clinics, since they go hand in hand. It takes education, training, and experience to produce a competent lymph-cleanse therapist capable of working with touch (massage), light, sound, and homeopathies to empty and reinvigorate a stagnant lymphatic system. I strongly suggest this therapy for anyone with a protruding gut or some other form of inflammation. I would make lymph cleansing mandatory for all cancer patients who routinely experience diminished lymph function from their toxic medications and a compromised immune system.

A good therapist should be able to open a clogged system within one or two sessions. How long it stays unclogged depends on many factors, including but not limited to diet, exercise, stress, and healing effort. Suffice to say that, as is the case with colonics, lymph cleansing is a lifetime activity for those with compromised lymph function.

In the ionization therapies section in chapter one, I discuss a simple way to maintain a highly functional lymph system. If, however, you already have a compromised system, a few visits to a lymph-cleanse therapist is a good way to begin your healing journey.

Chapter Nine

Liver-Gallbladder Cleansing

The blood tests requested by Dr. Gordon Tessler when I first visited him in 1982 revealed that all my liver enzymes were above normal, indicating a stressed and sluggish liver. "Your whole body is toxic, and your liver is working overtime," he said, "but I don't want you doing any liver flushes until we get your colon straightened out and your adrenals working again."

It took several months of coffee colonics and enemas, dietary changes, and food supplements before Gordon gave me the go-ahead to do a two-day liver flush. I suffered no complications from this procedure, so he had me do one liver flush a month for the next five months. By the time we did a third blood panel, the liver enzyme scores had returned to normal, and I was feeling considerably better.

I don't think anyone really knows how many functions the liver performs on a day-to-day basis: anywhere from 190 on up, depending on what book you read. Appendix I lists a few of the liver's major functions, which include the breakdown of every carbohydrate, protein, and fat entering the body; the detoxification of all poisons; the breakdown of all hormone residues; and the arranging and rearranging of proteins into amino acids and amino acids into proteins.[9-1]

Chinese medicine treats the liver and gallbladder as one unit, as they work together to process and emulsify fats. The liver is considered a vital organ—we simply could not survive without it. In Western medicine, the gallbladder is regarded as expendable, as many doctors quickly remove it when it becomes clogged with stones, which are small, hard, pathological constructs composed chiefly of cholesterol, calcium salts, and bile pigment formed in the gallbladder or bile duct.

It takes the entire digestive tract from the mouth to the small intestine to break down and separate food into its nutrient constituents: proteins, carbohydrates, and fats. These get routed to the liver, where they are disassembled and reassembled into forms the body can utilize in the production of energy and the replacement of tissue.

The liver can become congested from an intake of toxic and fatty foods, overindulgence of alcohol and drugs, overeating, constipation, and physical and emotional trauma. A liver that can't clear its own wastes will quickly bloat, harden, and swell from the accumulation of stuck toxic substances.

How do you know if your liver is sluggish? Start with the shape of the gut. A bloated gut is a sure sign of a sluggish liver, poor dietary habits, possible digestive problems, and toxicity in the small and large intestines. Elevated liver enzymes, as determined from blood tests, are an indication of a malfunctioning liver under stress.

Most Americans older than forty have sluggish livers, especially if they drink alcohol regularly. Fat (cholesterol) and metal (calcium) combine to form globules that clog the liver and gallbladder.[9-2] As a general rule, stones in the liver mean that there are stones in the gallbladder, but stones in the gallbladder do not necessarily mean that there are stones in the liver.

Fortunately the liver is a resilient organ that can regenerate itself if its host changes the eating and lifestyle habits that created the problem. If you are a newcomer to living a healthy lifestyle, I suggest you consult with a nutritionally oriented doctor who will test your blood chemistries for imbalances, analyze your food allergies (most people have them), and run urine and hair tests for metabolic errors and heavy-metal levels. These tests will provide you with a comprehensive evaluation of your health status, a profile of your specific health challenges, and a protocol for addressing them. You will probably have to pay cash for these tests, but they are not prohibitively expensive, and they will provide a reliable laboratory record of your progress.

> ***Caution:*** Liver flushes can be tricky if you are new to detoxification. Work with a doctor or practitioner who can evaluate your risks until you have completed at least two flushes. You do not want to do a flush if your liver energy is weak or if you are carrying large stones in your gallbladder as they could get trapped in its narrow opening, creating pain and possibly necessitating surgery to remove them.
>
> That is where the IonCleanse and food-supplements supports come into play. The proper food supplements will strengthen the liver, thus raising its energy level, which in turn increases its ability to mobilize toxins. The IonCleanse provides the internal relaxation that enables toxins to move and gives them a little extra push to leave.

When my liver crashed on December 8, 2004, the result of a lifetime of sustained stress and heavy alcohol intake, the medical doctor I visited called it nonviral hepatitis, pending more extensive tests, but a medical intuitive called it cirrhosis, a far more serious pathology that often requires a liver transplant. At first I did not agree with the medical intuitive's diagnosis, but my painfully slow recovery, still ongoing, has proven her right. I am still recovering six years later, but my energy level is half what it was ten years ago, when I was able to play an entire game of full-court basketball.

I employed an infrared LED light therapy device broadcasting Global Scaling Energy Waves, along with a milk thistle dandelion supplement from Herb Pharm and detoxifying footbaths in a continuing effort to regenerate my liver. To date I have been partially successful, as my energy level is slowly improving, but I am no longer the powerhouse of my late forties and fifties.

I have to give some credit to Alpha Lipoic Acid Drip Therapy, a series of intravenous drips developed by Dr. Burt Berkson, a medical doctor and leading FDA alpha-lipoic acid researcher in Las Cruces, New Mexico. I highly recommend Berkson's protocol for anyone with diabetes, cancer, rheumatoid arthritis, HIV, chronic fatigue, or liver disease.

I took ten treatments over five days, resulting in a seven-pound weight loss and a substantial increase in energy. As I sat in his treatment room with a needle in my vein for two hours each session, I had the opportunity to interview upwards of fifty patients with serious ailments who had been taking his therapy over many months, and every one reported an abatement of symptoms and an increase in energy. I also recommend his book *Alpha Lipoic Acid Breakthrough*.[9-3]

Chemical Detoxification

The liver processes toxins. Alcohol, allopathic medications, heavy metals, chemical residues, and inhalants from tens of thousands of industrial and petrochemical products stress the liver from the moment we come into life, including the time spent in the womb. Add to this toxic soup our cultural tendency to overeat, which overloads the bloodstream with fat and glucose, and the liver stresses even further. Nonalcoholic liver cirrhosis is becoming more frequent in our culture.

Never in human history has the liver been required to perform more work, and the strain is evident in the girth of our citizenry. Americans are the fattest group on the planet, and probably the fattest who ever walked—er, rode—upon the earth. As a fitting testimony to our cultural weight gain during the twentieth century, the architects who refurbished Yankee Stadium in 1980 reduced the number of seats from 65,000 to 55,000 to accommodate the four-inch expansion in the American derriere since the stadium had been originally built in 1920.

Statistics tell us we are living longer—but are we living better? Today heart disease, cancer, diabetes, and Alzheimer's disease account for more than 80 percent of deaths in the United States, versus 12 percent in 1900, and many Americans die broke , mostly from health-care costs. These four conditions involve a buildup of toxins somewhere in the body—arterial plaque for heart disease, tumors in cancer, glycation in diabetes, and amyloid plaque in Alzheimer's disease—that ongoing detoxification protocols can probably eliminate if begun while the body is still in decent health.

> ***Important note:*** Detoxification is not a treatment for severely impeded arterial blood flow. If you are experiencing symptoms that relate to impeded blood flow, you should seek medical treatment.
>
> Accumulated fat from overeating and poor food choices compounds the disease problem by speeding up the onset of chronic degenerative disease, resulting in a diminished quality of life, a shorter life span, and higher disease-maintenance costs. One would think that as a society we would be more invested in teaching healthy lifestyles, instead of encouraging indiscriminate consumption of pharmaceutical drugs to mitigate the symptoms of disease.

Since toxic accumulation accompanies most diseases, it appears that eating a healthy diet and periodically detoxifying the body will greatly reduce the incidence of chronic degenerative disease and increase healthy life span.

The Organ of Anger

Chinese medicine recognizes the role of emotions in the health of the body. According to teachings that have survived for more than 2,500 years, grief is held in the lungs, anger in the liver, fear in the kidneys, worry in the stomach, and joy in the heart. Obviously, the greater the intensity of an emotion, the greater the amount of stress in its corresponding organ.

Angry individuals who transcribe these emotion-organ links to physical events will likely experience liver problems over the course of their lives, because any deviation in liver chemistries will only increase the amount of toxic by-products the body must process. My research has shown that an angry person is more likely to be attracted to cigarettes, alcohol, and drugs—poisons that might neutralize the emotional pain but that add to the body's toxic burden.

I was an angry adolescent who discovered cigarettes at age thirteen and alcohol at fifteen. I started having liver problems at twenty-one —that was when a doctor gave me my first warning about cirrhosis. I discovered marijuana at twenty-seven and cocaine at thirty-five, hence the elevated liver enzymes and lung cancer at forty-three.

I was able to cut my alcohol consumption way down because of marijuana. However, because of business stresses and abstinence from marijuana, my alcohol intake escalated when I was in my early sixties. I didn't think I was drinking that much, but I didn't think about the weakness of aging and past cumulative damage, which is why three years after I reintroduced alcohol into my system my liver crashed.

My story is typical of many recovering alcoholics and drug addicts I've worked with over the years. Because they were angry personalities who took to some form of drug relief early in life, these addicts benefited greatly from the many months of food supplements and detoxification rituals required to reconstruct their organs and nervous systems.

Statistics have continuously shown that recidivism is much lower with recovering addicts who take supplements and detox regularly. L. Ron Hubbard, founder of Scientology, was the first to recognize the benefits of supplements and detoxification in the recovery process, and many programs now incorporate these modalities in their curriculum. While Hubbard's program ignored the emotional aspects of addiction, it did help me rebuild my vitality and physical strength, which enabled me to cope with the stresses of dependency. It took three years of physical rehabilitation before I could tackle my pent-up anger and rage.

A Powerful Liver Cleanse and Gallbladder Flush

This flush takes five days.

1. For each day, do a half-hour castor-oil pack treatment on the liver as follows: cut a piece of chamois of sufficient size to cover the entire liver, which extends from the center of the body to its right edge. Cover the chamois with a thin layer of castor oil and place it over the liver. Cover the chamois with a strip of wax paper, and place a heating pad set to medium heat over the wax

paper. Lie down and turn the pad on for thirty minutes as you maintain a stationary position.

2. Consume only raw salads and fresh vegetables or low-glycemic fruit and vegetable juices throughout the entire five-day period. Each day drink several glasses of filtered water with the juice from a lemon wedge. (See Chapter Seventeen: Water.)
3. Shortly before bedtime on the evening of the fifth day, drink eight ounces of virgin olive oil combined with juice from four or five whole lemons. Lie in bed on your right side, knees pulled up in the fetal position for at least thirty minutes. Go to sleep. You will probably awaken in the middle of the night for one heck of a malodorous bowel movement. That odor and the strange objects you will view in the bowl are the toxins and gallstones the flush has removed from your body.

Ideally, you should do this cleanse twice a year.

Chapter Summary

Keep in mind the following key points about the liver:

1. The liver is responsible for the breakdown of every carbohydrate, protein, and fat entering the body; the detoxification of all poisons; the breakdown of all hormone residues; and the arranging and rearranging of proteins into amino acids and amino acids into proteins.
2. As the primary organ for neutralizing poisons, the liver is particularly vulnerable to one's bad habits. Junk food, pesticides, drugs, alcohol, and trans fats eventually wear the liver out and cause it to fail.
3. As a general rule, stones in the liver mean that there are stones in the gallbladder, but stones in the gallbladder do not necessarily mean that there are stones in the liver.
4. If you are new to total body detoxification, do not attempt your first liver flush on your own. Work with an alternative practitioner who can monitor and evaluate your blood chemistries. You don't want a large stone getting caught in the gallbladder tube. That can be painful and may require surgery to remove.
5. Those with serious liver problems should investigate Alpha Lipoic Acid Drip Therapy. Call Berkson's clinic in Las Cruces, New Mexico (phone number 575-524-3720), and ask for a

location near you. Be prepared to travel, as only a few doctors in the United States offer this therapy.

6. Virtually all chronic degenerative diseases involve some form of toxin buildup in the body. Eighty-eight percent of the US population dies from diabetes, heart disease, cancer, or Alzheimer's disease, all of which involve toxin buildup. I hypothesize that an ongoing total body detoxification program would reduce that mortality rate to where it was in 1900: 12 percent.
7. Anger and its related manifestations of hatred, frustration, resentment, and envy impair the liver's ability to perform its many tasks and greatly increase the toxic load it must handle. Any attempt to detoxify the liver should be accompanied by a resolve to change the mental-emotional structure holding you to an anger-based way of interacting with life. (See Chapter Nineteen: My Personal Program.)
8. Liver and gallbladder flushes are essential for maintaining optimal function of these organs, especially if you travel by air, eat less-than-optimal foods, and are under stress. I recommend that anyone over fifty completes two flushes each year.

Chapter Ten

Detoxifying the Kidneys

The primary function of the urinary system and the kidneys in particular is to maintain the body's homeostasis in the following ways:

1. regulation of blood, water, and interstitial fluid volume (make it consistent)
2. reabsorption of required substances: water, sodium ions, potassium ions, bicarbonate ions, urea, uric acid, proteins, glucose, and creatinine
3. excretion of excess substances
4. excretion of toxic substances
5. regulation of body pH
6. regulation of normal blood pressure

The kidneys filter out wastes, the ureters convey wastes from the kidney to the bladder, and the bladder stores wastes until excretion. In addition to waste removal, the kidneys regulate body pH by excreting hydrogen ions (H^+), thus making the urine more acidic, and adding or withdrawing bicarbonate ions (HCO_3^-) to maintain normal pH.

The kidneys try to keep blood pressure within a normal range, but since they are sensitive to stress, they don't always succeed, hence the high rate of blood-pressure prescriptions among Americans. Prolonged or severe fight-or-flight reactions can stop blood flow to the kidneys for too long, killing the tubules (acute tubular necrosis) and finally the kidney itself.

I will cover emotional and traumatic impacts later in this chapter, but let it suffice for now that this is another example of the profound impact of stress on the body's health and well-being. By emotional and traumatic impacts, I refer to chemical and food insults, violent and abusive traumas, and the excessive daily stresses of the American lifestyle. Diabetics experience the highest rate of kidney disease because of the complications of insulin resistance and glucose metabolism inherent with that disease. Kidney diseases (and diabetes) are on the rise. Hundreds of thousands of people now require continuing dialysis.

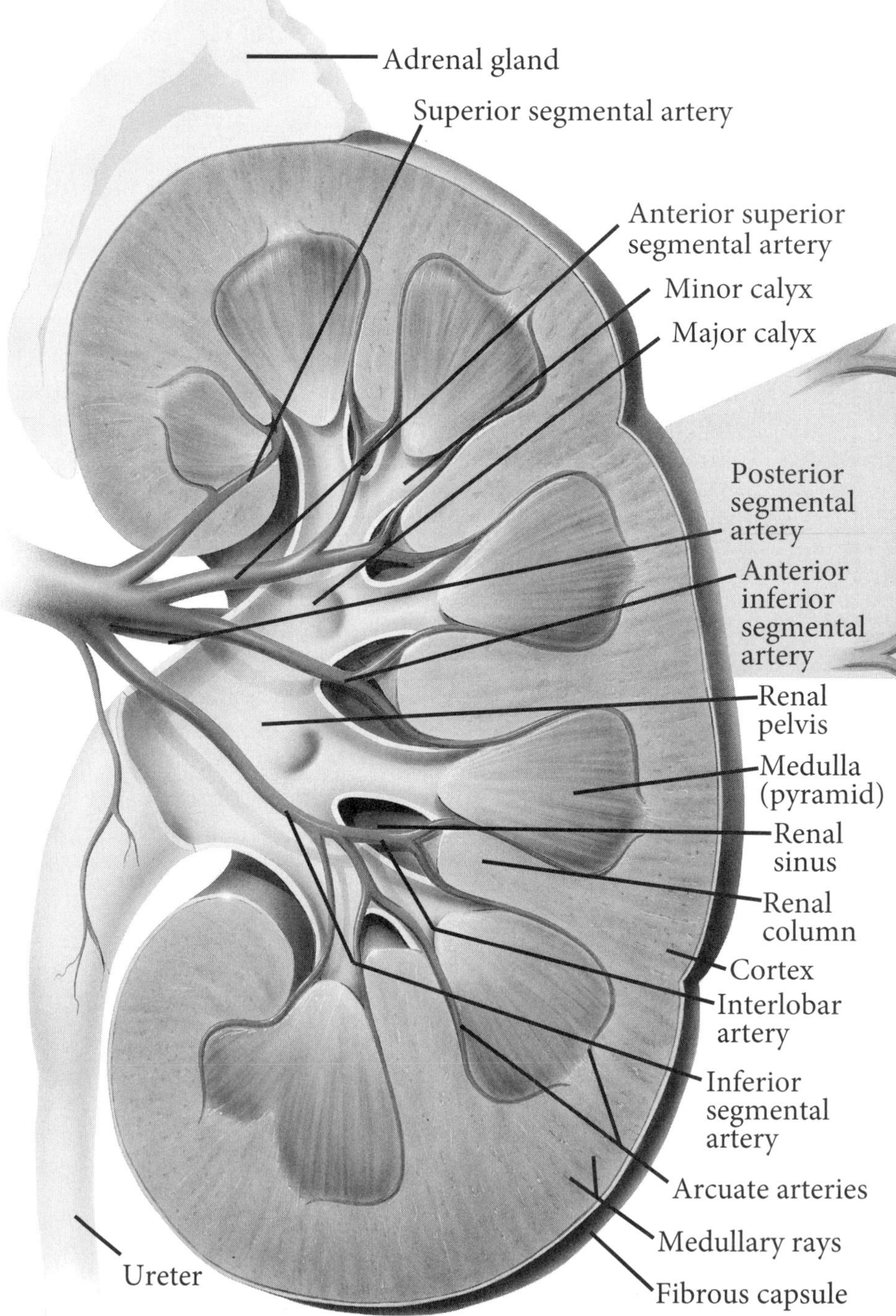
Sectioned Left Kidney
Adrenal gland
Superior segmental artery
Anterior superior segmental artery
Minor calyx
Major calyx
Posterior segmental artery
Anterior inferior segmental artery
Renal pelvis
Medulla (pyramid)
Renal sinus
Renal column
Cortex
Interlobar artery
Inferior segmental artery
Arcuate arteries
Medullary rays
Fibrous capsule
Ureter

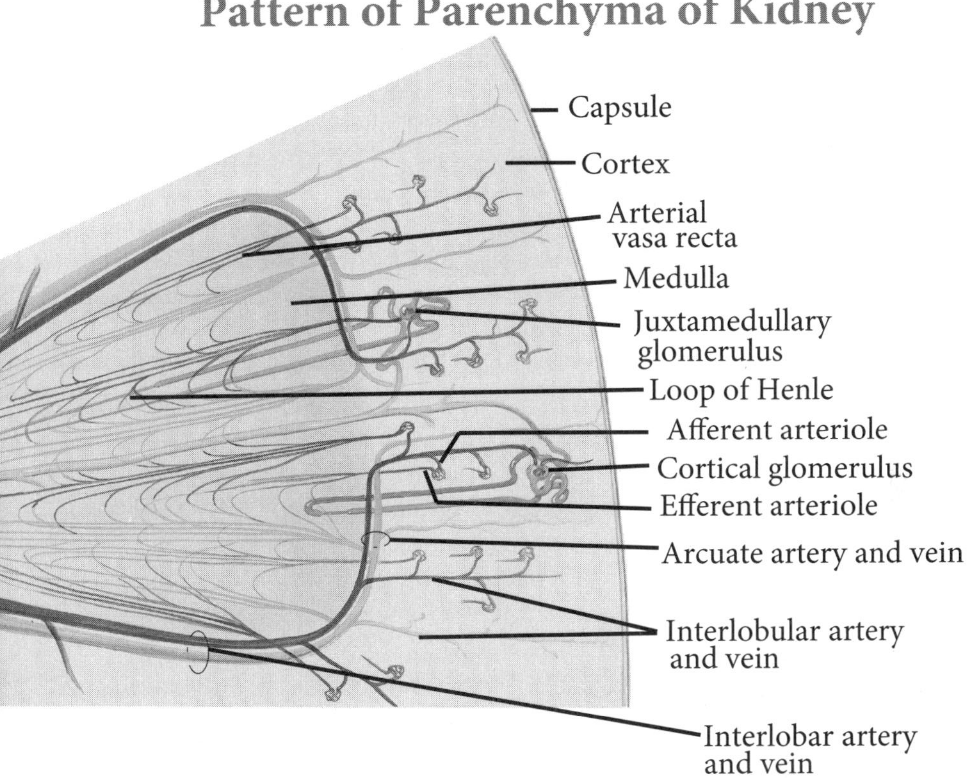

Figure 8: Renal artery has five named segmental branches.

A quart of blood per minute passes through the renal artery (figure 8). This flow represents 20 percent of the heart's output and is responsible for the kidney's dark-red color. Inside the kidneys the blood is passed through filters called *glomeruli*. The glomeruli are a small cluster of tiny blood vessels inside a small bag called Bowman's capsule (about the size of a pinhead). These filters connect to tubules and nephrons that transport the filtered blood back to the heart via the renal vein and transport the waste products to the bladder. When the blood passes through the glomeruli, some of the fluid is forced through the blood-vessel walls into the bag, taking with it the nitrogenous wastes, salt, and glucose. This fluid is drained via the bag to the nephrons, where 99 percent of the excess water is reabsorbed by the body, thus concentrating what is left into urine.[10-1]

Dr. Mark Braun, a pathologist at the University of Indiana, states on his website that "kidney disease is in large part a replay of microvascular disease," or in layman's language blood is not able to get into the tissues. He continues, "We see time and time again conditions that impact the functioning of capillary-size blood vessels will be the principal causes of renal damage."[10-2]

He did not elaborate further on the probable causes of vascular blockage, but it appears safe to speculate that these blockages are caused by advanced glycation end products and arterial plaque. In his book, *Let's Stop the #1 Killer of Americans Today*, Dr. Harry Elwardt said, "Advanced glycation end products (AGEs) are well known for their destructive activities in diabetes, where they contribute to vascular disease, kidney failure, eye damage and other kinds of dysfunction, including the nerve damage known as peripheral neuropathy."[10-3] Glycation is defined as the bonding of proteins and lipids to sugar molecules, forming a brown, paste-like substance that coats the internal organs and passageways.

The kidney chart in figure 8 shows the complex system of arteries that conduct blood and fluids in and out of the left kidney—an organ smaller than the heart, about the size of a small fist. Look at these arterial pathways; it's easy to see how a small amount of plaque and AGEs can impede blood flow and shut down life-sustaining kidney functions.

Arginine pyroglutamate, an amino acid, has been shown to be the best form of arginine for dissolving arterial plaque.[10-4] Heart disease and stroke are manifestations of modern civilization's emphasis on fast-food diets and high-stress lifestyles. I recommend a six-week course of arginine pyroglutamate every two years as part of an ongoing detoxification program to maintain high physical and mental function and to prevent plaque accumulation around the heart and kidneys.

If you are new to total body detoxification, I recommend that you have your circulation thoroughly tested and supplement with arginine pyroglutamate for as long as necessary to restore it to optimal function. (Wouldn't it be great to track healthy change taking place in the body as you age instead of having to hear the usual bad news?)

If you are concerned about arterial blockage and kidney vascular disease, read Elwardt's excellent book—especially chapter six, which talks at great length about the use of arginine in a health-building program.

Since diabetics experience the highest rates of kidney disease, I suggest that heavy supplementation with supercarnosine (1,000 milligrams [mg]) per day) accompanied by exercise and a healthy diet will lower glycation buildup. Supercarnosine is a supplement containing benfotiamine—a thiamin derivative, thiamin—otherwise known as vitamin B1, and carnosine, which is a potent antioxidant. Tests have shown that high-dose supplementation of carnosine is required for maximum effectiveness, and low-dose supplementation is not effective at all.

Aging individuals with a fasting glucose level above 85 mg/dl (milligrams per deciliter) as well as diagnosed diabetics should consider a hemoglobin A1c blood test to assess long-term blood-sugar levels and to help identify the level of age-accelerating glycation occurring in the body.

Having been addicted to drugs and alcohol, my body does not metabolize glucose effectively even though I exercise daily. My A1c score was 5.7, with anything over 7.0 being critical and below 5.0 being optimal. I plan to take supercarnosine (from Life Extension) and retest every year until I get my score below 5.0. Those who crave carbohydrates should test their glycation score every two or three years, especially if there is weight gain involved.

Dialysis is allopathic medicine's solution for keeping a person alive when kidneys fail. Dialysis is defined as the process by which uric acid and urea are removed from circulating blood by means of a dialyzer. I've heard from a few patients that it isn't a pleasant process and must be done for the remainder of one's life, but it's better than the alternative. I would do everything I could to avoid it or correct the need for it. If I were diagnosed with less-than-optimal kidney function, I would use supercarnosine to dissolve the advanced glycation end products and L-arginine/arginine pyroglutamate to dissolve arterial plaque under the guidance of a nephrologist or experienced health professional. I would also adopt a low-carbohydrate diet, drink plenty of clean, fresh water, and start a daily exercise program. If your doctor is warning you about the need for dialysis, your kidney function is probably unable to sustain life. It is best to take care of your kidneys while they are still functional.

A New Way of Life

Diabetes and kidney disease are on the rise because of a combination of factors relating to lifestyle, diet, and stress. DNA loses its ability to replicate accurately as we age, resulting in metabolic inefficiencies in the way our bodies process and utilize nutrients, especially simple carbohydrates.

A young body may get away with a less-than-optimum diet for a while, but beyond thirty years of age, its margin for error declines precipitously. The mistakes accumulate and take their toll in the form of plaque and AGE buildup. The greater the amount of trauma and stress in one's life, the faster the rate of DNA decay and the earlier the onset of metabolic errors. Eventually even minor bad dietary habits start creating discomfort and symptoms.

When I was in private practice, I encountered a number of clients complaining of gradual weight gain, three to four pounds a year over a ten-year period. It is as if they awakened one day to find forty extra pounds on their once-svelte bodies, a phenomena referred to as metabolic syndrome, syndrome X, or insulin resistance.

Metabolic syndrome, which affects approximately 25 percent of the adult population in the United States (a percentage that continues to grow), is loosely defined as a combination of medical disorders that increase the risk of people developing cardiovascular disease and diabetes. Time to cut down on the carbs, especially breads, pastas, sodas, and desserts, and rev up the exercise!

Defining metabolic syndrome as a combination of medical disorders assumes that it can be treated by medication and totally ignores the dietary, lifestyle, and aging factors involved in the condition. I have metabolic syndrome (as do most recovering alcoholics and drug addicts), and I deal with it by exercising to improve insulin utilization, cutting down on carbs to reduce insulin production, and consuming food supplements such as high-dose vitamin D, resveratrol, and supercarnosine, which as well as offering other benefits, improve insulin utilization.

A recent study showed that diabetes is significantly more prevalent in people with low serum levels of vitamin D,[10-5] and another study indicated that supplementation with 8,500 IU of vitamin D3 daily significantly increased serum 25-hydroxy vitamin D levels and improved insulin sensitivity. [10-6] These products are available through Life Extension and many local health-food stores.

Will I ever cure my metabolic syndrome? I doubt it. But will I be able to live a high-quality life free of heart disease and diabetes? Absolutely yes. I use the expression "no room for error" to describe the lifestyle choices I must make to deal with the metabolic inefficiencies of aging and the accumulated damage of lifestyle and dietary errors. I don't consume alcohol anymore, and

I have no trouble keeping bread and pasta out of my life, but I do have an occasional craving for a Ben & Jerry's ice cream. When I succumb I awaken with two to three extra pounds around my waist—a visible reminder to get back on the program. Bad lifestyle habits, like addictions, stress, poor food choices, and lack of exercise, will defeat all efforts to build health and wellness.

You can take food supplements and exercise every day, but if you drink alcohol regularly, smoke cigarettes, or overindulge in sweets, you will succumb to the same risks of obesity, liver failure, lung cancer, and diabetes as others who are not exercising or consuming food supplements. Exercise is great for physical health, so it may stave off those outcomes for a while, but sooner or later the body will succumb.

The Organ of Fear

In Chinese medicine the kidneys store and react to the emotion of fear. Obviously no medical studies exist to prove this statement, but simple observation confirms that fear-stimulating situations cause people to release urine uncontrollably. Chronic fear responses also cause the lower part of the spine to curl up under the body, a position that increases physical pressure on the kidneys and bladder. Fear in the form of anxiety causes carbohydrate cravings, which will eventually cause glycation buildup around and through the urinary system.

All humans are fearful of some phenomena. Death, disease, debilitation, lack of money, feelings of helplessness, trauma, brutality, war, or a letter from the Internal Revenue Service are but a few of the events that cause fear to grow within one's psyche. So great is the power of posttraumatic stress disorder, a common occurrence among veterans returning from war zones, that it can render its victims comatose.

A number of therapies for treating overt trauma and stress have evolved since World War II. All traumas get buried in the physical body and play back their fearful messages throughout life, whether the trauma came from a war zone or a dysfunctional household. Unresolved traumas will influence daily behaviors and eventually cause disease. Diffusing fear messages, whether from trauma or circumstance, is the most important step in achieving wellness.

Chapter Summary

1. The primary function of the urinary system—the kidneys in particular—is to maintain the body's homeostasis in the following ways:

- regulation of blood, water, and interstitial fluid volume
- reabsorption of required substances: water, sodium ions, potassium ions, bicarbonate ions, urea, uric acid, proteins, glucose, and creatinine (a protein metabolite)
- excretion of excess substances
- excretion of toxic substances
- regulation of body pH
- regulation of normal blood pressure

2. The kidneys regulate body pH by excreting hydrogen ions (H^+), thus making the urine more acidic and adding or withdrawing bicarbonate ions ($HCO3^-$) to maintain normal pH.
3. The kidneys are sensitive to stress, which impedes their ability to keep blood pressure within a normal range.
4. Diabetics experience the highest rate of kidney disease because of the complications of insulin resistance and glucose metabolism inherent in that disease.
5. It appears that most kidney disease is caused by blockages to the capillary-sized blood vessels contained in that organ.
6. These disturbances are most likely caused by arterial plaque similar to that found in heart disease and the buildup of AGEs (advanced glycation end products) formed from proteins and lipids in the presence of high glucose blood levels.
7. Consuming 1,000 milligrams per day of super carnosine and arginine pyroglutamate for periods of time has been shown to reverse the buildup of AGEs and arterial plaque that contribute to kidney disease.
8. Will the taking of super carnosine and arginine pyroglutamate obviate the need for dialysis? I don't think so, and I cannot imagine any practitioner willing to work with you with that goal in mind. I suggest that you begin working with a nephrologist the moment you notice your kidney scores dropping. Kidney failure is life threatening.
9. Metabolic syndrome is a glucose and insulin metabolic disorder that is a precursor to obesity and diabetes. It is easily neutralized by greatly reducing the intake of refined carbohydrates, regular exercise, stress-reducing activities, and detoxification rituals.

Chapter Eleven

Heart Disease

Poetry and song have celebrated the heart as the organ of love for three millennia, but twenty-first-century medicine celebrates it as the organ of money. Take, for example, the estimated direct cost of $475,000,000,000 (that's *billions*) to treat the 1,255,000 people who will be struck by some form of heart disease. That's $378,500 per patient. Cancer, by comparison, will cost $228,000,000,000 (again, *billions*).[11-1] Adding these costs to the cost of insurance premiums, emergency-room visits, doctor visits, prescription-drug care, and the treatment of diabetes and Alzheimer's disease, disease and health care has become a multitrillion dollar industry. In its present form, the way allopathic medicine is practiced in the United States is financially unsustainable.

These statistics show me that as a nation we don't love ourselves very much. If 1.25 million people are experiencing heart attacks each year and their number is growing, how many more millions are in the ticking-time-bomb stage? I see a high obesity rate almost everywhere I go. With all the ads on TV, every adult in the United States knows about heart disease risk factors, so why isn't there a massive public effort being exerted in the education and counseling of people who are at risk?

Consider this for a government health-care and bailout plan as one inexpensive idea: free omega-3 fatty acids, lysine, and vitamin C, along with nutrition and exercise coaching for every person even remotely at risk for a heart attack. Let us say arbitrarily that 30 million people are at some identifiable level of risk, and it would cost $1,000 per year ($400 for supplements and $600 for education and coaching) for each person.

You will read below that high-dose vitamin C and lysine supplementation will dissolve arterial plaque in six weeks. The amount required to accomplish that would cost less than $50 at a health-food store. Omega-3 fatty acids play numerous beneficial roles in ameliorating several risk factors contributing to arterial disease. *Life Extension Magazine*[11-2] lists seventeen risk factors, all of which can be improved by supplementation and dietary and lifestyle changes.

Let us say arbitrarily that the program results in a 25-percent reduction in the heart attack rate. Roughly speaking that would generate a reduction of $118.75 billion in treatment costs on an investment of $30 billion. This would be a net expense reduction of $88.75 billion per year and would result in a significantly healthier population whose improved vitality would further reduce health-care costs and make gains in economic and social productivity. Why aren't we doing this on a massive scale?

This book won't be read by a large majority of those at risk for heart disease. That's unfortunate, so it is up to those who do read this book to convey the message that heart-disease risk factors can be greatly decreased through education and counseling that result in permanent lifestyle changes.

Meet Dr. James Howenstein

An article appearing in a recent issue of *Nexus Magazine* by Dr. James Howenstein grabbed my attention.[11-3] Here was a medical doctor with thirty-four years of hospital and clinical experience talking about treating heart disease with alternative methods:

> Natural therapies are far more effective than drugs, which are unable to reverse arteriosclerosis. *Knowledge of the efficacy of natural therapies has been systematically suppressed by the powerful pharmaceutical industry, which controls what is published in conventional medical journals, and by the news media, which conveniently ignore health breakthroughs that would hurt the earnings of the pharmaceutical companies.*

Further into the article, he wrote:

> *Nobel Prize winner Dr. Linus Pauling proposed an effective therapeutic program using the amino acid lysine and vitamin C that reverses arteriosclerosis in six to eight weeks. Yet this therapy remains largely unknown to US citizens.*

One paragraph later, Howenstein wrote:

> *The use of alternative health therapies would promptly heal patients with arteriosclerosis. These therapies include: eliminating toxic metals from the endothelium with long-term oral chelation; treating endothelial infections with turmeric; taking high doses of lysine and vitamin C; supplementing with N-acetylcysteine and L-arginine; lowering homocysteine values with pyridoxine, folic acid, vitamin B12, and trimethyl-glycine; taking vitamin K2 (which removes calcium from arterial plaque and places calcium in bone); adopting a low glycemic*

diet (avoid foods that raise blood sugar rapidly, such as pasta, corn, bread, rice, bananas, white potatoes, and wheat); and curtailing sugar intake. Excessive sugar intake is now regarded as the number one risk factor for heart attacks in women and the number two risk factor in men.

Another worthwhile quote from this article:

Dr. Linus Pauling's high doses of vitamin C and lysine can rapidly reverse angina pain, hypertension and claudication… Any therapy based on repair of narrowed arteries is doomed to failure because it does not deal with the root cause of arteriosclerosis, which is a degenerative metabolic disorder caused by toxic metals, infections, deficiencies of vitamins C and K2, excessive intake of sugar, trans fats, gingivitis, and dangerous levels of homocysteine.

Homocysteine is an amino acid normally created by the body in cellular metabolism and the manufacturing of proteins. Elevated concentrations in the blood are thought to increase the risk of heart disease by damaging the lining of blood vessels and enhancing blood clotting.

The chart in figure 9 shows a narrowed coronary artery with about half its circulation blocked.

What are the odds that it will close completely within one year, three years, or five years? What would be the benefit to the individual as well as to all humankind if that artery were attended to now with lysine and vitamin-C detoxification protocols? This is the direction that we, as individuals and as a society, will need to take in the future as the current medical system prices itself out of the market. We simply cannot afford the present system—health insurance coverage or not.

Based on Howenstein's article, which was 100-percent supported by Dr. Harry A. Elwardt's book *Let's Stop the #1 Killer of Americans Today,* I strongly recommend that you add the IonCleanse footbath and food supplements—especially antioxidants, minerals, fatty acids, and herbal supports—to a total body detoxification program. This will greatly reduce your risk of heart attack.

Based on my personal experiences with healing addiction and two life-threatening conditions and the life changes they forced me to make (if I wanted to live), I believe that an ongoing total body detoxification program will greatly reduce the incidence of disease in the body and greatly improve quality of life for all who practice this discipline.

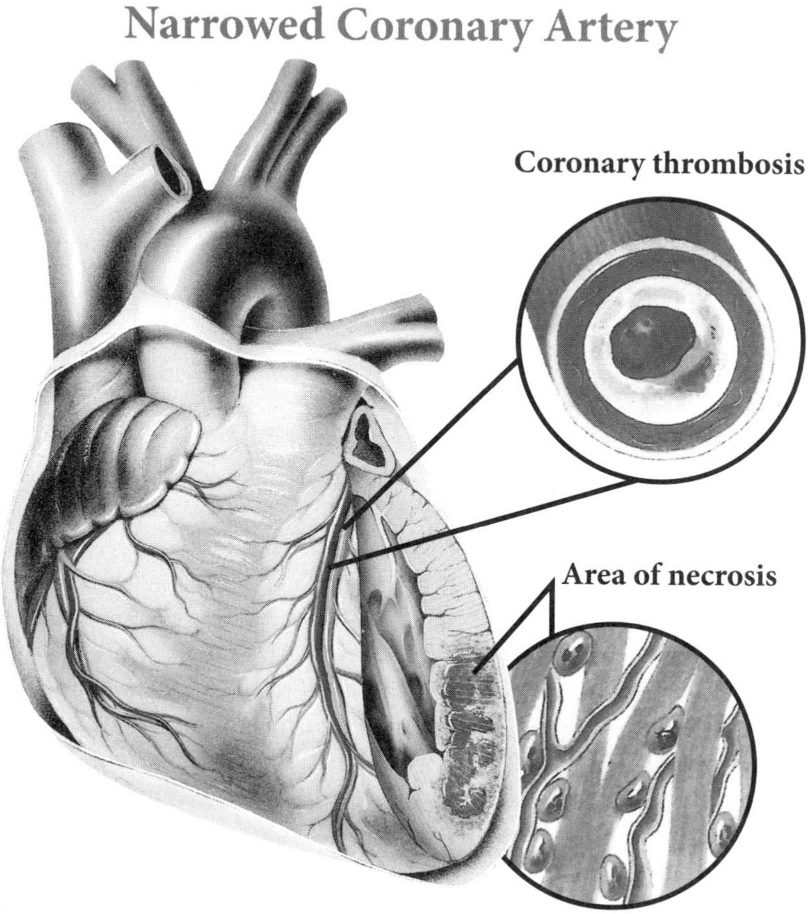

Narrowed Coronary Artery

Coronary thrombosis

Area of necrosis

Figure 9

Mild Cognitive Impairment (MCI) and Alzheimer's Disease

Mild cognitive impairment (MCI), a diagnosis made from an MRI (magnetic resonance imaging) scan of the brain, emanates from plaque buildup in the brain. In his excellent book *Brain Longevity*,[11-4] Dr. Dharma Singh Khalsa discusses the seven stages of Alzheimer's disease and how the progression of the disease can be delayed and in some cases staved off indefinitely through the taking of supplements, detoxification, and yoga. He classified the first four stages of the disease as "early stage," indicating that if diagnosed during these stages, Alzheimer's disease can be reversed or avoided almost indefinitely. The late stages of the disease are indicated by physical deterioration of brain structures and therefore cannot be reversed.

The common medical diagnosis for early stage Alzheimer's disease is MCI, which will eventually lead to full-blown Alzheimer's disease in the future for most patients diagnosed with this. Allopathic medicine has no protocol for reversing MCI, the plaque buildup in the brain that is similar to that of heart and kidney disease.

I was diagnosed in November 2009, with plaque on my brain, a fortuitous diagnosis resulting from an MRI, which I had taken as a result of attending a seminar on Dr. Ryke Geerd Hamer's research on brain lesions and disease. With that scan as a baseline, I have embarked on a journey to dissolve most if not all of that calcification buildup. I will describe my program in the following paragraphs, but before I do I will outline Hamer's brilliant work, because it will enable you to gain a deeper insight into the disease process.

Hamer was a radiologist and researcher in Germany. Over the course of his practice he viewed tens of thousands of MRIs and the case histories of those traumatized patients. By correlating his research by brain area, trauma type, and location of lesions, he concluded that when people experience an unexpected, dramatic, emotional shock, for which they have a limited coping strategy, that shock becomes imprinted in their subconscious and can subsequently manifest as health issues. Hamer found that these imprinted shock-conflicts, as they are now called, can physically manifest as small calcification spheres within the brain tissues, and these show up as light-colored rings in brain CAT (X-ray) scans.[11-5]

Hamer went on to discover that, depending on the nature of the originating shock-conflict, the calcification rings would appear in specific regions of the brain. Through extensive studies Hamer produced a series of brain maps identifying specific types of shock-conflict where the corresponding rings would appear. Using a CAT-scan image, he was able to identify the original shock-conflict from these maps, solely based on the location of the calcification ring within the brain.

Hamer extended his work to show that for each shock-conflict region in the brain, there is an associated reflex or relay area within the physical body where symptoms were likely to manifest from the trauma. He effectively showed the link between trauma and pathology.

Yet despite his outstanding contributions to medical science, Hamer has been imprisoned in Spain and Germany on two occasions for practicing unauthorized medicine, and Germany presently has a warrant out for his arrest. Hamer currently resides in Norway, where there are no extradition laws.

Peter Fraser, a physicist and founder of Nutri-Energetics Systems, used his knowledge of the human body-field and bioinformation delivery techniques to determine that original shock-conflicts result in energetic oscillations within the brain, which disrupt a specific part of the human body-field called the morphic field. His research enabled him to produce five "infoceuticals"—combinations of trace minerals in homeopathic solutions—to release the original shock-conflict memories.[11-6]

This is a significant development in the achievement of healthy, disease-free longevity in general and helping MCI in particular. Without having access to Fraser's proprietary information, I can only speculate that he has found a way to neutralize the ionic patterning of the shock-conflict mass in the brain. Once the ionic patterning is dissolved, its impact on the morphic field is also neutralized.

The *morphic field* is the energy field surrounding and permeating the body-field of all living things. It contains all of the information necessary for the organism to replicate and repair itself.[11-7] A disruption or distortion in this field means that its host organism will suffer some form of abnormality, such as a disease or addiction, because it no longer has access to its original, untrammeled energetic blueprint.

All shock-conflicts—be they chemical, emotional, or physical—impact the body's nervous and acupuncture systems and alter the thought patterns of their victims. In other words shock-conflicts have a global impact on physical and mental functions in that they set in motion a series of distortions that over time exert a significant influence on health. Hamer's discovery of shock-conflicts creating plaque buildup in the brain provides direct evidence that disease and emotional content are related to one another, and Fraser's infoceuticals offer hope that these life-threatening calcifications can be dissolved.

My Program for Dissolving and Releasing Brain Plaque

I have extensive plaque buildup and the brain scan to prove it. The program I propose for myself is as follows:

1. I will continue to take the food supplements I'm now taking, adding Fraser's infoceuticals and 8 grams per day of arginine pyroglutamate to the menu. Arginine pyroglutamate has been shown to dissolve arterial plaque and can penetrate the blood-brain barrier.
2. I will do ionic footbaths twice a week, simultaneously lasering my head with a multidiode cold laser. Several doctors have told me over the years that laser and IonCleanse footbaths have increased the arterial blood flow of many of their clients. It's

important that the lasering be done while in the footbath as the osmotic pressure of the bathwater will help to pull neutralized calcifications through the blood-brain barrier.

3. I will be mindful of the thoughts and energies that are surfacing and actively neutralize them. (I will describe a number of ways of accomplishing that task in my next book, but I suggest that you work with a professional until you become familiar with the process.)

Because of the high levels of radiation involved in brain scans, I will wait a few years before getting a second scan, at which time I expect most of the calcification to have been dissolved.

Radiation and Uranium Toxicity

It appears that each new advance in the production and delivery of energy brings with it a new set of toxins that pollute and weaken the body. We are well aware of the threats to health posed by the widespread use of fossil fuels, and Chernobyl showed the world how catastrophic a nuclear power plant failure can be. The recent multiple power plant failures in Japan nearly destroyed a substantial portion of that country, and their full impact has yet to be determined. Radiation from the Chernobyl accident traveled as far as southern Spain, causing increases in cancer rates in the countries it passed through.

The nutrition evaluation report in appendix V was compiled from an analysis of blood, hair, and urine from a healthy thirty-year-old male. Notice the high levels of uranium in the hair analysis. This young man sits in an office five days a week surrounded by three computers. He uses the latest smartphone and owns a television that broadcasts in high density—toys no successful young adult should be without. All of these devices contain numerous semiconductors, each containing small amounts of depleted uranium. His body is a stationary target for the radiation and uranium residues escaping from these devices. At the levels of toxicity indicated in the hair analysis, it won't be long before he manifests disease symptoms.

He has since put up radiation shields on all the computers and devices and has begun a long-term program to rid his body of the uranium and radiation. His program includes twice weekly IonCleanse sessions supported by daily intake of chlorella (an excellent heavy-metal and radiation detoxifier), Zeo-Tox (another heavy-metal detoxifier), a high-dose intake of a variety of antioxidants, and magnascent crystallized iodine to neutralize the radioactive iodine and caesium that are the most common elements of radiation fallout. Chlorella can be purchased at most health-food stores, Zeo-Tox from www.amajordifference.com, antioxidants from www.lef.org, and magnascent crystallized iodine from www.A2Zhealthproducts.com.

This is the first time I have seen uranium levels this high in a hair analysis. Cell phones and high-density televisions did not exist when I was in private practice, and computers were just coming into vogue. Our present-day civilization requires a computer on every desk, a cell phone in every ear, and an HDTV in every living room. My generation was not exposed to these technologies; however, this younger generation walked into them, and present-day students have been surrounded by them since birth. Electronic pollution and radiation are hazardous to human health. Yet the powerful corporations selling these devices have been able to confuse the issue by structuring their own studies showing that their products are not a danger to human health. Yeah, right! Cancer rates have increased dramatically during the twentieth century because of increased exposures to chemicals and heavy metals, and I have a feeling, based on this young man's hair analysis, that cancer rates will continue to climb. At a bare minimum, I recommend that school-age children and adolescents have a hair analysis done every four years if they are symptom-free, and students of any age with symptoms get one every year. The forms to initiate this program can be obtained from www.amajordifference.com.

Part III

The Importance of Nutrition and Supplements

Chapter Twelve

Antioxidants and Other Vital Nutrients

At a bare minimum, I advise anyone doing any sort of detoxification to consume large amounts of antioxidants, fatty acids, and minerals. Detoxification accelerates anabolic (building up) and catabolic (breaking down) activities throughout the body, which require additional nutritional support in the form of supplements.

Free Radicals

The following quote, taken from the bestselling book, *Grow Young With HGH* by Ronald Klatz, expresses exactly what I want to say about the power of free radicals to harm the body:

> *The constant bombardment of free radicals from the breakdown products of food and oxygen is a major contributor to aging and the diseases of aging, such as heart disease, cancer and autoimmune diseases.*[12-1]

And from *Prescription for Nutritional Healing* by Phyllis A. Balch:

> *A free radical is an atom or group of atoms that contains at least one unpaired electron. Electrons are negatively charged particles that usually occur in pairs, forming a molecularly stable arrangement. If an electron is unpaired, another atom or molecule can easily bond with it, causing a chemical reaction. Because they join so readily with other compounds, free radicals can effect dramatic changes in the body, and they can cause a lot of oxidative damage.*[12-2]

Metal rusting in a junkyard is an accurate example of oxidative damage. Biochemical processes, including the conversion of food to energy and the utilization of energy for sports and exercise, lead to the formation of free radicals that under normal circumstances can be kept in check. Free radicals do perform vital functions, such as destroying viruses and bacteria and producing hormones and energy. But excess free radicals—caused by poor dietary choices, X-rays, and exposure to environmental pollutants—can cause serious damage by changing protein structures, damaging genetic material, and destroying cell membranes.

As the body ages, DNA structural repair becomes inefficient, resulting in metabolic errors that reduce functional efficiency in all body systems. This inefficiency creates increased toxic buildup, which in turn creates more free radicals. This free-radical creation process may be the most significant contributor to the physical deterioration experienced by the aged.

Cancer and Vitamin C

Dr. Linus Pauling, recipient of two Nobel Prizes, recommended vitamin C in excess of 10 grams per day to ward off disease and maintain a healthy immune system.[12-3] Most mammalian species manufacture vitamin C internally in daily quantities comparable to Pauling's recommended dose for humans. This would indicate that nature places a high value on the neutralizing of free radicals in wild species whose habitat may not contain supplemental sources of that nutrient.

Compare Pauling's nutritional assessment of human need for vitamin C with the FDA's recommended dietary allowance (RDA) of 75 milligrams per day and 120 milligrams per day suggested as adequate intake.[12-4] Unfortunately because access to the media is expensive and due to the repressive tactics of the FDA and the medical industry, the value of food supplements in maintaining disease-free states is not recognized by most of the general public.

Pauling makes two points in *Cancer and Vitamin C*: (1) a high-dose intake of vitamin C daily (10 to 12 grams of sodium ascorbate) will extend the length and quality of life for patients with advanced cancer, and (2) the same dosage will delay the onset of cancer and heart disease in healthy individuals.[12-5]

When I was diagnosed with lung cancer in 1982, I had nothing to guide me except that pronouncement by my oncologist acquaintance Marty that all his patients died. My personal research led me to Pauling's books and the Vale of Leven lung cancer study performed between 1971 and 1976. In the study, 125 lung-cancer patients were studied; fourteen were treated with high-energy radiation, seventeen with chemotherapy, and twenty-four with 150 milligrams of ascorbate daily. Seventy patients received only narcotics to control their pain. The average survival times after the date of first hospital admission were 184 days for the radiotherapy group, 90 days for the chemo group, 187 for the ascorbate group, and 68 days for the untreated group. A later study showed much longer survival times when doses of 10 to 12 grams per day were administered.[12-6]

These studies influenced me to follow the orthomolecular (vitamin and food supplement) and detoxification route. I added more fruits and vegetables to my diet along with high doses of vitamins, minerals, and fatty acids—habits I continue to this day.

A 1955 study of 577 people fifty to ninety years of age in San Mateo, California, showed that persons with high vitamin C intake had a 40 percent lower mortality rate than those who did not supplement. This 40 percent lower mortality rate translates to eleven more years of healthy life.[12-7] Most of the vitamin C participants eventually succumbed to heart disease and cancer. Imagine what they could have achieved if they had been simultaneously undergoing a total body detoxification on a regular basis.

Healing Mechanisms of Vitamin C in Heart Disease and Cancer

Quoting directly from Pauling in *Cancer and Vitamin C*:

> *Cardiovascular illness (heart attack, stroke, circulatory disease) can be nearly completely prevented by proper intake of vitamin C, because the deficiency of vitamin C is involved in several specific ways in initiating and exacerbating cardiovascular disease.*
>
> *It is recognized by all cardiovascular researchers that an initial step in atherosclerosis (hardening of the arteries) is a tear in the wall of an artery... We pointed out that the walls of the arteries are strengthened by fibers of the protein collagen. Collagen is synthesized only with use of vitamin C. With a high intake of vitamin C much collagen is synthesized and the arteries are strong. With a low intake of this vitamin only a small amount of collagen is synthesized and the blood vessels are so weak that they develop lesions. Accordingly Dr. Rath and I stated that the primary cause of cardiovascular disease is a deficiency of vitamin C in the blood.*[12-8]

Any arterial clearing and strengthening program should include at least 800 international units of vitamin E daily. Vitamin E prevents cell damage by inhibiting the oxidation of fats and the formation of free radicals.

In relation to vitamin C and cancer, Pauling reports a study completed in January 1990 that involved 134 patients with advanced cancer, 101 of whom were put on a supplement regimen that included 12,000 milligrams of vitamin C, 800 international units of vitamin E, 1,500 milligrams of niacin (vitamin B3, either nicotinic acid or nicotinamide), and minor amounts of selenium, zinc, and calcium. The thirty-three patients in the control group who refused to do the protocol survived an average of a few months after registration in the study, whereas the ones who followed the protocol lived an average of sixteen times longer, with many still alive when the study concluded.[12-9]

In all of Pauling's books, he mentions the many times he presented data to the FDA and medical authorities only to be ignored or rebuffed by arguments with no scientific basis. The studies cited above, while not measuring up to a standard that would allow for a scientific claim, present compelling evidence that should have led to full-blown research efforts, which would have allowed the FDA to endorse treatment. In order to qualify under FDA standards, a study must be designed and approved by the FDA, no matter the credentials of the persons conducting it or the number of people in the sample. Under this rule the FDA can delay clearance of a drug, device, or procedure for years without recourse to any other authority.

Unfortunately it is not in the interest of the FDA and the medical-pharmaceutical establishment to support the development of health-improvement protocols (or disease-healing protocols.) Doing this would diminish profits made from the treatment of sick people with protocols that deliver questionable results. I don't know of any supplement distributor that has the several hundred million dollars necessary to fund a definitive study that would make it possible to launch large-scale advertising and public-education campaigns. Instead we have evolved a system that permits advertising of prescription medications with potentially life-threatening side effects to treat acute symptoms. Health care in the United States is big business.

In 1966, Dr. Ewan Cameron, a surgeon with thirty years of experience with cancer patients, wrote that the resistance of normal tissues surrounding a malignant tumor to being infiltrated by that tumor would be increased if the strength of the intercellular cement (also called *ground substance*) that binds the cells of the normal tissues together could be increased.[12-10] This intercellular cement contains collagen fibrils and very long molecular chains, called glycosaminoglycans, that give it strength, like steel rods reinforcing concrete.

Some, and probably all, malignant tumors liberate an enzyme, hyaluronidase, which causes the glycosaminoglycans to be cut into smaller molecules, thus weakening the intercellular cement. Moreover some (and perhaps all) malignant tumors also liberate another enzyme, collagenase, which causes the collagen fibrils to be split into small molecules, further weakening normal tissues, which makes it easier for the tumor to infiltrate these tissues.

Until 1971, no one had found a way to strengthen the intercellular cement until Cameron and Dr. Douglas Rotman suggested, on the basis of chemical arguments, that increased concentrations of vitamin C would stimulate normal cells to produce increased amounts of hyaluronidase inhibitor, which would neutralize malignant-tumor secretions.

Cameron's thesis was never proven, but it stimulated a 1971 study in which large doses of vitamin C were administered to advanced cancer patients. The following is an excerpt from this 1974 report:

> *Subjective evidence of benefit is usually apparent by about the 5th to 10th day of treatment, and in many patients, this response can be very striking indeed. The patient then enters a stage of increased well-being and general clinical improvement, and during this phase objective evidence accumulates to confirm that some retardation of tumor growth has been achieved. The objective evidence of benefit varies with the individual clinical presentation, but may take the form of relief of particularly distressing pressure symptoms such as pain from skeletal metastases, a slowing down of the rate of accumulation of malignant effusions, a trend towards improvement in malignant jaundice, or relief from respiratory distress, and is accompanied by a slow fall in the ESR [erythrocyte sedimentation rate] and serum seromucoid concentration. This phase of clinical improvement may be very transient, or it may last for weeks or months, and in a few patients may be so prolonged and accompanied by such convincing evidence of objective benefit as to indicate that permanent regression has been induced.*[12-11]

Recovering from Chemotherapy

We are all familiar with the agonizing side effects of chemotherapy, the standard form of treatment for many cancers. Several alternative clinics have told me that they have used ionizing footbaths and supplements to reduce and eliminate the side effects of chemotherapy with great success. I have spoken to two oncologists (neither of whom was willing to go on record) who felt that removing these residues improved the results of their chemo treatments, because lowered side effects improved patient morale and attitudes.

For a listing of clinics that use ionizing footbaths, go to www.amajordifference.com. For more information on orthomolecular medicine, visit www.orthomed.com and www.righthealth.com. For a listing of physicians who practice orthomolecular medicine, e-mail center@orthomed.com.

I opted for an alternative approach after my lung cancer diagnosis, because according to my oncologist acquaintance, the chances of my survival at that time were close to zero. I was not interested in spending thousands of dollars for chemo and radiation treatments that may or may not have bought me time. Presently the American Cancer Society's website reports a 15 percent survival rate for those with stage-four lung cancer.

Cancer is obviously a life-threatening disease, potentially affecting everyone on the planet. In an ideal world, oncologists and alternative doctors would be researching orthomolecular support protocols that might improve chemotherapy results and reduce its nasty side effects. However, with the politics (and economics) of medicine being what they are, this won't happen any time soon.

I would like to see a cooperative blending of allopathic and alternative medicine because both schools of thought have something to offer.

Wouldn't it be nice to know the impact on longevity and well-being by combining detoxification and supplement protocols with chemotherapy? Would reductions in chemo side effects improve cancer survival rates? Would a national education and counseling program dramatically reduce diabetes and heart-disease rates and costs?

Our society spends far too much on war and defense and virtually nothing on programs that would seriously benefit everyone and offer tremendous health-cost savings. Eventually our entire health system—from the food we eat to the delivery of medical services—will have to radically change, but it may take a collapse of the old system to stimulate this change. For the time being, change will take place, one reader, one person, at a time.

Other Antioxidants

In *Prescription for Nutritional Healing*, Balch devotes several pages to the more commonly known antioxidant subgroups, of which there are several thousand. Each subgroup has its own unique blend of micronutrients and enzymes that target different metabolic tasks and organs. I have selected a few of the more commonly used antioxidants to illustrate their diverse contribution to human health.

Alpha lipoic acid (ALA): Supplemental ALA has been used in Europe for over three decades to treat peripheral nerve degeneration and to help control blood-sugar levels in people with diabetes. It also helps to detoxify the liver of metal pollutants, block cataract formation, protect nerve tissues against oxidative stress, and reduce blood cholesterol levels.

Alpha lipoic acid plays a crucial role in the generation of cellular energy and is a significant immunologic stimulant that increases circulation; it has been approved in Japan to treat congestive heart failure.

Melatonin: A hormone produced in the pineal gland, melatonin is one of the few antioxidants that can penetrate the mitochondria, the cells' power plants, and protect them from free-radical damage. Laboratory studies with nonhuman subjects have shown that supplemental melatonin can inhibit cancer growth and protect against degenerative diseases.

Vitamin A and the carotenoids: Carotenoids are a class of compounds some of which can be converted to vitamin A by the liver. Over six hundred different carotenoids have been identified thus far. Vitamin A and the carotenoids prevent night blindness and other eye problems. They also enhance immunity, help to heal gastrointestinal ulcers, and are needed for maintenance and repair of epithelial tissues—that means tissues that cover inner surfaces and passageways in the body. They are important in the formation of bones and teeth, aid in fat storage, and offer protection against colds, flu, and some infections. The body cannot utilize protein without vitamin A, which is also a well-known wrinkle eliminator.

Flavonoids: Flavonoids are healthful plant pigments. These are especially potent antioxidants and metal chelators. More than four thousand chemically unique flavonoids have been identified.

Other common antioxidants include bilberry, burdock, curcumin, garlic, ginkgo biloba, methionine, N-acetylcysteine, Pycnogenol, silymarin, superoxide dismutase, and zinc.

As I researched Balch's book, I realized that most of these antioxidant nutrients (as well as all other macro and micronutrients) can be readily obtained from diets rich in raw, organic foods, but not from the junk that passes for food sold off supermarket shelves. How many symptoms and diseases could be avoided if our society focused on growing nutrient-rich food instead of the genetically modified, pesticide-laced, and depleted foods that have become a significant part of the American diet?A recent article in *TIME* magazine titled "America's Food Crisis and How to Fix It" spoke about the factory farming of animals among other large-scale, food-producing operations that add more pollution to the environment and destroy the habitats of natural food sources all in the name of providing food of questionable nutritional value to the American public.[12-12] Given the burgeoning disease rates of the American population over the latter part of the twentieth century, not only is the present health-care system economically unsustainable, but our food-producing system is unsustainable as well.

Essential Fatty Acids (EFA)

Essential fatty acids (EFAs) are beneficial fats that the body cannot manufacture from other dietary fats or nutrients. Research suggests that a lack of EFAs, ordinarily found abundantly in flaxseed oil and other unrefined polyunsaturated vegetable oils, play a significant role in the development of chronic degenerative diseases such as heart disease, cancer, stroke, and multiple sclerosis.[12-13]

Experts estimate that approximately 80 percent of the population is deficient in EFAs, specifically linoleic acid and linolenic acid, from which components of nerve cells, cellular membranes, and hormone-like substances, known as prostaglandins, are formed. Prostaglandins and EFAs play an important role in the following:

- producing steroids and synthesizing hormones
- regulating response to pain, inflammation, and swelling
- mediating immune response
- dilating and constricting blood vessels
- directing endocrine hormones to their target cells
- being the primary constituents of cell membranes
- regulating the rate at which cells divide (cell mitosis)
- maintaining the fluidity and rigidity of cellular membranes
- transporting oxygen from red blood cells to tissues
- keeping saturated fats mobile in the bloodstream
- preventing blood cells from clumping together
- being the primary energy source for the heart muscle

The above functions have a global impact on every body part and system. A deficiency in EFAs will eventually lead to serious breakdowns.

According to modern pathology, an alteration in cell membrane function is the central factor in the development of cell injury and death.[12-14] Without healthy membranes, cells lose their ability to hold water, vital nutrients, and electrolytes. They also lose their ability to communicate with each other and to respond to signals from hormones.

Consider type 2 diabetes, for example, in which insulin levels are typically elevated, indicating a loss of sensitivity to insulin by the cells. The type of dietary fat profile linked to type 2 diabetes is an abundance of saturated fat and an insufficiency of EFAs.[12-15] One of the key reasons appears to be the fact that such a dietary pattern leads to reduced membrane fluidity, which in turn causes reduced insulin binding to receptors on cell membranes or reduced insulin action.[12-16]

Conversely omega-3 oils appear to improve insulin sensitivity,[12-17] and population studies have shown that frequent consumption of small amounts of omega-3 oils protects against the development of type 2 diabetes.[12-18]

EFAs and Multiple Sclerosis (MS)

Multiple sclerosis (MS) is a debilitating condition of progressive nervous-system disturbance characterized by a gradual destruction of the myelin sheath that surrounds nerves. People with MS are thought to have a defect in essential fatty-acid absorption or transportation. Central to this defect are deficiencies of the omega-3 oils, which play a critical role in the structure and function of myelin. Chronic deficiencies can result in permanent impairment of the formation of normal myelin.[12-19]

In 1977, Dr. Roy Swank, professor of neurology at the University of Oregon Medical School, reported on a thirty-four-year study that provided conclusive evidence that a diet low in saturated fats and high in EFAs maintained over many years tended to halt the disease process. His dietary recommendations were to:

- eliminate butter and hydrogenated oils and intake no more than 15 grams of animal fat per day
- consume 3 to 4 grams of polyunsaturated vegetable oils per day
- take at least 1 teaspoon of cod liver oil daily and eat fish at least three to four times a week[12-20]

The results of the study were astounding. Minimally disabled patients who followed his dietary recommendations experienced little disease progression if any at all. Only 5 percent of those in the study did not survive over the time that it took to complete the study, but 80 percent of those who failed to follow the diet recommendations did not survive the study period. The moderately and severely disabled patients who followed the dietary recommendations also did better than those who didn't. In addition to dramatically reducing the death rate, the diet was also shown to prevent worsening of the disease, and it also greatly reduced fatigue.

A recent issue of *Nexus Magazine*[12-21] reported that a Dr. Paolo Zamboni completely relieved the symptoms of forty-seven patients (out of sixty-five operated on) with relapsing and remitting MS by performing a simple operation to unblock restricted blood flow from the brain:

> *Zamboni has put forth the idea that many types of MS are actually caused by a blockage of the pathways that remove excess iron from the brain. He reopens these pathways by simply clearing out a couple of major veins to reopen the blood flow, the root cause of the disease.*

The article goes on to state that more than 90 percent of people with MS have some sort of malformation or blockage in the veins:

> *Iron builds up in the brain, blocking and damaging these crucial blood vessels. As the vessels rupture, they allow both the iron itself and immune cells from the bloodstream to cross the blood-brain barrier into the cerebrospinal fluid. Once the immune cells have direct access to the immune system, they begin to attack the myelin sheathing of the cerebral nerves and MS develops.*

Based on Zamboni's hypothesis and the information presented in this book, I propose a three-to-six-month detoxification program using the IonCleanse, arginine pyroglutamate, omega-3 fatty acids, a daily intake of Zeo-Tox for heavy-metal removal (available from A Major Difference, Inc.), and cold laser to dissolve the venal blocks causing the MS. Take 3 to 4 grams a day of arginine pyroglutamate, do a footbath every third day, and laser the brain area during the footbath. (I am doing this program to dissolve plaque buildup in my brain.)

Based on Swank's research cited above, the fatty acids prevent or slow plaque buildup and should be included in everyone's daily food intake. MS has long been regarded as a life sentence of debilitating nerve degeneration. Nothing about this program is harmful, so with no physical risk and the relatively low cost of this protocol, the MS sufferer has nothing to lose and a new life to gain.

I base this suggested protocol on the assumption that all diseases emanate from or cause toxic buildup somewhere in the body. In this case it is iron (or possibly some other metal) buildup in the brain because of lack of circulation. If the cause is congenital (a structural obstruction), nothing may help except an operation, but if the vein or artery has been closed by plaque, my suggested protocol may restore normal blood flow. It's definitely worth a shot. You will know within a month or two. I also suggest that you participate in some form of yoga, tai chi, or bodywork class after you begin the cleanse if you are able.

Unfortunately for those suffering from MS in the United States and Europe, no alternative-health company or doctor can afford to jump through the FDA hoops to gain approval for this protocol. It would cost millions of dollars and take several years, if ever, to obtain that approval. Many notable people, among them US congressman Ron Paul, have proposed an elimination of medical licensure and the creation of a subclassification of non-FDA-approved alternative medical treatments, but I don't think I will see that in my lifetime. Word of mouth through the Internet may be the only viable way of broadcasting this valuable information.

Minerals

As is the case with EFAs and antioxidants, minerals are systemic to every function in the body. Every living cell on this planet depends on minerals for proper structure and function. Minerals are needed for the proper composition of body fluids, the formation of blood and bone, the maintenance of healthy nerve function, and the regulation of muscle tone, including the heart.

Like vitamins, minerals function as coenzymes, enabling the body to perform its functions, including energy production, growth, and healing. Because all enzyme activities involve minerals, they are essential for the proper utilization of vitamins and other nutrients. Minerals help maintain balance in the body; if a level of one or two minerals is low, that can have a negative impact on the functions of all the other minerals.

Nutritionally, minerals belong to two groups: bulk or macrominerals and trace or microminerals. Bulk minerals include calcium, magnesium, sodium, potassium, and phosphorus, and these are needed in larger amounts than are the trace minerals. Trace minerals include but are not limited to boron, chromium, copper, germanium, iodine, iron, manganese, molybdenum, selenium, silicon, sulfur, vanadium, and zinc. The supplements mentioned later in this book will provide adequate supplementation of all minerals. Refer to the "Minerals" section of Balch's *Prescription for Nutritional Healing* for more information on minerals.

Chapter Summary

In this chapter I have attempted to show the vital role that certain nutrients play in healing the body and reducing mortality. Our society's consumption of denatured foods, the shortage of reliable, unbiased research, and the lack of publicity regarding the studies cited in this chapter mean that most people will suffer needlessly from the ravages of a chronic degenerative disease at some point in their lives.

The average American family of four spends in excess of $20,000 per year on health care, including insurance coverage, doctor and hospital visits, and medications. A generous food supplement allotment of $6,000 to $7,000 per year would serve that family much more effectively than the $20,000 spent on fending off diseases that could be avoided with adequate supplementation of what is probably a nutritionally inadequate diet.

Detoxification amplifies the need for higher levels of supplementation and herbal support, because all the activities discussed above are accelerated. High-grade nutrition is essential for effective detoxification.

Chapter Thirteen

The Impact of Modern Technology on an Ancient Healing Technique

Most of what I say in this chapter is based on my personal experiences with the technologies described, the shared experiences of thousands of health-seeking people, and a thorough review of available research.

First I should introduce you to two important players in the businesses of medical devices, alternative medical devices, and registered devices: the Food and Drug Administration (FDA) and the Federal Trade Commission (FTC).

To be classified as *medical* or *alternative medical*, a device has to pass FDA safety and medical-claim standards. This clearance gives the device's manufacturer the right to make a claim that the device causes a specific change in the body that is beneficial to the patient. For new technology this process can take years and cost from $300,000 to several million dollars. For predicate devices—meaning devices that perform exactly the same function as the original cleared device whether manufactured by the same or a different manufacturer—clearance takes four to five months with less than a $100,000 outlay.

Having *FDA clearance* is a good marketing tool—it is a gold-standard accreditation, the one that distinguishes a product from cheaper replications that can't meet the FDA's rigorous safety and manufacturing standards. Anyone who holds this clearance can sell his or her product anywhere in the world and bill it as an approved device for treating a particular medical problem. On the other hand, a device that bears an *FDA registered* designation means that it has met all safety standards for a device that makes no medical claims, a useful classification for distinguishing a safe device from its unsafe competition. Registered nonmedical devices are forced to operate within narrow advertising and marketing parameters.

The FTC rigorously monitors the websites and marketing statements of companies engaged in the sales of nonmedically approved devices. In other words it keeps an eye on what companies (and people) say about their own products. A manufacturer can *claim* anything it wants about its product as long as it can prove the statement. If it's not proven by passing FDA-designed test procedures, then the claim cannot be used to sell the product. User testimonials also count as claims, and if a manufacturer uses them to sell a product, they might be in violation of FDA and FTC regulations.

This labyrinth of rules favors larger companies and severely penalizes smaller ones, because only large companies can afford the time and financial outlays to obtain clearance for a new drug or device. It also favors illegitimate manufacturers that can cut and run when faced with FDA regulations they might not pass; if they make illegal claims or can't meet safety standards, all they have to do is move locations and change product names and they are right back in business. Manufacturers that are in it for the long run, on the other hand, must simply deal with the obstacle course.

Before you buy a registered nonmedical device, look at the firm that makes it. How many years has it been in business? What are its return and warranty policies? How does it handle customer support? Does it have FDA and (if necessary) electrical safety clearances? The latter is especially important when purchasing a footbath device. Most offered for sale over the Internet are unsafe and can damage the body's electrical system—especially cheap units from China.

A Very Brief History of Detoxification

Ancient cultures—most commonly the Chinese, the ayurvedic doctors of India, and the Native American medicine men—have used fasting, colonics, and sweating rituals for centuries to help the body get rid of toxins. Colonics have grown in popularity throughout the United States over the past fifty years, and sweat lodges are still a part of Native American healing rituals.

Fasting, or the organized cessation of food intake for a specific period of time, is effective at deep-body cleansing. However, few individuals possess the blood-sugar-regulating capability to sustain a fast long enough—at least ten days—for it to be deeply effective. Theoretically fasting throws the body into starvation mode, forcing it to cannibalize whatever material it can consume within itself: fats, mucous, catarrh, microbes, microorganisms, and gases are dissolved or released through urine, feces, skin, and breath. However, fasting wreaks havoc on blood-sugar levels of diabetics, persons with low blood sugar, and those with weak adrenals—which accounts for most people in the United States.

Fasting has never worked for me. Drug addicted, hypoglycemic, and burned out from a stressful lifestyle, my adrenals and other blood-sugar-regulating mechanisms could not cope with even minor interruptions in food intake. The longest I ever fasted was three days, during which all I could think of was eating food. I knew I would hurt myself if I continued the fast, so I stopped.

However, I know people who don't mind not eating for a week or two. Good for them! I can imagine that they are freeing their bodies from the ongoing need to process food and waste, they are cleaning and recharging themselves, and they are going back to a higher state of health without any concern about FDA and FTC regulations. Fasting may be the best way to detoxify the body—if one could do it for ten to twenty-eight days at a time!

Footbath Publicity

Ionized footbaths have attracted a significant amount of attention in the media, perhaps because of their phenomenal success worldwide. Granted some of the attention has come from unsubstantiated claims made by overenthusiastic practitioners, and some of it has come from vitriolic criticisms by representatives of the medical establishment.

But the bulk of the attention has come from word-of-mouth advertising by those who have achieved astonishing healing results, especially with fibromyalgia, arthritis, and some forms of inflammation. The following testimonial, taken from Oprah Winfrey's website (www.oprah.com/community/message/991573#991573), describes the results achieved by many practitioners, most commonly chiropractors. It was posted by an herbalist who was tired of hearing inane criticisms from uninformed people. The author did not reveal his or her identity but gave me permission to use the quote:

> *I too was skeptical that ionic foot spas could actually produce any real results. I am an herbalist and in my practice, I suggest many ways for my clients to detox the body… I then researched ionic technology and the effects of negative ions on the body. It seems that bodies that are acidic are deficient in negative ions, and that when the body becomes charged with negative ions, it begins to balance the pH factor… During the course of this balancing, the body does purge itself of toxins, metals, and impurities that the abundance of positive ions in the body caused to bond to cells. Whether there is any real organic material in the foot spa water or not, I have seen first hand that the body rids itself of impurities through the urine and bowels during periods of ionic detoxing. But because of the pungent odor of the water after the footbath, I tendto believe the oils and sediment in the water are in fact organic and toxic in nature. Being an herbalist, I am a great believer in the effects that plants can have on our bodies. But I have found that no amount of herbal detoxing was completely effective in some conditions such as joint pain, fibromyalgia, and autoimmune disorders, just to name a few. I have found that using ionic technology in addition to typical herbal detoxes has given nearly all of my clients with chronic disorders 99 percent relief and restored 100 percent of my clients back*

to a normal pH factor. It has been particularly helpful to clients with lower back pain due to kidney weakness and toxicity.

This is a powerful testimonial—and it is similar to what I have heard from hundreds of practitioners over the years. Unfortunately no manufacturer or distributor can carry such a testimonial on its website without running afoul of the FDA or the FTC. This deprives consumers of valuable information and opens the door for unethical and irresponsible manufacturers to sell cheap and unsafe equipment.

I believe that water ionization is the best detoxification assistant on the planet today. Fasting requires powerful, healthy adrenals, which few people possess. Colonics are excellent for removing impacted fecal matter from the bowel, a key aspect of any detoxification program. Herbs and herbal food supplements remove toxins from the organs and the tissues they support, but as the body ages, it does not process toxins as efficiently as it once did; an herbal formula may be effective in stimulating liver or kidney releases, but the pathways out of the body may not be sufficiently operational to complete the release. Osmotic pressure from water ionization, however, ensures that the neutralized toxins get out of the body. As I write this, I have completed more than six hundred footbaths on myself, and I anticipate that I will continue doing them for the rest of my life. I find them especially helpful when I fly. Air travel tires me fairly easily, and my fatigued body tends to bloat for a few days after a flight. One IonCleanse footbath takes out the bloat and raises my energy level so I'm back to normal within a day or two. Not bad for a busy guy who is seventy-one.

During my founding years with A Major Difference, Inc., I talked with thousands of doctors and their patients about their spectacular results with IonCleanse-centered therapies for fibromyalgia, pain, gout, arthritis, fatigue, and edema—virtually the entire gamut of modern human ailments.

Many of the patients had lost hope of ever finding relief. The earliest testimonial of a miraculous cure came from my friend's fiancé, who is a doctor and a former boxer immobilized by severe osteoarthritis. He was able to walk without pain after five footbaths.

Similarly a chiropractor from Montgomery, Alabama, called to say that her ankles were back to normal size for the first time in twenty years. Several parents of children with autism called to report remission of certain symptoms. Patients with fibromyalgia diagnoses have reported significant symptom reduction by combining colonics with footbaths.

The simplest explanation for these so-called miracles is that removing toxins improves health and vitality and reduces symptoms.

The IonCleanse Footbath and Arginine Pyroglutamate for Dissolving Arterial Plaque

In chapter twelve, I discussed Pauling's findings with respect to cancer, heart disease, and vitamin C. Dr. Harry A. Elwardt, in his excellent book *Let's Stop the #1 Killer of Americans Today* (See 10–3), also offers a number of alternative ways of treating heart and kidney conditions that do not have the debilitating side effects of allopathic therapies. He cites an impressive number of studies on the effects of arginine-derived nitric oxide on a multitude of health functions. [13-1] He reports: "There have been over 69,000 studies, dating back to 1927 and they continue to study the effects of arginine derived nitric oxide in the top medical centers around the world."[*13-2]

So now you have heard it from two authoritative sources: we do not have to succumb to the disease epidemic that is plaguing Western civilization. We can live healthy, vital lives for our entire life spans if we make doing so a priority.

By doing so you are engaging in an activity that will give you an economic return greater than any other investment, and you are getting the greatest amount of pleasure and peace as well.

As we age the toxins that have accumulated in our bodies grow in quantity and influence to a point where they begin to shut down parts of the body. Muscles atrophy and stiffen. Range of motion decreases. Reverse these processes, and you could perhaps live to be 100 without illness.

Elwardt recommends arginine pyroglutamate in daily quantities of 5 to 6 grams. He does not say how long to take it, but Pauling mentioned six weeks along with large doses of vitamin-C therapy. My suggestion is that you work with a qualified health professional and get an arterial scan every two or three years as needed. I also recommend adding vitamin C and omega-3 fatty acids to the pyroglutamate program. These nutrients complement and support one another.

The goal here is to reduce arterial plaque in the body, which is formed from a buildup of metal and fat. Nitric oxide is one of the breakdown products of arginine metabolism, and since it is an oxide, it carries a negative charge. Once inside the body, these negatively charged particles attach themselves to the positively charged metals in the plaque, thus neutralizing their bonds and freeing them to flow into the bloodstream, where they can be released through urine, feces, and ionization footbaths. So simple! So easy! Eliminate arterial plaque, and you may significantly reduce your chances of heart disease.

---

* L-arginine pyroglutamate is a delivery system for arginine. Arginine is involved in the synthesis of nitric oxide, so the supplement is taken to, among other things, increase nitric oxide production in the body, hence the term *arginine-derived nitric oxide.*

Since arginine accelerates detoxification, I strongly recommend the addition of ionized footbath sessions to speed the release of toxins from the body through the pores of the skin. You can rent or buy a safe and reliable device from www.amajordifference.com.

Far-Infrared Saunas

Light waves are measured in nanometers, which is shorthand for a billionth of a meter. Red light travels in the 600- to 800-nanometer range and is visible to the human eye. The infrared light range begins at 800 nanometers and is largely invisible to the human eye.

Steam saunas have been used as health-building therapies for centuries by Native Americans and Scandinavians, and the infrared variety—a recognized medical device—has been in use for several decades in the United States.

Some of the documented benefits of infrared sauna include: [13-3]

- increased speed of metabolic processes
- statistical improvements in blood pressure
- statistical improvements in heart strength
- improved function of impaired vascular cells
- relief from chronic pain
- relief from depression

Some of the undocumented benefits include:

- release of fat-soluble toxins
- increase in body temperature
- improved blood flow to organs and glands
- increased speed of metabolic processes
- increased heart volume and rate

Another unproven idea going around the alternative-healing world involves petrochemical residues. The theory is that they form a shellac-like coating over internal organs and cells, thus limiting their ability to function. This statement isn't a stretch. Dr. Theo Colborn, in her landmark book *Our Stolen Future*, discussed in great detail the enormously debilitating effects of petrochemical residues entering the body and occupying cell receptor sites normally reserved for hormones. She labeled these residues *hormone disruptors* and stated that their presence threatens our species' ability to reproduce itself. She believes that we are doomed to extinction.[13-4] Unless I (your author) have some form of detoxification plan that she does not know about.

In addition, Ronald Klatz and Carol Kahn state in their pioneering book on antiaging *Grow Young With HGH* that many people require hormone injections because normally produced hormones do not get to cell receptor sites due to toxic blockages. Colborn is certain that these toxic blockages are mostly comprised of the residues from petrochemicals above all other possible sources.

I believe that far-infrared sauna sessions are essential for dissolving these shellac-like petrochemical layers and that every couple contemplating procreation should engage in an intense, three-month detoxification program with this technology before conceiving, in order to reduce the possibility of birth defects. Colborn mentions a direct correlation between a 1,667-percent increase in birth defects since 1980 and petrochemical toxins disrupting the gestation process at key stages of the fetus's maturation. In her aforementioned book, she states, "It's just a matter of when and where the disruptors enter the process." Ridding the body of these hormone disruptors should be a primary consideration for intelligent couples seeking to bring healthy offspring into the world, and far-infrared saunas can be a key to this process.

Far-infrared saunas can also aid in weight loss, which is a great concern to many people today. Fat becomes soluble in water at 110 degrees Fahrenheit, and so combining sauna sessions with IonCleanse footbaths and massage, especially around and over fatty tissue, will speed the removal of dissolved fat from the body. An interesting scientific experiment would be a before and after database of changes in water-fat content after a sauna-massage-IonCleanse session, supported by appropriate supplements. Just remember that before attempting to sit in a high-temperature environment for any length of time, you should consult a professional practitioner for an assessment of heart, thyroid, and adrenal statuses and always drink plenty of water before, during, and after a sauna session. Remember, detoxification requires energy—the level of which is determined by how well those organs are functioning.

In his excellent book *Achieving Victory Over A Toxic World,*[13-5] Dr. Mark Schauss discusses an observation that metabolic rate and internal temperature are lower in laboratory rats exposed to toxins.

A few years ago, the American Medical Association debated whether to drop the average healthy body temperature of patients from 98.6 degrees Fahrenheit to 98.0 degrees—not because it was healthier to be lower, but because fewer and fewer people were coming into doctors' offices with the higher temperature.

Body temperature and metabolic rate are thyroid functions, and toxins, along with a lack of iodine in the American diet, severely impede the function of the vital thyroid gland.

Since the body is at rest most of the time, a slow-resting metabolism means less energy produced from carbohydrates and a higher fat accumulation from the conversion of unprocessed carbohydrates to fats. Exercise and activity burn the glucose that is produced from carbohydrates. The glucose that is not burned up converts to fat, which is one of the many reasons exercise is so important.

Fever is the body's way of fighting infection and the presence of viruses, fungi, and bacteria. Long, high-temperature sessions in the sauna have helped reduce the debilitating effects of these microorganisms.

A lower body temperature, a sluggish thyroid, and a slow metabolism combines to impede digestion which increases toxin buildup in the colon and creates an environment conducive to the proliferation of microorganisms. I strongly recommend the inclusion of far-infrared saunas in all detoxification programs for the sauna's ability to heat the body, which speeds up metabolism, kills microorganisms, and dissolves accumulated layers of petrochemical toxins.

I have been using infrared saunas for the past five years with excellent results. The interior has gotten up to 150 degrees Fahrenheit in twenty-five minutes—more than enough heat to liquefy fat and fight microorganisms and infections. A two-person sauna runs on 110V, a four-person on 220V. Several companies sell far-infrared saunas over the Internet.

Low-Level Cold-Laser Therapy

Cold-laser simply means that the laser light source does not generate enough heat to burn or cut tissue. *Low-level* means 5 milliwatts (mw) of power or less. These instruments are FDA-cleared for use in treating joint pain and carpal tunnel syndrome, but many doctors use them to stimulate the lymph system during footbath sessions. Figures 6A and 6B in Chapter Six show that neurolymphatic reflex points (NRPs) are densely packed around the chest and groin and on both sides of the spine. A person can stimulate the points in the front of the body with the laser, which should double the outflow of toxins in the footbath.

From years of experience, I recommend three five-minute passes over these points with a single-diode 5 milliwatt laser for maximum results. The light will easily pass through clothing and stimulate an inch or two of tissue, which is more than sufficient to unclog the nodes. Persons with chronically blocked lymphatics should definitely use cold-laser or far-infrared instruments on a regular basis, along with periodic massage.

Used appropriately, cold-laser light will increase oxygen utilization and speed up cell replication and metabolism.[13-6] In chiropractic offices it is used to quickly dissolve any myofascial buildup around wounded and stressed muscles, thus restoring their range of motion. However, overuse, even at this low level of energy output, will heat and inflame tissue.

I have used low-level cold-laser therapy during my IonCleanse sessions when I did not have the time for a sauna. While not as intense as far-infrared sauna, it does increase the amount of toxins dislodged from the fat and lymph. Single-diode lasers can be purchased at www.amajordifference.com.

Closing Comments

The FDA and FTC regulate all devices that come in contact with the body. FDA clearance assures a degree of safety and a degree of effectiveness, but the clearance process, which can be time-consuming and expensive, often prohibits small companies from pursuing it, thus assuring that many devices will never get the recognition they deserve. It is illegal for device manufacturers to make unsubstantiated claims about curing diseases, so as a consumer, you should shy away from those that do. When purchasing footbath devices, ask for safety-test reports and *stay away from units made in China*. These units are usually of poor quality and electronically unsafe, and the metals used in the dissolving plates have not been certified to any standard.

Large amounts of arginine pyroglutamate—5 to 6 grams a day—have been shown to dissolve arterial plaque. In addition Pauling has demonstrated that 10 to 12 grams per day of vitamin C will clear an artery of plaque within six weeks. The evidence that these supplementation programs work effectively is compelling. Everyone older than fifty should get an arterial assessment every two or three years. When plaque begins to build, the arginine, vitamin C, nutrition, and IonCleanse protocols would be an excellent way of dissolving it. However, remember that the ionized water footbaths are an essential addendum to any full-body detoxification program, because the extreme toxic burden the human body must handle every day is greater than what its organs of detoxification can process;the older we get, the less efficiently our organs of detoxification function; and high stress levels from ordinary daily living lessen the body's ability to detoxify itself. The relaxation response set up by an ionization footbath device provides the extra energy the body needs to release toxins efficiently.

Far-infrared saunas are the most efficient way of dissolving shellac-like petrochemicals that have layered themselves over the surfaces of your body's internal cells and organs. These petrochemicals block hormone uptake and utilization, thus impairing gestation and accelerating aging.

Low-level cold lasers are an inexpensive and efficient way of accelerating the detoxification process, especially when they are used to stimulate the liver and lymphatic systems. It is not known whether they have any impact on petrochemical buildup. I think they do not, and I prefer using far-infrared for that reason. Petrochemicals are always finding their way into the body and need to be removed regularly.

Chapter Fourteen

Winchester's Protocol: The Body-Mind-Spirit Connection

I was introduced to Dr. Ted Winchester in the spring of 2005 by a mutual acquaintance who was seeking to open an alternative-healing center. Winchester, a practicing chiropractor for twenty-five years, had recently sold his Gunnison, Colorado, practice and had relocated to the Denver Tech Center, a cluster of new office buildings twenty miles southeast of downtown that housed mostly high-tech and software-development firms. By the time I met him, he was already operating at close to full capacity, a rare achievement for any alternative-health practitioner.

We agreed to exchange services, but as I had been suffering from upper arm, shoulder, and neck pain, my visits to Winchester were more frequent than were his visits to me. He was using an ionized footbath manufactured by a competitor that was known to make shoddy products. He also used a cold laser both for myofascial work and to accelerate the detoxification process. I loaned him an IonCleanse, and within a short period of time he had two of them going virtually full-time.

"I only adjust the body when there are obvious subluxations," he told me. "Over the years I have found that most body pain is caused by mental and emotional factors. Let's see what's going on with you." So instead of cracking my spine and neck, Ted sat me down on his treatment table and began a series of inquiries by having me touch different points on my body while he used my arm as a muscle-testing feedback device.

He told me, "Pain is oftentimes related to emotions held in organs and chakras. Identify the organ, the emotion, and the chakra, and we can then explore the issue or conflict causing the problem. Once we do that, you then have information that will lead you to making new choices and decisions in your life. And then the pain goes away."

Made sense to me. After all I had been doing mental-emotional work with my clients for almost twenty years. It came as no surprise that body pain was related to mental-emotional issues. But chakras? How were they involved in the process?

"Chakras seem to govern various aspects of a person's life," Winchester explained. "For example, the heart chakra involves one's ability to give and receive love. The throat chakra governs expression. The first chakra, family and tribal issues, and so on. I ask the body what chakra imbalance is involved in the pain, and once I identify the chakra, I then ask the body a few questions to help me identify the specific issue.

"Once I identify the issue, I then ask the patient to consciously identify how that issue relates to events in his or her life. I then confirm the patient's issue identification through muscle testing—a strong test confirms, and a weak test disaffirms. If the issue is a trauma, I then remove that trauma by palpating the spine. If the issue is a conflict, I have the patient resolve the conflict in his or her mind. I then confirm the resolution by palpating or retesting the range of motion of the impacted muscle groups. I might repeat this procedure two or three times if I determine that other chakras and issues are implicated in the problem.

"Pain, or any other symptom for that matter, can involve a number of issues, and muscle testing is the only way to effectively identify the issues causing the problem unless the trauma or issue is so big and obvious that the person can't help but know it.

"I also use muscle testing before and after footbath treatments. I muscle test all patients for organ and meridian blocks and weaknesses before I put them in the footbath. When I got the IonCleanse, I found that it corrected most or all of the blockages in one session—a fascinating discovery in that it shows that all energy blocks and weaknesses are directly related to toxin buildup.

"Here's the best part: for the first few visits, the patient presents the same energy blocks over and over. As we get into the emotional work and the patient becomes more aware of his or her issues, the blocks lessen, and the symptoms clear up. Everything is connected or related: body, emotion, mind, spirit.

"If a chakra is out of balance, it causes a problem in the body. The body responds to that problem by creating a symptom. The symptom shows up as an energy block or weakness in an organ or meridian. As a result, toxins accumulate in the area related to the symptom. Removing the toxins begins to reverse the process. I say 'begins,' because one has to alter the internal mental-emotional process underlying the symptom in order to permanently heal the symptom, and the information needed to make the mental-emotional change is held in the chakras, our direct link to spirit. At least that's how I see it."

Winchester's clinical procedures conform to four of my five basic laws of detoxification, and it's worthwhile to repeat those here:

The first law of detoxification states:

> ***It takes physical energy and a powerful commitment to detoxify the body. If either is missing or in short supply, the body will not detoxify to the level required for healing.***

It never came up with me, but many of Winchester's new patients do not take supplements, are under severe stress, and don't drink enough water. Supplements—especially omega-3 fatty acids, minerals, and antioxidants—provide an energy lift and in themselves help to detoxify the body. Stress and high levels of toxins weaken the adrenals, and virtually all of Winchester's new patients have low adrenal function, and many have low thyroid function.

The adrenal glands govern many important body functions, including but not limited to:

- blood sugar level regulation
- production of several hormones, including
- cortisol production, which can reduce or increase inflammation
- mineral balances
- organ function

The thyroid gland governs the body's metabolism of nutrients, which means it can impact multiple organ and endocrine functions that usually result in distortions in blood-sugar levels—either too high (hyperglycemia or diabetes) or too low (hypoglycemia). This distortion severely impedes the body's ability to manufacture energy and release toxins.

In addition to the blood-sugar problem, digestive waste from an incomplete breakdown of nutrients increases, thus compounding the rate of toxic buildup in the body. People under severe stress or experiencing ongoing fatigue require at least two weeks of adrenal and other nutritional supports before initiating a detoxification program. I also recommend a few colonics before taking on the complete program to make sure the bowel is working properly.

Winchester conducts muscle tests for organ and gland weaknesses prior to initiating a detoxification footbath to ascertain the patient's readiness to begin a detoxification program and also to determine what organs and glands require nutritional support. Muscle or kinesiological testing is a recognized method of stressing various muscles to gain information about body structures—organs, glands, bones—that the practitioner can use as a course-of-treatment guide.

Since the IonCleanse will strengthen all or most weaknesses indicated by the testing, retesting the patient for nutritional support after the footbath will not give an accurate assessment of nutrition requirements. Winchester knows from his years of clinical experience that weak organs and glands are related to the patient's mental-emotional pattern, which will not change until the emotional overload is removed from them, a process that will take time and conscious effort to achieve. Meanwhile the nutritional support will enable these weak and toxic organs to sustain healthy function.

The second law of detoxification states:

> ***You cannot detoxify beyond what you are willing to release emotionally.***

Unless a patient has been subjected to severe heavy-metal or chemical exposures, Winchester states that there is always an emotional component to the toxic buildup behind the symptom. To permanently heal the problem, the patient *must* deal with the trauma or emotional process that caused the toxic accumulation and created the symptom.

I will say more about this in the last chapter of this book, and emotional healing will be the subject of my next book.

The third law states:

> ***Total body detoxification is an essential component of any consciousness-raising and healing effort.***

Winchester's clinical modus operandi adequately illustrates this point. Change what you have been thinking and feeling, and your symptoms will abate. Continue on in your old patterns, and your symptoms will return again and again to remind you that you need to look at something inside you.

You are distorting your energy field. It's an automatic biofeedback system: distort your energy, and you create a symptom. Once patients realize that their symptoms are connected to their emotional responses to stresses, they empower themselves to heal, because they are willing to make the necessary life changes to correct the problem. That, I believe, is what Spirit intended for all of us to do when It created us.

The fourth law states:

> ***Suppressing emotional pain and trauma creates energetic blocks in the body that attract and hold toxins. These energetic blocks trap body wastes and fluids, thereby restricting the flow of toxins out of the body. These toxins will be released only when the blocks are dissolved, and the only way to dissolve the blocks is to get in touch with and release the emotional pain they hold.***

Viewed in the context of Winchester's clinical practice, this law naturally flows from the other three. Suppressing emotional pain increases internal stress, which causes the adrenals to secrete higher levels of cortisol, which creates inflammation and in turn creates metabolic errors, impeding the flow of toxins out of the body. Over time this causes the fifth law to come into effect:

> ***The greater the amount of toxins stored in your body, the more sensitive you are to environmental onslaughts and the less capable you become at coping with stressful situations. Conversely, the lower the toxic levels in your body, the less reactive and better able you are to cope.***

Coughs, colds, fevers, pain, and fatigue emanate from some form of toxic buildup, as do allergies and most forms of mental and behavioral disorders. In other words you get sick more easily. I wonder how many "problem children" would not be problems if they ate wholesome food and went through a rigorous detoxification program for three months.

My twenty-seven-year-old son, Neill, discovered that when he detoxes in February and March, his spring allergies are minimized. The body is always creating and attracting debris of some sort, even in a relatively young person living in a nonindustrial area. Neill is relatively young, eats healthy foods, and takes high-quality supplements. If he has problems from not detoxifying his body, imagine what is happening to people with mediocre or poor diets.

Winchester's clinical practices drive home the body-mind-spirit connection and the applicability of the five laws of detoxification. Regardless of religious affiliation, we are all subject to physical laws. Anger, fear, anxiety, hatred, resentment, and worry alter the body's biochemistry, cause it to operate inefficiently, and lay the groundwork for the buildup of toxins, which lead to disease.

Consider this chapter to be your owner's manual—a guide to what you must do to transcend the ravages of aging and disease and what you must do to lead a happy, healthy, and productive life. Every other way leads to disease and disability.

The Adrenal-Thyroid-Pancreas Axis

No clinical discussion of detoxification would be complete without mentioning the adrenal-thyroid-pancreas axis, as Winchester and other integrative medical practitioners refer to it.

As was mentioned above, the adrenals regulate blood-sugar levels. As the adrenals weaken, their ability to produce cortisol lessens, causing blood-sugar levels to drop. Low blood-sugar levels mean that the body has an energy-production problem, and one of the ways it deals with that is through carbohydrate cravings, which add to the pancreas's stress load.

As a second way of coping with unstable blood sugar, the thyroid will upregulate for a short period of time, similar to raising an automobile engine's RPMs into the red zone. The thyroid has a limited ability to do this, so it too will crash. The body is now operating in metabolic syndrome mode, a twentieth-century phenomenon that eventually leads to full-blown diabetes (which is raging out of control in Mexico and gaining epidemic-like momentum in the United States). The Centers for Disease Control and Prevention presently forecasts that one in three children born in 2000 will become diabetic at some point in his or her life.[14-1]

A secondary problem that is plaguing women throughout the world is the increased use of halogens in the form of chlorine, bromine, and fluorine in commercial products and drinking water. These halogens occupy receptor sites in the thyroid that are normally reserved for iodine and form electromagnetic bonds with metals in the body that render them unavailable for use in the body's anabolic activities.

A recently published study in Japan showed that women who supplemented their diets with 19 milligrams of iodine daily had an 80-percent lower incidence of breast cancer. Breast-cancer rates have increased by 400 percent in the past twenty years because the fat tissue in breasts acts as a magnet for petrochemical and halogen residues. Here again is another example of chemical use run amuck. Do we need any more incentive to engage in a continuous program of detoxification to keep the levels of these dangerous chemicals as low as possible?

Iodine, by the way, is a nutrient vital to thyroid function, and our diets provide very little. I recommend supplementing with iodine, not kelp—as one would have to eat several bowls of kelp a day to ingest 19 milligrams of iodine.

Special Notes

Winchester schedules separate seminars for licensed health practitioners and laypeople in major cities throughout the United States. Call his office in Denver at (303) 221–0195 for more information or to book a reservation.

He has recently completed an instructional video containing his entire level-one seminar entitled *Dr. Winchester's Level One Seminar for All Alternative Healing Practitioners*. It contains instructions on clinical detoxification, nutrition support, therapy localization through muscle testing, and eighty pages of downloadable PowerPoint slides and published research, all of which are accessed from the DVD (that's twelve hours of chiropractic-accredited seminar material on a single DVD, suitable for practitioners of all healing disciplines). This video can be purchased at www.amajordifference.com.

Winchester also offers live webinars for lay practitioners seeking certification as footbath therapists through the same website.

I took applied kinesiology for eighteen months (see discussion in chapter sixteen) to get fully certified by Boulder Graduate School (later merged into Naropa University.) Two weekends of Winchester's beginning and advanced courses would have given me a better, more-efficient system for working with clients and patients than that eighteen-month course.

Closing Comments

Dr. Wayne Tashea, my foremost detoxification teacher and probably the most knowledgeable practitioner in the world of detoxification protocols, is a former acupuncturist who practices in Anchorage, Alaska. He abandoned his acupuncture practice when he realized that most of his patients were so toxic that they were not responding favorably to his treatments. Tashea combines his own unique form of homotoxicology with essential oil and alcohol-based solvents to create the most potent detoxification session I have ever experienced. He developed a unique way of identifying the toxins being emitted into the footbath, finding a solvent to accelerate their release, and making a homeopathic remedy to continue the releasing process after the session was over.

When Tashea speaks, I listen, and Tashea says:

> *Acupuncture and Chinese medicine were developed at a time when there were no chemical toxins on the planet and far less stress than today's fast-paced lifestyles. Acupuncture can't begin to touch what's inside people's bodies now. A more intense intervention is required to make a real dent in the toxic buildup.*

Winchester says something similar:

> *In my twenty-six years of clinical practice, I have noticed that people are getting sicker younger, and their symptoms are more severe. I recommend more nutrition support now because the symptoms are more deeply imbedded. Adrenals are chronically overstressed, and the overall body condition is weaker. Recovery takes longer.*

In this book I have suggested that ionizing footbaths be combined with a low-level red laser or infrared saunas and nutrition support in an effort to intensify an ongoing detoxification as a way of remaining healthy throughout the whole of life. I have great respect for Chinese and ayurvedic medicine as well as aromatherapy, but without support from light and ionization technologies and nutritional intervention, they may not be enough to bring a depleted body back to full health in today's environment.

Ayurvedic, Chinese Medicine, and Aromatherapy

Ayurvedic medicine was developed in India more than 2,500 years ago, and Chinese medicine, of which acupuncture is a part, was developed a century or two later. Ayurvedic medicine focuses on the stimulation of organ, gland, and chakra points on the body, with oils and aromas to strengthen organs and cleanse the body. It emphasizes diet, herbs, massage, relaxation, and aromatherapy in a total body-lifestyle approach to healing.

The acupuncture segment of Chinese medicine recognizes the energetic or electrical nature of the body as superseding the chemical aspect. Its early practitioners identified energy flows that run up and down the body like railroad tracks, with tiny energy vortexes spaced a few inches apart from each other in a manner similar to stations along railroad tracks. They named the railroad tracks *meridians,* and the stations are acupuncture points into which they would insert thin metal needles to adjust and stimulate the flow of current. The Chinese combined needling with herb and food diets into a medical practice that sustained a healthy culture for two millennia, until modern foods and industry invaded China.

The basic premise underlying Chinese medicine is that symptoms are caused by blocked, deficient, or excessive energy flows along these meridians. Restore or normalize these flows, and the healing process can begin. Herbs are used to strengthen organs and support the release of trapped toxins, which are the chief cause of pain, inflammation, and disease.

Where Winchester uses muscle testing to identify energy blockages, the Chinese read pulses located along the distal aspect of each wrist, just above the hand. Reading pulses is an art that takes years of practice to master, because unlike Western medicine, which recognizes only one or two pulse rhythms, Chinese medicine recognizes nine pulses, each having several different characteristics that, when analyzed by a master, give information about all organ and gland functions in the body. Muscle testing will achieve similar results in a much shorter practice time.

Aromatherapy, the use of aromatics and essential oils, is used by massage therapists and other types of energy and body workers to promote relaxation, reduce inflammation, and stimulate detoxification. I have experienced several sessions with some dedicated practitioners, but to be truly effective, the practice needs to be included in a holistic approach to detoxification that includes awareness of body energetics, adrenal strength, herbs, food selection, and lifestyle choices.

I strongly encourage everyone to take active responsibility for his or her health and supplement choices. One of the most effective ways of doing that is to learn muscle testing, and the easiest way to learn that art is by purchasing *Dr. Winchester's Level One Seminar for All Alternative Healing Practitioners.* It is structured in such a way that most people could become proficient in a relatively short period of time. Muscle testing is an essential skill for all alternative-health practitioners in that it assists them in making supplement determinations for their clients.

Laypeople will save hundreds of dollars a year by avoiding supplements they don't need, and they will improve the quality of their supplement selections through their ability to identify those the body really wants at any given time. Supplement requirements change monthly, so the ability to muscle test is the perfect way to monitor those changes.

Chapter Summary

This chapter is essentially a summary of Winchester's practice methodologies. I suggest you reread it several times or whenever you want to refresh your memory.

Chapter Fifteen

The Spiritual Connection

I met Dr. Bruce Lipton, a cell biologist and medical-school instructor, at a 1986 seminar on the immune system given by Dr. James Privitera, a genius in his own right who invented the live-cell microscope, a method of observing the shapes and activities of live blood cells under a high-powered microscope.

Privitera was an excellent and inspirational presenter, but Lipton stole the show. The doctor sitting next to me leaned over in the middle of Lipton's lecture on "The Effects of Nutrition, Light, and Emotions on the Immune System" and whispered in a hushed tone, "This guy is the second coming of Christ." I couldn't agree more.

I was in the midst of a healing journey through lung cancer and in need of a broader perspective to help me understand the powerful physical and emotional detoxes I was going through. I highly recommend reading his incredible book *The Biology of Belief* to get the full impact of what science has to say about how we are intimately connected to Spirit and how thoughts profoundly affect health and well-being.[15-1]

Lipton gets to the point of his book on page three of the prologue:

> *First, the science of Signal Transduction focuses upon the bio-chemical pathways by which cells respond to environmental cues. Environmental signals engage cytoplasmic processes that can alter gene expression and thereby control cell fate, influence cell movement, control cell survival, or even sentence a cell to death. Signal transduction science recognizes that the fate and behavior of an organism is directly linked to its perception of the environment.*

To drive his point home, he offers a second opinion from a different science:

> *Second, the new science of epigenetics, which literally means "control above the genes," has completely upended our conventional understanding of genetic control. Epigenetics is the science of how environmental signals select, modify, and regulate gene activity. This*

new awareness reveals that our genes are constantly being remodeled in response to life experiences. Which again emphasizes that our perceptions of life shape our biology.

On page sixteen of the prologue Lipton writes:

Understanding on a scientific level how cells respond to your thoughts and perceptions illuminates the path to personal empowerment. The insights we gain through this new biology unleash the power of consciousness, matter, and miracles.

This statement clearly summarizes a lifetime of research, both academic and personal, into humankind's spiritual origins and the path each of us must take to resolve our physical, mental, and emotional dilemmas. Lipton negotiated his personal transformation by observing the behavior of microscopic forms and applying the concepts and lessons of those observations to his own life—with extraordinarily beneficial results.

I never got better than a C in any science course, but Lipton and I got to the same place in our transformational journeys through two different paths. His tantalizing descriptions of tiny proteins being shaped by invisible energies, such as electromagnetic impulses and emotions, enabled me to visualize and put into language what was happening to me as I struggled to release the pains ravaging my body and mind.

His playing field was the microscope and laboratory; mine was lung cancer, drug addiction, and over twenty-six years of challenging, transformative work. I came to know my spiritual origins in the same way that Lipton came to know his. Although our life paths were different, our inner journeys were similar, starting with a reassessment of who we are and the real purpose of life and working with modalities that would peel away the stored nervous-system messages that accompanied our old programs.

At some point we both came to the realization that we are the creators of our reality; that what we think and feel has a cosmic effect on the physical body and the flow of our lives. We have both discovered the power we have to alter cell function consciously by changing the thought processes that power the nervous system and the messages it carries to the cells.

These realizations require the body to make powerful readjustments that will stress its physical resources. Everyone's path is different, but the destination is always the same: to know and accept yourself as the God-creator of your life. We are all made from the same God and energy stuff.

How We Have Been Programmed

After hearing my story, a business consultant I recently hired shared some of his old Alcoholics Anonymous experiences and ended by saying, "I still have a difficult time understanding the concept of Spirit and what is meant by spiritual transformation."

"I think I have an answer for you," I told him, "but it's a bit complex. Are you ready for something different in your life?"

"Sure, go ahead."

"It would be helpful if you saw yourself as the creator of your reality. You are not an accident of birth, a victim of circumstances, a curse of God. You came into this life at the behest of your soul to transform yourself from an angry victim of circumstances to a fully functioning, self-aware human being. That's the opportunity you afforded yourself when you chose a life of sobriety. You decided to liberate yourself from the story you inherited from your parents and environment. If you hold yourself to any other belief, you permanently relegate yourself to the role of victim, with no power to change yourself."

As I spoke I became aware that his story was my story and was everyone's story, in one form or another. I continued, "Your story—you know, the one you told yourself before you checked into AA, the one about how you were beaten by your parents and told you will never amount to anything—is what you chose to experience as the vehicle for your learning. Until you decided to change your story, you misbehaved in school, got yourself fired from a few jobs, and went through a few painful breakups in your relationships with significant others. Your imbibing accelerated with your screwups until you finally gave up and checked into a drug rehab.

"Your story, with all its agony and angst, had imbedded itself in every thought and emotion that pulsed through your nervous system. It held you in behavioral patterns that were destroying your life: hating your parents for their abuse, blaming them and others for your failures, being afraid to take chances lest you fail and expose yourself to ridicule, to jealousy of others' good fortune, and worst of all, to hating yourself and your existence.

"Your programming began the moment your father's sperm joined with your mother's egg. His mental-emotional patterns were incorporated with your mother's patterns to form an energetic framework for your life patterns. While in the womb, you absorbed your mother's emotional response patterns to the stresses she was experiencing in her life so that on the day of your birth you came in fully programmed to respond to your family's mental and emotional environment. This prelife experience in the womb profoundly influenced your long-term health and behavior. As Lipton states in his book: “The quality of life in the womb…programs our susceptibility to coronary artery disease, stroke, diabetes, obesity, and a multitude of other conditions in later life.”[15-2]

Lipton also states from a later study: “Recently, an even wider range of adult-related chronic disorders, including osteoporosis, mood disorders, and psychoses, have been intimately linked to pre- and perinatal developmental influences.”[15-3]

The way that I see it, your programming in the womb electronically imprinted your brain and nervous system and through them imprinted your organs, glands, and muscles with a set of emotionally based responses to circumstances and conditions that influence your family's life. You entered life programmed to respond to stresses in your environment, and this programming will continuously play throughout your life, shaping your beliefs, attitudes, and perceptions; your life choices; your metabolism; your body shape; and the diseases you have. *Spirituality*, or *personal transformation* as I prefer to call it, is ridding yourself of the angers, fears, and hatreds that have ruled your life and adopting new beliefs, attitudes, and perspectives that are congruent with spiritual law and make you fully responsible for your existence.

I did not share in my parents' lives during their final years, but my wife's parents spent their final years in our home, providing me with an incredibly moving and informative experience. Barbara's mother had been a control freak her entire life and her father, a postal worker for thirty-five years, never made an effort to improve his prospects or take responsibility for his family. Mom was rendered immobile by Parkinson's disease during the last five years of her life to the extent that she needed someone to take care of all her personal needs. Her last words to me, spoken three years before her passing were “this is painful.” She had gone from being in control of everything in her environment to not being able to control anything, especially her own body. Dad spent the better portion of his last five years struggling to walk his stiff and wasted body twenty feet from the sofa to the bathroom to relieve himself, every step a titanic effort.

As I said above, every lifetime, whether the being is aware or not, is an opportunity for transformation. In my mother-in-law's case, four years of paralysis forced her to let go of the fears and anxieties that controlled her life; for my father-in-law it took five years of dragging his weak body to the bathroom to program effort into his being. I watched in amazement how Spirit supported him as his wasted body appeared to have no strength to travel the twenty feet. To his credit he never gave up on that task. As I understand from my sibling's descriptions of my parents' final years, their journeys appeared to be similar to my in-laws' journeys. As I mentioned earlier, my brother, who lived with them until they required professional care, described that in their later years "they became more of what they always were."

I believe that the end-of-life journeys of my parents and in-laws provided them with the opportunities to subconsciously neutralize the life programs that held them in debilitating patterns of control and paralysis. Their issues and traumas caused their bodies to distort into shapes and diseases that brought them face to face with their soul-dictated life challenges. These were ignominious life endings when viewed from a human perspective, but they were effective and successful endings when viewed from a spiritual perspective. These souls left this lifetime prepared to take the next step in their evolution, free of the burdens they came in with.

Now, thanks to the efforts of many yogis, gurus, quantum physicists, and scientific researchers including Lipton, we have a body of scientific and esoteric knowledge that enables us to understand and cultivate our divine connection. The human evolutionary process has always acknowledged a god or gods of some sort, usually possessing human attributes that required a special and privileged order of priests to act as an intermediary between them and ordinary people. Some priests throughout history have used this office to manipulate the fears and superstitions of the populace for power and personal gain. Now, with this new knowledge, humans can shed the yokes of ignorance and superstition and can claim their direct connection to God or the "All That Is" of which they are an integral part. Of course staking that claim requires a willingness to take full responsibility as the creators-in-spirit of all our life experiences. Any other perspective holds us in helplessness and victimhood.

Most beings are unaware of just how intimately connected to Spirit they are, even though they may acknowledge that God is out there. That's okay. They chose their life circumstances, by which I imply that their physical, mental, and emotional circumstances perfectly express what their souls created them to experience at any one specific time and place. The life experiences of people who are unaware of a conscious spiritual connection are just as valid a vehicle for growth and transformation as are the experiences of those who are aware of their divinity.

This "new" information gives us the wherewithal to thrive in a toxic bowl that has the ability to sustain life that is under assault from a number of sources. Imagine being able to live your whole life disease-free, being able to control and influence your environment in a positive way, and being able to create an effective and dynamic life that flows and cooperates with the universal law.

Remember the 1981 Fram oil-filter commercial in which the mechanics say, "You can pay me now, or you can pay me later"? If we want to enjoy healthy, energetic, and meaningful lives, our only choice is to undertake this spiritual and physical cleansing. Toxin buildup equates to disease; no toxin buildup equates to health. And not so ironically, deep detoxification—the kind required to maintain lifetime health and vitality—requires that we transmute the angers, fears, and hatreds that subconsciously govern our lives.

This "new" information gives us options that our parents did not have. We can change who we are or any aspect of who we are by taking responsibility for our lives and working through our emotional turmoil to effect change within ourselves. We are more toxic than any generation in human memory, and despite the Environmental Protection Agency's assurances, the body has zero tolerance for toxins. Every toxin affects electrical (nerve) function in some tiny way, but multiply "tiny" by a lifetime of exposures to several different toxins and we become a species incapable of reproducing itself. That's extinction, and we appear to be headed that way.[15-4, 15-5] The adversity we are facing as a civilization demands that we evolve through the consciousness that created these crises, and everything is in place for us to do so.

By age forty-three, my life was a junkyard filled with failures: estranged from my family, fired from several promising positions, a criminal record and prison time, more broken bones than I could count, numerous addictions, and finally a terminal-disease diagnosis. I hated humanity for its shortcomings and corruption, but I hated myself more for my inability to succeed. I was blessed with a high intelligence and ability to organize numbers and probabilities, but this just added poignancy to my failures. How could I be so smart and be such a failure at the same time?

My healing journey put me in contact with modalities that talked about energy concepts and the role of emotions in the disease-addiction process. These concepts made intuitive sense to me, and since they appeared to work when I employed them, I learned everything I could about them. It wasn't until I joined a structured meditation group that I began to learn about the creative force of negative emotions and the role I played in the creation of my life.

My sense of victimhood was so powerfully ingrained in me that it would take a dozen years before I could fully accept that I was the creator of my life. Before I crossed the line from victim to creator, nothing made any sense to me. Now that I am on the other side, I see my life and everyone else's as an opportunity to attain a oneness with the All. That is, an opportunity to live in peace and harmony and to love myself and my fellow humans, who are also part of the All That Is.

If you are up to the task, I can state with authority and conviction that this path is the only one that makes sense. You will be glad you followed it.

Chapter Sixteen

The Electrical-Chemical Relationship

Dr. Ted Winchester's protocol demonstrates the intricate relationship between the body's electrical and chemical natures.

Applied kinesiology, otherwise known as AK or muscle testing, was originally developed by Dr. George Goodheart, DC, in 1964 as a way of using muscles as primary-feedback mechanisms to determine how a person's body is functioning.[16-1] Goodheart chose the term "kinesiology," because the word embodies the study of motion, form, and muscle movement. Using this type of testing, he could diagnose the viability of individual muscles and the effectiveness of the various therapies used to treat the particular muscle.

In the 1970s, another chiropractor, Richard Versendaal, expanded AK to include the measurement of organ and gland performance by muscle testing reflex points located along acupuncture meridians—an electrical energy network that forms the basis of Chinese medicine, which is a healing modality that has sustained a huge population through famine and pestilence over three millennia.

Versendaal discovered that imbalances in reflex points could be ameliorated by mega doses of nutrition supplements, which in effect causes the strengthening or rebalancing of electrical pathways with food or chemical substances. He called his approach *contact reflex analysis*, and he has trained thousands of practitioners worldwide in this healing method. All of the practitioners I have interviewed over the years happily attest to the system's effectiveness in dealing with problems presented to them by very sick clients.

Significant in the clinical practice of AK is the ability to make a determination of the client's ability to benefit from a particular supplement or group of supplements by testing the weakness or strength of indicator muscles. (The deltoid muscle, located in the front of each shoulder, holds the arm in place when it is extended straight ahead. In the presence of foods or supplements that benefit the body, it will continue to hold the arm in that position, but in the presence of substances that are toxic to the body, it will become weak and incapable of continuing to support the arm. That makes it a perfect indicator muscle.) Like food allergies, which can vary from individual to individual, one person's superfood may be another person's poison. An AK practitioner will introduce one supplement at a time into the body's energy field. A weak muscle test indicates that the supplement is not appropriate at that time. The reason is not important. The supplement could contain an allergen peculiar to one out of a hundred people. AK will catch that most of the time. A miscue by an alternative practitioner may slow the healing process but won't seriously harm anyone, because the substances used are generally safe.

As an aside I wonder how many pharmaceutical medications would pass a muscle test with all those nasty side effects mentioned in television ads.

Allopathic medicine is well aware of the electrical nature of the body—for example witness the use of electrocardiogram (ECG) and electroencephalogram (EEG) testing and the use of electrodes to revive the heart or alleviate certain mental conditions. However, it completely ignores this electrical aspect when it comes to treating symptoms of depression and chronic degenerative disease, largely, I believe, because of the dominating influence of a pharmaceutical industry that donates hundreds of millions of dollars to medical schools. Psychiatrists are not sure how electroshock therapy works—whether by stimulating mood-altering neurotransmitters or by stimulating other neuroendocrine chemicals. But they claim an 80 percent success rate at relieving severe depression—far higher than pharmaceuticals.[16-2] Nutrients high in omega-3 fatty acids have been shown to ease depression and relieve some neurodegenerative and mental-emotional disorders,[16-3, 16-4] but their relatively low profit margins don't generate the profits that patentable drugs earn.

Chinese medicine treats the electrical nature of the body with the needling of acupuncture points and treats the chemical nature of the body with herbs and foods. These methods have worked effectively for 2,500 years, but most Western doctors either denigrate the discipline or ignore it entirely.

Chiropractors are trained to put the body's main energy-system component, the spine, back into alignment. Composed of bones called vertebrae that are sandwiched between cushioning discs, the spine extends from the base of the skull down the entire length of the torso. It acts as a conduit through which the twelve cranial nerves attach to their organ, gland, and muscle destinations.

The integrity and positioning of spinal vertebrae determine the overall mobility of the body and the strength of electrical signals that travel through the nerves to power the body. These cranial nerves must snake through tiny holes in the discs in order to get to their designated terminals. Compressed discs and subluxated (crooked) vertebrae squeeze the nerves, thereby reducing the amount of current they can carry, which results in diminished function of those aforementioned organs, glands, and muscles.

Since Versendaal's discovery, many practitioners from varied disciplines have modified and expanded Versendaal's work to fit their clinical needs, all with excellent results. I have studied AK for eighteen months as part of my master's degree program at Boulder Graduate School. I have also attended Winchester's beginning seminar in which he introduces his system of using muscle testing to determine the impact of toxic accumulations on the neurological system, the nutrition required to support the energy reflex points weakened by those toxins, and the immediate impact of his ionized detoxification protocol on strengthening those weakened points. His methodology allows the practitioner to accomplish three things in the time it takes for an average office visit:

1. complete a neurological examination in less than fifteen minutes[16-5]
2. determine a nutrition protocol to support the removal of toxins causing the neurological impairment in those reflex points that tested weak during the muscle-test evaluation
3. retest all the weak reflex points after a thirty-minute footbath to demonstrate that the release of just a small amount of the body's toxic load was sufficient to restore most or all of the reflex points to normal function

Not a bad result in a one-hour visit.

Versendaal, Winchester, and all AK practitioners are tapping into the body's electrical system to gather information about the impairment of toxic accumulations on nervous-system activity and energy flow. My teachers did not link weak reflex points to toxic accumulation; neither did Versendaal, although he intuitively understood the relationship of toxins causing weak reflex points.

The addition of ionic footbaths to Winchester's detoxification protocol made it possible to measure energetic changes in the body resulting from a single footbath: he could evaluate how many weak reflex points existed before the footbath and how many were cleared up as a result of the thirty-minute session. Winchester's discovery has made it possible to simplify AK protocols to the point that a practitioner can effectively start using them the next day in his or her practice. He has just completed a DVD entitled *Dr. Winchester's Level One Seminar for All Alternative Healing Practitioners*, available exclusively through www.amajordifference.com.

The nutrition-support evaluation is essential, because the toxic accumulations that are removed in the first footbath are just the tip of the iceberg. The patient will leave Winchester's office with all mental, emotional, and lifestyle habits in place and will continue to attract and accumulate toxins in exactly the same pattern that created the symptom until those habits are modified. Meanwhile the organs and glands associated with those weak reflex points will need to be supported until the detoxification process is complete: a perfect example of chemistry in the form of nutrition supplements being used to restore electrical function and support stressed organs.

Chapter Summary

Applied kinesiology (AK), or muscle testing, is a method for using points on the body as feedback mechanisms for determining information about the energetic condition of the body. Introduced in 1964, it has become a recognized and accepted way of determining energetic imbalances throughout the body. In the early 1970s, Dr. Richard Versendaal discovered that organ reflex points in the AK system corresponded to acupuncture points in the Chinese medicine system. Acupuncture points are situated along electrical pathways that travel up and down the body. That meant that AK practitioners were tapping into the body's electrical system in a uniquely American way—a giant step forward in the practice of complementary and alternative medicine. AK allows practitioners to accurately access a client's nutrition requirements and their exact dosages, and AK acts as a filter, because it rejects substances that are harmful or inappropriate for the body. AK allows practitioners to connect the dots between energy flows (or the lack thereof) and stressed organs. Sooner or later stressed organs will weaken and fail, and as I have said throughout this book, all diseases and symptoms emanate from a buildup of toxins. Removing toxins from the body is the best way to avoid disease.

Chapter Seventeen

Water

I almost left this chapter out of the book, but then I thought that a few words about what kind of water to drink might be an appropriate add-on. After all, there are several different kinds of water to consider: distilled water, reverse-osmosis water, plain tap water, filtered water, and clustered water.

I dutifully researched each category and the processes that went into their creation. Wow! Water is a complex subject, and since it comprises over 70 percent of the physical body, I came to the conclusion that water, above all other elements, exerts the most powerful influence over our physical health and mental-emotional well-being.

At birth the human body is 75 to 80 percent water. In a seriously ill older person, that percentage dips to less than 50 percent. These ratios apply equally to vegetation and animals. Water, which occupies 75 percent of the earth's surface, is the only substance on the planet that can exist in three states: liquid, solid, and gas. Without water, life as we know it would cease.

All toxins are delivered into the body through the medium of water. If you eat, drink, breathe, or bathe, you are taking in toxins, because every molecule on earth has been impregnated with some form of toxic substance.

Worse than the systemic planetary pollution is the concentrated effort of municipal water authorities to add chlorine, fluoride, and chemical-masking agents to drinking water under the guise of preventing disease and tooth decay. As I stated earlier in this book, these known poisons seriously disrupt endocrine and immune function by occupying cell receptor cites normally reserved for hormones produced by the body. I don't know what insanity drove virtually every civilized country to adopt these tactics of water treatment, but to paraphrase a well-known poem: mine is not to reason why, but I must adapt if I want to live a healthy life.

The Nature of Water

Scientists worldwide have been studying water for decades to fathom its marvelous and mysterious properties. Not only is it the most copious substance on earth, but the amount on the planet now is the same as it was when the planet was formed. Billions of humans, trillions of insects, countless mammals, and acres of land consume it every day, yet its quantity never changes. Try holding water in your hand; it is essentially a soft substance, yet it will eventually erode the hardest and thickest rock.

The chemical structure of water (two hydrogen atoms attached to a single oxygen atom) never changes, but its structure (the way its molecules are organized) changes with the environment surrounding it.[17-1]

The first hint of this phenomenon occurred in 1956 in a top secret military laboratory in Southeast Asia, when scientists, who had been discussing ways of modifying poison gases for biological warfare, suddenly became ill in spite of having eaten no food for several hours.[17-2] The water they had been drinking was analyzed and found to be chemically normal, but the examining doctors concluded that the scientists had been poisoned by bad water.

Over the next twenty years, scientists from a number of countries, especially Japan and Russia, began to discover the effects of thoughts and words on the crystalline structure of water. They discovered that each water cell has 440,000 information panels that record the memory of every environmental, atmospheric, and emotional contact made by that cell—from the particles that it touched as it fell to earth, to the rust and resins in the conduits that transported it, and finally to the emotional content of the humans that consumed it.

Each contact rearranges the crystalline structure in a predictable way, with poisonous, negative thoughts causing the crystals to deteriorate and happy, loving thoughts causing them to form highly organized and beautiful structures, like those seen in frozen snowflakes.

Dr. Konstantin Korotkov, from the Russian Academy of Natural Sciences, studied the effects of magnetic and electrical fields on water. He came to the conclusion that human emotions were the strongest element of influence in the formation and destruction of water structures.[17-3] He discovered that the emotion of love increased water's energy level, while aggression and hate diminished it. Dr. Masaru Emoto, of *What The Bleep Do We Know!?* fame,[17-4] has demonstrated—in seminars all over the world—the destructive effects of electromagnetic radiation and the impact of positive and negative emotions and words on crystal structures.

Musical impressions on water, from compositions by Bach, Mozart, and Beethoven, show the buildup of strong crystalline structures, while impressions from hard rock create structures similar to negative emotions. In a slightly different experiment, Emoto placed rice kernels covered by plain water in three glasses. Each day he said, "Thank you" to one glass, "You are an idiot" to the second glass, and totally ignored the third one. At the end of the thirty-day period, the kernels fermented in the thank-you glass, turned black in the you-are-an-idiot glass, and rotted in the ignored glass.[17-5] Anger may be debilitating, but isolation apparently is worse. Over the course of my life, I have found that humans respond similarly to emotional inputs.

Dr. Alexander Solodilov, also from the Russian Academy of Natural Sciences, subjected water to magnetic fields hundreds of times weaker than earth's magnetic field. The offspring of fish living in the treated water were born with patterned stripes and spots, whereas none existed in their parents. Behavior changes in swimming patterns occurred simultaneously in the entire school.[17-6]

How much does toxic water influence the present craziness and dysfunction displayed by governments and financial institutions throughout the world? Based on the growing record numbers of ADHD, autistic, allergic, and emotionally troubled children in the United States, I conclude that accumulating toxins weaken each successive generation, which then produces weaker offspring, who go on to produce still-weaker offspring.

The closing statement from *Water: The Great Mystery* DVD puts into perspective humankind's present predicament:

> *The system of the universe exists as a single perfect organism. All of its parts, including us and our earth, are inseparably bound together by huge streams of information, and on our planet, water plays the key role on how that information is exchanged. In effect, it is the order through which all nature is governed.*[17-7]

It appears, then, that we are biological information units, sending and receiving emotions as we move through life. It is difficult enough to cope with the toxicity entering us from the electromagnetic and chemical pollution of our environment. But when our own inner messages—based on fear, anxiety, and anger—enter the mix, erratic behavior, drug addiction, and chronic degenerative disease become a certainty.

Science Net Links[17-8] estimates the number of cells in the human body at somewhere between 30 and 100 trillion. At 70-percent water content, that's a whole lot of deteriorated and crumbling crystalline water structures in a chronically angry and fearful human host. Altering that ecology—changing one's attitudes and addressing those angers and fears—will allow deteriorated water structures to recrystallize, thereby paving the way to health and wellness.

Structured water can be formed from light, sound, magnets, quartz crystals, and pyramids.[17-9] For those with a curiosity about the chemistry of water structures, the website Nature'sAlternatives.com features a lengthy article—including some excellent academic references—by Norman Mikesell on the biochemical changes in water, resulting from exposure to different vibrations and frequencies.

Commercially it has been shown that plants exposed to artificially produced structured water grow faster and larger than their untreated counterparts grow. Kirlian photography shows an energetic increase of forty thousand times in structured water over ordinary water, and structured water has been shown to alter the pH of blood.[17-10]

Finally the Buddhist monks use prayer in the form of repetitive mantras to correct the crystalline structure of bad water in the body.[17-11] Prayer is a practice common to all religious and spiritual traditions that, when performed with respect and reverence, shifts brain-wave activity to lower frequencies and creates a peaceful inner environment. When accompanied by a sincere desire to forgive and let go of past judgments, insults, and injuries, permanent healing can be achieved. To do so requires that the energetic content of the water in the body be changed, and to accomplish that the thought content of the body must be changed.

What Kind of Water Should You Drink?

Distilled water is pH neutral and completely devoid of minerals. Reverse-osmosis water is one stage above distilled on the dead water scale. Both are chemical-free and microorganism-free, and both will pull minerals out of the body. As I will describe below, reverse-osmosis water may be your only viable option because of the abundance of harmful chemicals and heavy metals—particularly arsenic, aluminum, and fluoride—in your local water. Forty percent of all bottled waters are right out of the tap, and they contain large amounts of petrochemical toxins drawn from the cheap containers housing them. Most community water supplies are treated with chlorine to kill off microorganisms, but the chlorine breaks down into disinfection by-products (DPB's)—chloroform, haloacetic acids, trihalomethanes, chlorite, and bromate to name a few—which can cause serious organ and nervous-system damage.

In my opinion the water delivered by most municipal systems in the United States is unfit for human consumption. Household tap water is usually heavily chlorinated to neutralize microorganisms. Having administered footbaths at seminars and conventions throughout the United States, I can state categorically that no municipal water system delivers clean water, with the water in Phoenix and Fort Lauderdale being the dirtiest I've seen. (That statement was accurate up to 2007 when I stopped traveling to shows.) Some municipalities put so much chlorine and chlorine-masking agents in the water that it will not ionize. Water that does not ionize will not be absorbed into the cell; as a result the host body will never receive enough hydration to maintain proper electrical function.

At a teaching seminar in London, England, I noticed that the footbath water was not drawing toxins out of the people we were treating. Later that day I walked into the seminar room to find three competent chiropractors standing at the podium and scratching their heads over the failure of their treatment techniques on the audience of practicing doctors. One of our hosts shared with us that London water contained an exceptionally high amount of chlorine. His comment helped to explain our dilemma. I had noticed a heavy chlorine odor coming from the footbath water, and I realized that the municipality probably added additional chlorine each time it processed the water. Putting two and two together, I deduced that there was so much chlorine and there were so many chlorine-masking agents in the tap water that it failed to ionize.

I have encountered similar situations throughout the United States, and the use of chlorine and chlorine-masking agents appears to be on the increase.

Healthy water is supposed to provide electrical conductivity and deliver minerals into the body. Water that cannot ionize into H^+ and OH^- will not be assimilated. The body must be electrically charged for a chiropractic adjustment to take hold. The bodies of the English doctors were not carrying a sufficient electrical charge to maintain structural integrity because of the dead water they were consuming on a daily basis. To a lesser extent, daily consumption of distilled water will also significantly reduce the body's electrical charge.

Alkaline water is created by running filtered tap water through electrically charged plates (similar to ionic footbaths) that separate the water molecule into its ionic components: H^+ and OH^-. A portion of the H^+ ions are removed from the stream of water, thus reducing its acidity. The technology for accomplishing this has been around for over fifty years, and I have read many positive testimonials from people who have used the water. In theory, alkaline water is supposed to lower the acid content of the body, but I have a problem about drinking it around mealtime, because the stomach requires a high acid content to digest protein.

Hydrochloric acid and pepsin are highly acidic substances produced in the stomach to digest protein. Adding OH^- ions to that mix would neutralize the acids and impair protein breakdown. I've asked two companies who distribute alkalizing devices about that problem but did not receive satisfactory answers. After reviewing the claims and testimonials offered by these distributors, I believe that alkaline water has some merit that warrants drinking two or three glasses a day apart from meals, but no more than that.

That leaves us with plain tap water with all its gases, microorganisms, and toxic solids. There are several different makes and models of carbon filtering systems, and the better ones will effectively filter out the gases and toxic solids in the water. Your local installer will know the content of your local water and the best filter for the job.

I have installed a carbon-based filtering system that filters all the water coming into my Florida home, because the local water authority uses liberal amounts of chlorine to kill microorganisms. Since the system uses a salt compound to soften the water, the salt content at the tap is higher than I would like to drink, so I installed a reverse-osmosis device to remove the salt. Finally I use an electronic device to structure the tap water before I drink it. I alternate between drinking the filtered tap and reverse-osmosis water, and I take mineral supplements every day so that my mineral levels stay in a healthy range.

I do a lot of work to drink healthy, clean water that will properly hydrate my body. Including amortization of the initial investment, I estimate that my program costs about $500 a year to maintain—about $1.37 a day.

Countertop filters will also do a satisfactory job at one-third of the cost. Whatever you can afford to invest in a water-filtering service will be well worth the expense.

Ozonation of Water

As a society we should be focusing on ozonating water instead of chlorinating it, but the costs and logistics of mass ozonation are considerably higher when the health costs of chlorination are not factored into the equation.

Ozone, designated as O_3, is a highly unstable molecule that quickly degrades to oxygen (O_2). Ozone can be produced in large amounts using corona-discharge devices, ultraviolet light generators, or electrolytic and chemical reactions. UV-type generators are excellent for home use, while corona discharge is used in industrial applications.

Ozone will effectively remove bacteria, viruses, iron, manganese, and hydrogen sulfide from the water, but the insoluble metal oxides created by ozonation require postfiltration. Ozonation will improve taste and remove odors from the water.[17-12]

YouTube hosts several videos that show how to make ozonated water. Search for "ozone water" and Dr. Robert Beck. Beck is a physicist who designs healing equipment, including a low-cost ozone generator that can be found at www.toolsforhealing.com. You may want to listen to the Beck videos on YouTube, as he makes some interesting statements about curing AIDS and cancer using low-level microcurrents to sap viruses. I've known Beck for many years and highly recommend his work.

Chapter Eighteen

Contraindications

Generally speaking, people on allopathic medications should proceed cautiously with detoxification protocols, as allopathic and alternative medicine do not mix well. The FDA, along with state medical boards, discourages any use of alternative approaches to healing to the point of prosecution and license revocation of offending physicians. In other words your doctor can't even suggest an alternative approach that he knows will work for fear of losing his license.

I had a private nutrition and peak-performance practice in Denver for sixteen years. During that time I witnessed eight medical doctors administering chelation therapy get their licenses revoked for practicing unapproved medical procedures. Chelation—a procedure in which an amino acid (EDTA for short) is injected via IV into the body—is an effective and much cheaper substitute for coronary bypass surgery.

Detoxification should be the foundation underlying all healing procedures regardless of the disease. Allopathic medicine intoxicates the body to mask the symptom, thus increasing the toxic load, which results in a new set of symptoms popping up in a different location that will require a new medication to submerge the problem. Granted, allopathic medications will create a fairly quick measurable result—like reducing blood pressure or preventing blood clotting (as with Coumadin)—without the assist of lifestyle changes as required by alternative medicine. Allopathic medicine is the perfect vehicle for those who don't want to change anything in their lives and don't want to pay cash for services—about 80 percent of Americans.

However, a growing number of people who would normally be content with allopathic medicine have begun to notice the lack of positive results achieved with the drugs they or their parents have been taking and are looking for ways to get better. I get calls every week from people on multiple medications, asking what they can do to get toxins out of their bodies. This chapter is written for those individuals.

How to Detoxify around Your Medications

As I stated earlier, the average, healthy sixty-five-year-old American is on five medications, mostly for mental-health problems. If not healthy, he is averaging eleven medications. (I met a Vietnam War vet who was on twenty-three medications. Insanity!)

I loathe saying that someone on eleven medications should not detoxify, but that intake represents a serious commitment to the allopathic system. I have spoken to patients who got off that much medication, but this required efforts that spanned months of cooperative consultations among the patient, the medicating doctor, and the alternative practitioner. These patients had three things in common: (1) they were completely fed up with not getting better, (2) they were willing to do anything it took to get better, and (3) they were willing to take complete responsibility for the outcome of their actions. Come to think of it, that's exactly what I did to heal my cancer.

> ***Important:*** If you decide to get off your medications, work with your main physician. Tell your physician what you feel about the medications, and ask for help to wean yourself off them. Stopping your medications cold turkey may do more harm than good.
>
> For those on allopathic medications who are considering a detoxification program, there are two main concerns: (1) whether a certain blood level of the medication must be maintained, and (2) what the level of risk associated with the removal of the medication from the bloodstream is. Let us take it one condition at a time.

Immune-Suppressing Medications: These are typically taken after an organ-transplant procedure to prevent the immune system from destroying the newly implanted organ. Unless your doctor specifically approves, I do not recommend any detoxification procedure or herb that lowers the medication level in the blood. I suggest that periodic colonics, lymph massages, daily exercise, and dietary modification will go a long way toward extending healthy vitality.

Blood-Thinning Medications: These medications, which can be highly toxic, are intended to prevent life-threatening blood clots and strokes. I do not recommend any procedure or herb that would lower the blood level of these medications.

However, there is hope. Dr. Garry F. Gordon (his website is www.gordonresearch.com) developed a nutrition-supplement program for dealing with coagulation problems. Under normal circumstances coagulation is an essential life-sustaining process common to all mammals, whereby a damaged blood vessel wall is covered by a platelet and a fibrin-containing clot to stop bleeding. Because of a number of negative lifestyle and nutrition factors, however, arteries can become clogged, blood can thicken, and blood vessels can become fragile, setting the stage for increased production of blood clots. Gordon has been a pioneer in medical-based nutrition for several decades, and I highly recommend his program (which I have followed). His protocol includes garlic, vitamin E, omega-3 fatty acids, ginkgo biloba, and Essential Daily Defense, a chelating product.[18-1] As always check with your personal physician before going on this program.

Again I suggest that periodic colonics, lymph massages, daily exercise, and dietary modification will go a long way toward extending healthy vitality and probably reducing the threat of blood clots.

Beta-Blockers: These drugs are prescribed for hypertension, congestive heart failure, coronary heart disease, atrial fibrillation, and angina. As a general rule, do not do anything that would tamper with the blood levels of heart medications without consulting your doctor. These drugs can be beneficial for temporary relief, but long-term use can lead to a multitude of side effects.

You should talk to your doctor about going on a program that will build your health so that you can be weaned off these drugs as soon as possible. If your doctor does not cooperate (or cannot cooperate), look for alternative doctors on the websites given in this book for someone who can guide you. Meanwhile these medications should not prevent you from doing colonics, doing a lymph massage, and eating a healthy diet.

Calcium-Channel Blockers: These drugs are prescribed for hypertension, arrhythmia, and angina. Arrhythmias can be serious, but angina and hypertension conditions are not contraindicated for total body detoxification protocols unless your blood pressure is in the stratosphere. As always check with your doctor, as cleansing herbs will lower blood levels of most medications. Research has shown that people taking calcium-channel blockers have a 60-percent increased incidence of heart attacks.[18-2, 18-3] Again, these medications should not prevent you from doing colonics, lymph massage, and eating a healthy diet.

Pacemakers: People wearing pacemakers can and should do colonics and lymph massages, and they should take all the herbs and food supplements necessary to support detoxification. Use of electrical devices such as footbaths and lasers are contraindicated as they may introduce an electrical field into the body that could interfere with pacemaker function.

Seizures: As a general rule, people on seizure medication should not take detoxifying herbs or do footbaths because of the risk of lowering the blood levels of the medication, which may increase the incidence of seizures. However, I suggest that if there is reasonable evidence that the seizure activity may be related to heavy-metal buildup—particularly mercury such as in dental fillings and in some vaccinations—babies, children, and adults can do total body detoxification programs, with children and babies doing less-concentrated regimens. The downside, or side effect, of doing this program is a possible increase in seizure incidence, and the upside is that there may be a remission or lessening of symptoms if heavy metals are implicated.

The evidence that vaccinations may be a contributing factor in autism[18-4] and other neurological disorders is compelling enough for the government to take an objective look. However, I don't think that will ever happen because of the cozy relationship between the FDA and the pharmaceutical industry. The website www.generationrescue.org contains a number of studies pointing to the presence of above-average amounts of heavy metals present in the brains and tissues of autistic and ADHD children.

> *There is no evidence that a loosening in the diagnostic criteria has contributed to increased number of autism clients... We conclude that some, if not all, of the observed increase represents a true increase in cases of autism in California...a purely genetic basis for autism does not fully explain the increasing autism prevalence. Other theories that attempt to better explain the observed increase in autism cases include environmental exposures to substances such as mercury; viral exposures; autoimmune disorders and childhood vaccinations.*[18-5]

Heavy metals—arsenic, mercury, lead, cadmium, aluminum, beryllium, and nickel being the most common—cause significant nervous system and brain damage, and vaccinations contain thimerosal (a sodium salt derived from mercury), acetone (nail-polish remover), formaldehyde (embalming fluid), aluminum (heavy metal), carbolic acid, alum, and several other toxic goodies.[18-6]

A Recent Vaccine Court Ruling That Vaccines Do Not Cause Autism

On March 12, 2010, a special court formed in 1986 known as the vaccine court ruled in response to a five thousand-strong class action suit that vaccines do not cause autism. In response to this decision, Rebecca Estepp, mother of an autistic child and president of the Coalition for Vaccine Safety, stated, "The deck is stacked against families in vaccine court... Government attorneys defend a government program using government-funded science before government judges. Where's the justice in that?"[18-7]

The following is an excerpt from special master George Hastings's 120-page decision affirming the court's decision:

> *The evidence is overwhelmingly contrary to the petitioners' contentions. The expert witnesses presented by the responder were far better qualified, far more experienced, and far more persuasive than the petitioners' experts concerning the key points. The numerous medical studies concerning the issue of whether thimerosal causes autism, performed by medical scientists worldwide, have come down strongly against the petitioners' contentions. Considering all of the evidence, I find that the petitioners have failed to demonstrate that thimerosal-containing vaccines can contribute to the causation of autism.*

One would think that the rapid growth of autism cases over the past three decades would stimulate serious research efforts at identifying its cause. Rather than deal with this uncomfortable issue, the government formed the vaccine court to hand out cash awards to parents whose children were harmed by vaccinations—a direct admission that vaccinations did cause health problems.

Compare this response to the 1989 tryptophan scare, where between 5,000 and 7,500 people were severely harmed by a batch of genetically modified tryptophan made by a Japanese manufacturer. The FDA immediately removed all tryptophan products from store shelves and banned its manufacture for two years. Why doesn't the FDA stop vaccinations for three years and see if the rate of autism declines? That would put to rest any doubts about the safety of the vaccines.

I have spoken to many parents whose children were diagnosed with autism shortly after being vaccinated, so I have a problem accepting the judges' findings in the case quoted above. The judges' decisions did not convince me for this and several other reasons, including (1) the correlation between the rise of autism coincident with the rise in the number of required vaccinations, (2) the fact that many autistic children recover once the toxins have been removed from their bodies, and (3) the fact that many adults become quite ill after being given just one flu vaccination. If one vaccination can make an adult ill, what can thirty-six vaccinations before the age of six do to a child?

We are on our own in dealing with the onslaughts of vaccinations and the thousands of other chemicals in our daily environment. Do not expect help or effective advice from the FDA, the pharmaceutical companies, or your family doctor—unless that doctor practices alternative medicine—when it comes to treating toxicity-based neurological disorders.

Given the titanic financial resources of the government and vaccine manufacturers, it is not surprising that the petitioners lost their case. In my cursory review of the scientific literature involving vaccines and autism, I found hundreds of studies refuting the link between vaccines and autism, including a Danish study involving over a half-million subjects. Who or what could afford to fund such a study? Certainly not the petitioners in the cases cited above.

I even found studies that reported a rise in autism when thimerosal was removed from the vaccine. That's a hard one to accept, given that mercury toxicity can cause over one hundred symptoms—many of them neurological.[18-8]

I know of several children who have reversed their autism. Identifying and avoiding food allergens, rebuilding the immune system, and detoxifying the body have had a powerful impact on restoring normal function in a significant number of autistic and ADHD cases.

Troubled Children and Adolescents: A Possible Happy Ending

Anthony Elementary School in Leavenworth, Kansas, was the most violent school in the district, when principal Janine Kempker instituted an Eat, Exercise, Excel (EEE) program that involved giving the students food supplements among other logistical changes, including eating lunch in the classroom and having structured exercise periods. She based her program on the research of Dr. Stephen Schoenthaler, a professor of criminology at California State University–Stanislaus.[18-9] The following, taken directly from the Ocida.com website, summarizes Schoenthaler's research in nutrition and behavior:

> *Over the past twenty-five years, numerous studies have demonstrated that violence and impaired learning are caused in part by abnormal brain function that coincides with abnormal brain chemistry. When nutrition intervention is used along with certain therapies, blood chemistries normalize, brain function is ameliorated, and learning capacity improves. Violence typically ceases within days.*

Kempker reported that the program produced immediate results, and within a year the rate at which kids were sent to her office for discipline problems dropped 95 percent. In the year before the program, there were thirty-four in-school suspensions because of physical violence. The year after there was one.

Equally remarkable were the academic test scores at the school. In 2003, before EEE, 22.2 percent of fourth graders tested in the unsatisfactory or bottom category for math, while only 6.7 percent scored in the exemplary category. But in 2004, only 3.7 percent scored unsatisfactory, and 48.1 percent scored exemplary. Similar improvements were seen in fifth-grade reading scores.[18-10]

For more information about this experiment, a documentary by PBS was made titled "How to Turn Around a Failing School."

I am familiar with the company that made the E3MV product used in the Anthony experiment. E3MV is a proprietary blend of vitamins, minerals, fruit, and herb extracts for boosting brain function, but its nutrient content is far less than the content of formulations I use and recommend in this book. Imagine what a full-blown wellness program could do for troubled adolescents and adults if a small amount of well-prepared nutrition could change the lives of hundreds of children virtually overnight.

Brain Tumors

Each year more than two hundred thousand people in the United States are diagnosed with brain tumors, which are now the leading cause of solid-tumor cancer death in children and young adults under the age of twenty. Based on his observations and long experience with his patients, Dr. Keith Black, a neurosurgeon at Cedars-Sinai Medical Center in Los Angeles, says that a primary reason for the sharp increase in brain tumors can be found in our environment. "It's very well known that the risk of onset and development of cancer is a combination of one's genetics—the natural ability of one's body to neutralize toxins—offset by the quantity of exposure to those toxins."[18-11]

Over the past decade, Black and his colleagues examined the relationship between occupational exposure and brain tumors and found that in at least one area—plastics factories—employees exposed to vinyl chloride have a much higher incidence of brain cancer, regardless of any predisposed genetic protections. Similar results were shown for people working in textile plants (acrylonitrile), and people living near golf courses (nitrates in pesticides), waste dumps, and power lines.

Studies conducted in Sweden and Switzerland show a clear correlation between cell phone use and brain tumors, but Black said that there are other studies that refute the European studies. I have not seen any of those contradictory studies.

I get a severe brain buzz whenever I use a cell phone without an electrical block, so I have no trouble accepting the Swedish and Swiss statistics as valid.

To lower the risk of brain tumors I suggest, at a bare minimum, 2 to 3 grams of mixed antioxidants per day, 1 or 2 tablespoons of essential fatty acids, phytonutrients from fresh vegetables and fruit, and regular ionic footbaths. And put an electric block on your cell phone. They are inexpensive and they work. You can buy one at www.amajordifference.com.

Throughout this book I have repeatedly shown the link between toxin buildup and disease. Every human being on the planet, regardless of location, is bombarded by more toxins than our species has had to handle at any time in its history. Medically we are in trouble as cut, burn (radiation), and poison tactics exacerbate rather than heal toxic accumulations. *Burn* in this case means use of radiation devices, and *poison* applies to the use of any drug that produces significant side effects.

We are in trouble mentally and emotionally, because toxins impede our nervous-system function and reduce our ability to cope with stress, hence the staggering growth of autism, allergies, and adolescent behavioral problems. Spiritually we are in trouble because it is virtually impossible for a toxic nervous system and brain to rise above the downward pull of these toxins to attain the higher spiritual states of unconditional love and tranquility.

Based on the Anthony Elementary School results, one might ask why this program is not in every school in the country. But notice that there are no mainstream media references on the supplement manufacturer's website—just the PBS report that may have reached 2 or 3 percent of the population. One pharmaceutical ad for Fosamax, a medication for osteoporosis that has been shown to cause bone degeneration, will be seen by ten times as many people as the PBS program.

Given the present profit-driven model of health care and the cozy relationship between the government and the pharmaceutical industry, that model will not change any time soon. The only way to alter that situation is for those people who detoxify regularly to share their healing experiences on the Internet so that those seeking answers to their dilemmas may find support and inspiration. With networking websites such as YouTube and Twitter, the opportunity has never been better.

Chapter Nineteen

My Personal Program

My personal program evolved from the answer to a question I asked myself after I recovered from lung cancer: what do I want the rest of my life to be? Living is being—being happy versus being depressed, being healthy versus being sick, and being productive versus being dependent. My recovery from cancer and several addictions taught me that nothing is incurable, that with intention, focus, and the right knowledge, I (and everyone else) can create a healthy and vital aging experience. We do not have to suffer the ravages of aging if we make the attainment of health and vitality a priority.

Health affects mood, mood affects mind, and mind influences health. The condition of one is related to the condition of the others. In my journey out of cancer, addiction, and a failed liver, I discovered the core protocol for overcoming disease and maintaining healthy longevity. Healing cancer, Parkinson's disease, Epstein-Barr virus, diabetes—any disease—involves a journey into self; an inner journey that for me began with a question: "Why me?" That question led to a personal contract that I made with myself: "I am willing to change anything about me that needs changing." That journey of self-discovery and transformation, which I began in 1982, continues today, and it will probably continue beyond the boundaries of this lifetime.

My cancer experience provided me with the opportunity to cleanse myself of the fears, angers, and hatreds through which I created my life. From my present perspective, I am most grateful for that opportunity, because without it I would have lived a short, unhappy life.

Lifetime Healing Protocol

There are two distinct differences between younger people and older people: older people have more toxins in their bodies and less range of motion in their muscles and joints. From these observations, it appears that the best way to age healthfully and gracefully is to keep toxic accumulations to a minimum and maintain maximum joint and muscle flexibility. The following program will achieve those goals.

1. Make the attainment of healthy longevity your number-one priority. No matter what your starting point or station in life, improvement begins with forming an intention to make health a priority.
2. Begin your journey with a full-body detoxification program and maintain it for the rest of your life. You will come to love detoxification rituals for the incredible benefits they deliver. The more you learn about detoxification, the greater your ability to self-guide your routine.
3. Practice some serious form of yoga, tai chi, or chi kung for movement, balance, and range of motion. The practitioner should be competent enough to challenge you without causing injury. Your goal is to constantly improve your range of motion at any age.
4. Budget permitting, periodic chiropractic adjustments accompanied by soft forms of body therapy, such as the Trager approach, various forms of manual therapy and Feldenkrais, will reduce the impact of traumatic and stressed emotional patterns on the nervous system, thus enabling muscles to return to a more flexible form.
5. Work on reducing and eliminating your mental-emotional issues—those nagging feelings of anger, frustration, depression, anxiety, and fear that have become a permanent fixture in your life. Forgive those who have harmed you; ask forgiveness and make amends to those you have hurt. Use this healthy time to achieve peace and tranquility in your life. It's what you came into this life to do anyway.

I want the rest of my life to be healthy. That's my gift to me. With body and brain intact, I will always be able to take care of myself and thrive. I will continue to make positive contributions to society, and I will continue to publish and teach, because that's what I love doing. Health is the driver that makes these activities possible.

Here's what steps one through five look like in my daily life:

- I try to eat organic foods and nutrient-rich healing juice most of the time, and I supplement that with concentrated nutrient powders and supplements when needed. I like dessert more than is good for me, but I'm still a work in progress and will eventually overcome that addiction as I have the others.
- I practice yoga, tai chi, and chi kung daily for range of motion, flexibility, and balance.
- I work with light to moderate weights five times a week to maintain muscle mass and tone. I do moderate run-walk exercises two times a week to maintain aerobic ability.
- I meditate daily for thirty to sixty minutes to quiet my mind. I sleep better after meditation.
- I do body-centered therapies to take out old trauma patterns, and I get a chiropractic adjustment periodically to keep my spine aligned.

That's basically it: an hour and a half a day of exercise, movement, and stretching, and an average forty-minute meditation. I am always detoxifying: a thirty-minute session in the far-infrared sauna with a fifty-minute ionizing footbath afterward every two weeks; a colonic four times a year; and a high daily intake of food-based concentrations of antioxidants, vitamins, fatty acids, minerals, and specialty substances, including carnosine, to keep glycation levels down. Fortunately I can afford a Rolls-Royce program, and I have the background to knowledgeably choose the nutrition I need, which varies from month to month.

The above regimen will appear to the uninitiated to be a serious investment of time and money, but the older I get, the more sensitive my body becomes to stress, environmental onslaughts, and indulgences such as sugary desserts. Aging bodies have a greater need for food supplementation to augment diminishing life functions, including food enzymes for digestion, CoQ_{10} for heart-muscle support, and antioxidants to reduce plaque buildup and free-radical activity.

Regardless of your present vigor, time and toxins will diminish your life force. As this life force slowly dissipates, your body's immune and endocrine systems power down, just like a battery nearing the end of its charge. Metabolism slows. You tire quicker and seemingly gain weight for no reason. The older you get, the greater your body's nutritional needs to support organs and glands; the greater the amount of toxins in your body, the faster your energy level declines. You may need supplemental nutrition to rebuild and support several functions at the same time, depending on how depleted you are when you begin your program.

Make the attainment and maintenance of high-level wellness your number-one concern as you age. All other goals and objectives—relationships with family and friends, money, hobbies, activities—will fall into place. In good health your later years could be the most productive and happiest of your life. In poor health they will be the most burdensome and unpleasant.

My Supplement Program

I usually have a daily shake made from combinations of whey protein powder, for easily assimilated protein; GI Revive Powder, to clean and rebuild the bowel; PaleoGreens Powder, made from concentrates of green vegetables and grasses for phytonutrients; PaleoCleanse, for detoxification support; PaleoFiber, to speed bowel transit; Genesis PURE Nutrition, a nutrient-dense, liquid food supplement; and cocoa powder, a powerful antioxidant. I add sprouted peas, sunflower seeds, alfalfa sprouts, and low-glycemic frozen fruit, such as blueberries and strawberries, depending on what is available. I mix and match with one egg and unsweetened almond milk. I drink two to three 12-ounce glasses a day.

My daily supplements

Super MiraForte and prescription testosterone: These raise testosterone levels and metabolism. Testosterone is a crucial male hormone that influences many health functions, including bone density, muscle strength, and energy levels. You can buy Super MiraForte from Life Extension (LE). I take bioidentical testosterone five days a week and Super MiraForte the other two.

I highly recommend that women look into the Suzanne Somers's (www.suzannesomers.com) natural hormone replacement program. Natural hormone replacement benefits any woman older than forty, especially if they continually detoxify their bodies.

Multizyme: A vegetable source multienzyme for digesting proteins, carbohydrates, and fats. As we age, pancreatic production of digestive enzymes to digest cooked meals diminishes. I suggest digestive enzymes for everyone over fifty. You can purchase these through your local health food store, LE, and AMD.

Bitters or acai: Both stimulate hydrochloric acid (HCL) to aid protein digestion in the stomach. HCL production declines with age and increased stress levels. You can purchase bitters and acai at your local health-food store and acai at Genesis PURE.

Vitamin D: I take 5,000 international units a day as I am sensitive to sunlight. Vitamin D is a powerful hormone precursor—a deficiency that underlies many diseases—and most Americans are seriously deficient in this vitamin. A *precursor* is a substance that must be combined with other substances to make the final product. You can buy these from LE or your local health food store.

IntraMAX or Genesis PURE Nutrition: Over seventy-two vitamins, minerals, antioxidants, amino acids, and herbs in a highly assimilated liquid formula. AMD sells intraMAX, and Genesis PURE sells Nutrition.

Additionally, I take the following supplements for at least four months each year:

Cognitex with pregnenolone: This is a concentrated nutrient and hormone combination to stimulate and support brain function. You can buy this from LE.

Acetyl-L-Carnitine Arginate: For plaque dissolution and brain support. This is a powerful antioxidant. You can buy this from LE.

Adrenal Adaptogen Plus: For adrenal support, especially when I'm traveling. You can buy this from AMD.

CoQ_{10}: A powerful antioxidant for heart-muscle support. It increases endurance and helps my workouts. It has a high dosage only. You can buy this from LE.

Super carnosine: For lowering blood-sugar levels and reducing glycation rate. This is mandatory for diabetics and borderline diabetics. It has a high dosage only. You can buy this from LE.

Resveratrol: A potent regulator of insulin utilization and other documented aging benefits. I take this supplement at least eight months a year. Diabetics may want to take this full time. You can buy this from LE.

DHEA: A potent multiple hormone precursor that declines with age. Low levels of DHEA affect many body functions. Persons with low DHEA levels may want to take this every day for a few years. You can buy this from LE.

Vitamin K1 and K2: For rebuilding of connective tissue. I'm actually getting stronger, and my range of motion is increasing. You can buy this from LE or your local health food store.

Iodoral: An iodine supplement for thyroid function. Modern food sources are lacking in iodine. The body requires a minimum of 18 milligrams per day. Iodized salt doesn't count as it has little nutritive value. You can buy this from LE.

Fourteen supplement formulations: Including Genesis PURE Nutrition or intraMAX and four or five powder shakes is a high nutrient intake. Take about twenty-six to thirty-two capsules or pills per day of these supplement formulations—not much compared with supermodel Carol Alt, who consumes over 190 capsules and pills per day. I think Carol, as is the case with many health-conscious individuals, might be taking way more nutrition than her body requires, but judging from her bright looks and high energy, she's doing just fine.

Since I started taking Genesis PURE products, I have now added a daily juice regimen to my program. Because these juice products are grown in the most nutrient-dense soils on the planet, I may be able to reduce my need for encapsulated food supplements.

Free and Discounted Nutrition Evaluation Services

As I wrote earlier, Life Extension offers discounted blood chemistry testing and free health counseling from highly trained doctors at www.lef.org. Because doctors do not have access to a detailed health and dietary histories nor auxiliary tests, they will be limited in the scope of their recommendations. A Major Difference, Inc. (www.amajordifference.com) offers a discounted battery of blood, hair, and stool testing along with an in-depth health history that generates a comprehensive report detailing the results of those tests, along with supplement and dietary recommendations. This testing and report service is under the direct supervision of Dr. Ted Winchester and may be the best place for the health seeker who cannot find a local practitioner to begin the journey. Winchester is in the process of integrating tests for methylation deficiencies with his nutrition-evaluation service. Once people begin to understand the depth of damage that has been done on their bodies and the drop in mental, emotional, and physical abilities wrought on their brains and nervous systems because of petrochemical damage, those who can afford to make the effort will do so. What investment do you know of that offers a better return?

Food Considerations

Everything in my daily shake is uncooked, so you might say that I eat more than half my daily food intake in the raw state, with enzymes and micronutrients intact. The rest of the time I eat eggs once or twice a week, cottage cheese several times a week, steak, fish, or fowl accompanied by a vegetable salad for dinner every evening. I eat organic food as much as possible. (If the pesticides and radiation don't get you, the GMOs will.)

I keep the pastas and breads down to a bare minimum, if at all. I have a fondness for ice cream and cheesecake, my last addictions. I've overcome every other addiction, and I will overcome this one as well. I don't drink alcohol or soft drinks or eat junk food, frankfurters, packaged meats, or chips. My liver said "no more" to alcohol four years ago, and I don't miss it. There's nothing wrong with a glass of wine or two on occasion as long as your body does not talk back to you. If you feel uncomfortable after a few drinks or can't sleep, cut it down or eliminate it entirely.

Closing Comments

If I—with addictions to pot, cocaine, cigarettes, alcohol, and sugar and a diagnosis of lung cancer—can free myself of most of these burdens and live a healthy, productive, loving life, what will you be able to accomplish now that you have the road map I didn't have? My journey began with a lung cancer diagnosis. For you it might be a look in the mirror at an aging face, shortness of breath, a pain that won't go away, low energy, forgetfulness, depression, lack of focus, or a forty-pound weight gain. If you are first noticing these changes at age sixty, bravo! You have either lived a good life or you have a strong constitution. Reading this book will only improve your technique. If you are seeing these changes at age thirty, thirty-five, or forty, you need to make some changes quickly. The techniques and information in this book will quickly restore health and vitality.

Before my lung-cancer diagnosis, I knew nothing about healing except that when I got sick, I always got better. That was a young body doing its thing: it had a marvelous curing ability that served me well in my early years. At midlife, healing took on a different meaning as symptoms, such as cancer and depression, didn't just go away. My body had lost its ability to overpower bad habits so that I had to go deep within myself for a cure, and when I did that, I found that I was the problem creating the disease. I had to change me in order to heal, and that was not easy to do.

At some point, if you are lucky, you will be called upon to examine your life. Most people get to age thirty without too many problems, but beyond forty, physical issues and bad habits begin to have serious consequences. The body loses its youthful bounce and beauty. The lucky ones ask the questions that will lead them to positive change; the unlucky ones medicate their pain all the way to the cemetery.

The main message of this book is that you can change anything about yourself that you want to change if you are willing to work at it. Do not confuse this message with messages, like "you won't age" or " you won't get sick." I battled lung cancer, survived long enough to earn two graduate degrees, and found a successful business. More importantly I learned how to forgive and how to receive love. I survived a nasty liver crash that occurred in December 2005, and I went on to write this book. But as I write these words, I find myself battling a condition that has been variously diagnosed as a bladder infection, prostate infection, kidney shutdown with virulent tumor growth, and a blood clot sitting just under the heart. In other words I have a big problem, and once again my survival is in question.

I seriously abused my body-mind system, and my organs absorbed that abuse. But you, me, and everyone else must pay a price for the havoc we unleashed upon ourselves. All that fury gets stored someplace in the cells and nervous system. Perhaps that damage can work itself out without organ failure, but more likely an organ or structure says, "This is as much as I can take." That's just common sense. The correct question is "what would my life have been like if I hadn't taken care of my body the way I did?"

The truth is that you can exercise a serious amount of control over the quality of your life as you age. The less damage you did to your body as a young person, the greater the amount of control you can exert over your aging process. Whatever your issues and whatever you seek to change about yourself, your journey should begin with a total body detoxification program. In my personal as well as clinical experiences, I find that suppressed emotions surface when detoxification begins. As you strip away the endless layers and walls of toxins layered over your organs and cells, you will open pathways within yourself that will lead to new attitudes, insights, and self-knowledge. I call this process *a journey into Spirit*, a building of your conscious connection to your universal source.

Afterword

A Preview of Coming Attractions

As I wrote in the introduction, I started by writing an entirely different book—a relatively simple tour through the protocols, supplements, and regimens I have researched and practiced over twenty-five years of cleansing my body. Then my healing journey entered another realm, appropriately named the pain body by Eckhart Tolle. One day, out of the blue, I began to feel pain-filled energy bands struggling to get out of my body. I could feel an internal energetic outline of each layer slowly exiting through my tissues, like needles being stuck in me from the inside out. Each layer had its own unique theme and energetic flavor: an old trauma or an unpleasant event attached to an emotion or an attitude that I had buried deep inside me some years previously. Each layer held its own unique pain and wreaked its own unique havoc on my body and mind. Sometimes it was anger accompanied by an inability to sleep; sometimes it was anxiety accompanied by fatigue; sometimes it was constipation before a thought-form would surface into consciousness; sometimes it was marijuana, sugar cravings, and so on. As I write this, the journey goes on.

Basic Level One: Detoxification

I've come to think of total body detoxification as an incredible healing opportunity that can lead us directly back to our spiritual source. Many people will be led into the spiritual movement by environmental circumstances and health issues. Detoxification will reduce or relieve many different symptoms. Nutritional and herbal-support supplements will strengthen and empower the body to intensify its detoxification. Cleaning up the diet and eating organic foods will increase the amount of nutrients and reduce the toxins flowing in and out of the body. Get the adrenals working again by powering up the exercise and yoga. That's an excellent level-one program.

Intermediate Level Two: Detoxification

Time to talk about my favorite subject: emotions. The trick is what to do with them. We invent elaborate addictions and compulsions to avoid feeling them: work, power, money, food, shopping, drugs (including prescription), cigarettes, alcohol, and all other obsessive-compulsive behaviors too numerous to list. No one is exempt, as we are all biomagnetically patterned to respond to environmental stimuli in our own unique way. The greater the amount of trauma and stress in life, the greater the likelihood of an inappropriate adaptation response such as an addiction or illness.

Health seekers find their way to this level, because they are looking for a solution to a problem, be it a disease, an addiction, or other painful condition. They have exhausted all the standard sources—doctors, counselors, psychotherapists—in their search for a way out of their dilemma. Their intentions, formed from the pain of their lives, lead them here.

If you can accept as your credo that "you are the God-creator of your reality," your journey will move faster, and your pain will be less. By *God-creator* I mean that within parameters defined by your consciousness you use the energy of the universe to create your life. Until you awaken to this reality, you create a cauldron of beliefs, attitudes, perspectives, and emotions that lie beneath the level of your awareness. Learning to interrupt, challenge, and change these subconscious dynamics is the task of every human being and the purpose of every human life.

The term *God-creator* is intended to convey the power that you possess to change anything about yourself, regardless of how difficult or impossible that task may appear in the moment. Your life-creation is totally yours. It's not your parent's, not the government's, and not your boss's. The quicker and more completely you own that, the less resistance you will have to the inner work. Resistance causes most of the pain.

This is the level where you confront your issues in depth, being fully responsible for them. What issues outside of you are provoking anger, hatred, resentment, fear, anxiety, worry, grief, or depression? The emotional response to any dilemma is rooted within you; it is your anger, your resentment, your fear, your anxiety that you seek to change. Initiating this inner journey takes you into the pain body, as Eckhart Tolle calls it. On page 142 of his extraordinary book *A New Earth: Awakening to Your Life's Purpose*, he describes the pain body phenomenon:

> *The remnants of pain left behind by every strong negative emotion that is not fully faced, accepted and then let go of, join together to form an energy field that lives in the very cells of your body. It consists not just of childhood pain, but also painful emotions that were added to it later in adolescence and during your adult life, much of it created by the voice of the ego. It is the emotional pain that is your unavoidable companion when a false sense of self is the basis of your life.*[A-1]

The work on level two teaches you how to access the major mental and emotional themes that have been feeding your pain body since conception. I call this process *conscious interruption*. Taking full responsibility for your life forces you to stop blaming others or bad luck for your misfortune. Performing the releases described in my next book will enable you to discharge pent-up angers and fears and their supporting attitudes and beliefs so that eventually you regain full control of yourself.

If you have a lot of work to do, meaning that you have many deep-rooted beliefs anchored to some nasty emotions, you will be working on this level for a while. Looking back I would guess that I resided at this level for eighteen years. It would have taken considerably less time had I come to the realizations that I created my reality sooner and that my living drama was based on many false beliefs about myself and a host of angry emotions that constantly caused me to blow up my life.

The average human being has many of these mental-emotional dynamics (intention-vectors from a quantum physics perspective, thought-forms from a spiritual perspective, *samskaras* in Sanskrit, *tikkuns* in the Kabbalah, and cell memories from a medical-intuitive perspective) operating all the time, literally controlling all of life's major decisions. This level teaches you how to work with this inner web of tangled information and emotions and neutralize the ionic charges that have been driving the body-mind to disease.

I mentioned several different languages and words used by different cultures to describe the concept of thought-form, because while this concept may be new to our present-day culture, ancient cultures knew about the power of thought-forms thousands of years ago. I believe from the way that they feel when I release them that cell memories and thought-forms are electrically charged, meaning that they can and do profoundly influence body functions.

Separating from Emotional Charges

The main challenge in level two is acquiring the ability to separate one's consciousness from the emotional charge.

Alice came to me, because she found herself eating uncontrollably once or twice a week. She tried to eat according to a plan that, when she stuck with it, would cause her to lose weight. Somehow, however, her emotions would get the best of her from time to time, and she would eat the contents of her cupboard and refrigerator. We arranged that she would see me the day after each eating binge, and we would work to identify the trigger she claimed she could not feel.

In our next session, she described coming home from work and going on an immediate eating binge. I had her relax and slowly recount everything that had happened leading up to the binge.

Her morning and lunch period had been uneventful, but in the early afternoon, her boss had called her into his office and had criticized a job she had done. I walked her through that event several times before she could access her emotional response to it. At first she glossed over her emotional reaction because she did not believe her job was in jeopardy. Finally she recalled that he had called her "sloppy" and "careless," and she expressed anger at what she felt was her boss's harsh and unfair criticism. She had labored to get the job right in spite of confusing instructions from him.

"He always gives me incomplete instructions, and when I question him, he tells me to just do my best."

Upon further questioning she remembered that her father used to do the same thing concerning her grades in school. She had been a B student, and he had berated her for not getting As, even though she had thought herself to be a conscientious student. She recalled being angry at his criticism and was even able to connect it to her childhood eating binges.

I taught Alice how to do anger and fear releases, and within a few months she was able most of the time to feel the emotional upset as it occurred. The release work was relatively easy; feeling her anger in real time—meaning feeling her emotions as the event was occurring—took training and practice to master. Whenever she overlooked or ignored her anger, urges to binge became her road map to maintaining contact with her feelings until she could feel them in real time.

Advanced Level Three: Releasing Cellular Memories

Imagine for a moment that you are watching a movie about a person trying to overcome the effects of a severe trauma that caused amnesia. The film shows scenes of the trauma flashing in the victim's consciousness, indicating that the victim's memory is slowly returning. That would also be a fairly accurate depiction of how a cellular memory operates. A trauma or unpleasant incident occurs. The memory of that trauma, including the circumstances, the emotional response, and the odors and sounds of the place where it occurred become embedded in the victim's psyche. If you asked a neurologist or psychologist where the psyche is located in the body, both would probably say the brain, because traumas impact neurotransmitter production and brain-wave formation.

Referring back to chapter seventeen about water, we can put two and two together to come up with a more precise answer. Since humans are approximately 70 percent water, each molecule of water contains 440,000 memory compartments, and water remembers every place it has touched. It would appear therefore that trauma memories are held in all of the water cells in the body. Since the body is basically an electrical mechanism that functions by ionic exchange, we can further assume that these memories are held in an ionic or charged form, through which they attract and hold toxins in direct proportion to the intensity of the memory.

This charging process begins in the womb as the mother's emotional responses to life events become embedded in nervous-system patterns that will play throughout the life of the child. As the child transitions out of the womb, these patterns form an automatic-response mechanism for dealing with stress. Over the years one emotionally charged event after another layers itself over the same pathways, just like animals carve a path to a watering hole. Each new event increases the electrical charge in the body until the pathway breaks down from the overload, creating disease and disorder throughout the body and mind.

By early adolescence, these imprints have formed thick, energetic pathways that cause muscles to contract and misfire, disrupt metabolic processes, and create mental imbalances that further limit the individual's ability to handle stressful incidents appropriately.

By age forty these energetic (think electrical) pathways can number in the hundreds if a person is living a stressful life. Consider that an average human body has upwards of seventy trillion cells, 70 percent of which are water cells. Each water cell has the capacity to store 440,000 memories. No wonder we describe some individuals as powder kegs ready to go off at any moment. The body is capable of holding an enormous electrical charge.

I describe the human being as a biomagnetic energy center comprising beliefs, attitudes, perspectives, and emotional responses formed by experiences in the womb and reinforced by experiences after birth. The electrical nature of these mental-emotional dynamics creates an energy matrix that feeds on repetition and breeds habits. The only way out of this cycle is to break the patterns by consciously separating from the pattern and neutralizing its electrical charge. The operative word is *consciously*, as in one must become mindful of the emotions and attitudes driving behavior before effective modification can begin.

A View of Life from a Different Angle

Think about your life as a play that you wrote and orchestrated prior to assuming a human form. You chose your parents and their circumstances to kick-start the programs that will run your life. These emotionally based programs coupled with your parents' merged DNA form the structure and scope of your future life experiences. If you can accept this premise, it is a short leap to accepting that you and Spirit deliberately constructed a life path with some specific beneficent intention in mind.

You might ask: What is so beneficent about childhood starvation or cancer? And why does learning require the presence of pain?

I don't know is my response to the first question. Maybe it is karmic debt, defined as making restitution for something you did. Or maybe the disease helps the soul to break some attachments that no other experience can accomplish. On the matter of the second question, no one ever came to my practice saying, "I'm feeling fine. My life is good. My relationships with my wife and kids are great. I'm healthy and have a successful business. What can you do for me?" For my clientele, the journey begins with a need to change something. And that something is usually accompanied by pain.

Whether the pain is a speed bump or a brick wall depends on what it takes to get one's attention. (I was a slow learner who required a few brick walls to help me change direction.) A few people, including Princess Diana, manage to come to a place of understanding where they have the power to alter their symptoms and pain, but most plod along, dealing with their pain through denial and repression. The disease lying in wait for them twenty years hence will be the brick that forcibly initiates a life-altering course correction. At that point the victims, including myself, will be forced to reconsider some inappropriate life choices and attitudes. In the words of former baseball great Mickey Mantle, "If I knew I was going to live this long, I would have taken better care of myself."

Because I possessed a heavy pain body, it took me nineteen years to consciously get to level three. I'm sure that some layers were peeled off over the years, but I mark the day I entered level three when my marijuana cravings returned in 2005. Marijuana was my drug of choice for medicating and denying pain, and releasing cellular memories means feeling old pain and trauma. Looking back had I been able to take full responsibility for my life, I could have shaved fourteen years (or more) off my journey. Full responsibility is the key.

The German New Medicine

Earlier in this book, I mentioned the work of Dr. Ryke Geerd Hamer as it related to calcifications in the brain causing disease somewhere in the body. In his *Summary of the New Medicine*, Hamer discussed a theory of disease that he developed after viewing thousands of MRIs (magnetic resonance imaging). He discovered that the location of a calcification on the brain emanated from a traumatic event that would manifest a disease process twenty to forty years later.[A-2] From this theory he was able to connect a disease to its root cause—an act that was effective in reversing 85 percent of the chronic degenerative disease cases (including terminal cancer) presented to him.

As mentioned earlier, his cancer cures infringed on the domain of the medical and pharmaceutical industries that apparently enjoy the same monopoly and government protection in the European Union as they do in the United States. Hamer's theories indicate that traumas leave an indelible imprint on the brain—an imprint that is ionic in form and that affects tissue and organ function until it is dissipated. Apparently all that's required to dissipate it is the realization of what put it there, emphatically proving that the original cause of all diseases is based on emotional imprints from traumatic events.

Post-traumatic stress disorder (PTSD) is the most overt expression of trauma impacting the nervous system. It creates severe mental and physical problems for its victims unless treated. Trauma distorts the flow of neurons, which are tiny electrical charges that stimulate activity throughout the body. I infer from Hamer's work and the behaviors of PTSD victims that electrical patterns formed by these traumas create permanent ionic bonds that attract and hold specific types of toxins in some relationship to the type and intensity of the trauma. The pattern of electrical charges determines the organs that will be affected and the diseases that will be contracted in the distant future. Neutralizing these disruptive electrical patterns is essential in any healing program, because they will continue to attract toxins as long as they remain active.

Negative emotions such as anger, fear, and anxiety have effects on the body, similar to those caused by overt traumas. Someone cuts in front of you on the highway, and you let go with a string of expletives. To use a legal expression, you have memorialized the event by giving it an emotional content. Your rage imprints an electrical charge into your cellular memory, and it will grow in power, locking you into a debilitating behavior pattern that will intensify over the years. Those memorialized electrical charges will work *you* if you don't work at neutralizing *them*. That's the *German New Medicine*, and it apparently works.

The myriad of toxins that coat every organ and cell in the body reduce the nervous system's ability to handle stress messages and act as amplifiers of emotional content. The greater the amount of toxins in the body, the greater the emotional response to adversity. Since every toxin—be it physical, gaseous, or emotional—is held in ionic form, ionizing footbaths amplify the impact of all modalities in their efforts to transport toxins out of the body. Removing toxins increases the nervous system's ability to handle stress, thus reducing addictive tendencies and creating a space for making new choices. My experience tells me that total body detoxification is a necessary adjunct to any effort at clearing out the pain body. Detoxification of any kind—physical, mental, or emotional—requires energy. Physical toxins increase the amount of energy required for the cells to release trapped emotions and memories. Ionization provides that extra energy.

Scientists studying the impact of toxic accumulations being passed to succeeding generations report a reduced ability to deal with stress from one generation to the next for all species of mammal, whether water- or land-based.[A-3] Anyone wanting to live well in the future must detoxify on a regular basis.

Where Do We Go from Here?

My healing journey caused me to completely rethink who I was as a human being who had created cancer, several addictions, and an unhappy life. Twenty-six years after the cancer diagnosis, I have come to see myself as a conscious being capable of accepting full responsibility for his life, capable of dealing with the challenges and opportunities presented in his life, and capable of creating a healthy and productive aging experience. I live in a state of peace and tranquility most of the time. I handle change and adversity well. I love and forgive easily, and I don't create enemies anymore. I started out trying to cure a deadly cancer and ended up healing all of myself that was angry, fearful, and alienated from humankind.

As I slowly dissolved the layers of thought-forms and cellular memories that plagued my life, I discovered that I had developed an ability to come to a place of peace and tranquility within myself. In that place I feel free and unencumbered by imprisoning thoughts. In that place I know, understand, and accept that whatever is happening to me in the moment and whatever is going to happen to me in the future are part of a grander design that, over the long run, will serve only my highest good. Letting go of how I expect things to be and surrendering to the will of Spirit has been the most challenging part of my journey. It's gotten easier over the years. When I hit what I used to perceive as an obstacle, I surrender it to Spirit and virtually all the time, it leads me to something better. Ironically I now actively seek that peaceful place of surrender from where guidance and inspiration can flow into my consciousness.

My new life and consciousness grew out of seven years of intense detoxification of the physical body. And that facilitated thirteen years of more-intense emotional and attitudinal detoxification. My first blood, urine, and hair tests showed a clogged colon; a clogged and overstressed liver; high levels of cadmium, aluminum, and mercury; parasites; a high level of uric acid; and creatinine. I needed to release much of that toxic load and stop the intake of drugs and cigarettes that medicated the anger and hatred I carried throughout my being. It took three years of physical detoxification before I could consciously feel emotions and another three years to mindfully work with them. As I said I did not have an owner's manual, and neither did anyone I consulted. I was a totally blind man at the beginning of the journey, with Spirit obviously leading me to water. I'm glad I drank it, for I would not be here otherwise.

In adversity there is opportunity, and my recovery from two major diseases and several addictions testifies to the incredible ability we all possess not only to heal and improve ourselves but also to create a magnificent life well into what might be considered old age. Our in vivo exposure to our mother's nervous-system patterning sets the table for an opportunity to find our way back to a place of peace and oneness with our universal source. Several decades of intense toxic exposure have left our species weak and debilitated to the point that our ability to procreate is impaired. The generations that have recently come into the planet have no margin of error with respect to taking care of their health. They carry the remnants of toxic exposures dating back several generations and now must take on the added burden of the insanity that is modern civilization. These young people, like my son, must deal with their mental-emotional patterning at an early age if they are to survive and procreate (85 percent of males in the United States do not qualify as sperm donors).[A-4]

It is what we, acting individually and globally, decide to do now about the increasing threats to our future survival that will determine our destiny. The effects of petrochemical use will impact us for many generations unless we individually decide to keep their residues to a bare minimum through continuous detoxification. Athletic records notwithstanding, we are a species in decline. The last twenty-five years have produced significant increases in autism, allergies, bipolar disorder, stress disorders, heart disease, breast cancer, birth defects, obesity, diabetes, cancer, and a host of mental-emotional disorders. Everyone has been severely impacted. Our increasing use of toxic substances and the passing on of ancestral exposures to offspring has placed a growing burden on each succeeding generation that has made the word *extinction* part of our daily conversation.

From a spiritual perspective, the crises we are presently confronting—global warming, hormone disruptors, worldwide financial upheaval, perpetual wars, increasing disease rates—present humanity with an unprecedented opportunity to rethink its relationship with earth and for each person to realign with the natural law and right actions. We are clearly up to our eyeballs in serious problems that will not be solved by the same consciousness that created them.

The Miracle That We Are

Over my thirty-year (and counting) journey, I adopted two mantras to help me recenter and refocus when I had wandered off being in the now. The first mantra is "no matter what," which translated into an I-will-die-before-I-fail mentality when coping with the release of some painful emotions. My earliest self-confrontations were the most painful, because I did not yet understand the totality that I am.

The second mantra is "in adversity there is opportunity," emanated from my growing ability to take greater responsibility for my life and all its circumstances as my own creation. This helped me move through some unpleasant karma I had picked up along the road of existence.

From that perspective my painful childhood and the course of my life as an adult (until I began to take stock of myself) created an incentive for me to change whatever needed changing. Looking back at the effort I expended, the changes I negotiated, and the way my life is working now, I'd say my life has been a great, albeit challenging, opportunity to alter a hated-filled, self-destructive personality-ego into a loving one. That's a positive lifetime, which anyone can be proud of.

"In adversity there is opportunity" is exactly where we are as a species. How are we going to survive this age of intoxicating chemicals and denatured foods that are making each new generation weaker than the previous generation? The question begs the answer: we must rethink the aging process.

Lose the idea that you have to go limp, lame, and fat into an aging you do not want to face. I'm having fun, and I am optimistic that I will make a difference to many people who are ready to hear that they can perform the ultimate miracle: *create a healthy aging experience.*

Imagine adding twenty-five years of productive life to your expected life profile and perform a cost-benefit analysis of what health and vitality would mean to your wealth, your productivity, your value to family, community, and nation. What is your present value if you could be productively active from age seventy to ninety-five? Compare the value of that lifestyle to an expected life profile of someone who doesn't do much maintenance and someone who does none at all. The answer is obvious, and we haven't touched on quality-of-life issues yet. Possessing good health, faculties capable of decent mental function, and the ability to go to work every day gives me the wherewithal to determine the purpose and quality of my future life. I have come to a place of completely forgiving those who have trespassed upon me and a place where I can take responsibility for the instructive role they played in my life. And this is a great personal achievement that gives ongoing meaning and joy to my life. May it do the same for you.

I wish you a successful journey.

Bob Moroney
Ponte Vedra, Florida

Epilogue

Throughout this book I have tried to encourage cooperation between allopathic and alternative medicine, a merger that would decrease mortality rates and pain for all of humanity with a corresponding decrease in the cost of treatment for all chronic degenerative diseases. Alas based on information I have recently received, I do not think that will happen any time soon.

It appears that with the help of the FDA and various state licensing boards, big pharma and the allopathic medical industries are slowly gaining control over the practices of homeopathy, naturopathy, colon therapy, and every form of alternative-healing activity with a view to limiting their influence or eliminating them entirely, thus creating an environment in which the only available medical relief is from the allopathic industry.

Over the past century, governments, both state and federal—urged on by generous political contributions and a revolving-door employment policy that encourages regulators to seek employment with the companies they regulate—have given themselves the power to regulate everything medical in the name of protecting the public and the public interest.

The actions of the FDA and state licensing boards have forced thousands of practitioners out of business under threat of long prison sentences if they continued in practice, regardless of the results they were achieving, such as Hamer. The situation in Europe is worse: vitamin and food supplements are now regulated by a commission known as Codex Alimentarius, which mandates that all over-the-counter food supplements contain only minimal (ineffective) quantities of each nutrient and that supplements containing larger quantities be sold by prescription only. Production of many homeopathic remedies has been terminated by law.

The inevitable result of this suppression will be a worldwide decline in human health and an increase in disease and mortality rates, with a few government officials, regulators, medical doctors, pharmaceutical executives, and stockholders receiving obscene financial benefits.

One might be tempted to ask how could a protocol with a 15-percent chance of working be the only legally approved protocol for treating lung or pancreatic cancer? One might also ask why a society would incarcerate a doctor who can routinely cure these conditions, as Spain and Germany did with Hamer. Rationally these actions make no sense, but it is clear that the greed of a few has gained considerable control over the health and well-being of the many through legislative processes that will create more human suffering and casualties than Hitler ever did.

I cannot speak for Europe, but the United States still has some semblance of a constitution left, particularly the First and Fourteenth Amendments, which guarantee the rights of free speech and assembly. To counter the rise of these state boards and their suppressive attitudes toward alternative practitioners, a few legal services have sprung up that will enable individuals and practitioners to form private organizations based on the First and Fourteenth Amendments, where individuals and practitioners can contract privately to give and receive health care—or any other service for that matter—unless the individuals involved are engaged in some pervasive evil. This type of structure—ideal for naturopaths, homeopaths, colon therapists, medical doctors looking to expand their scope of practice, and other nonmainstream, unlicensed practitioners—places the practice under the domain of common law and removes it from the statutory purview of federal and state authorities.

Under common law you are free to contract with me regarding your treatment and care, and I am free to advise you without limitation on any process that will improve your health and well-being. Under statutory law I need the permission of the state to act as caregiver, and if I violate those state laws that limit my scope of practice (or violate the law entirely), I can be sent to prison.

We humans are a peculiar lot. We say we want freedom, but we continually ask the state for benefits and protection. State medical licensure creates a monopoly for those holding that particular type of license: medical doctors, psychotherapists, dentists, massage therapists, chiropractors, naturopaths, and so on. Chiropractors, once hounded and persecuted by the American Medical Association, are now doing to their competition what the medical doctors did to them. State medical boards, especially in California, Florida, and Texas, vigorously go after any practitioner who is dumb enough to make a medical claim. Medical doctors themselves are prohibited from practicing unauthorized medicine—a euphemism for alternative treatments—even if that procedure is more effective than the authorized one.

During the sixteen years I maintained a nutrition practice in Denver, Colorado, I watched eight medical doctors lose their licenses for administering chelation therapy to heart-disease patients. A course of chelation injections takes about one month, costs around $5,000, is noninvasive, and unblocks arteries just as effectively as bypass surgery with the same mortality risk. Back then the average bypass procedure cost $50,000. Who benefited from the chelation option? The patient, because of the costs savings and the avoidance of a complex surgery, and the public in general, because of the overall cost reduction to society and the gain in productivity from the patient's not losing any job time. Who lost? The hospitals, the surgeons, and the pharmaceutical and insurance industries. Follow the money!

Licensure creates monopolies, and monopolies do not care about social costs and human suffering. If you observe the uniform behavior of state licensing boards, it appears that even the heretofore persecuted behave exactly like the establishment power structure when they acquire monopoly protection. Monopolies stifle competition, increase costs, and slow innovation, and my use of the word *slow* is optimistic. The people of the United States have spent trillions of dollars on cancer treatment and research, and the odds of defeating lung and pancreatic cancer are virtually the same today as they were when I was diagnosed. Why bother to find real cures when there is so much money to be made the old-fashioned way? And now state medical boards, urged on by the pharmaceutical industry and Codex Alimentarius, are going after providers of health-building procedures, including colon therapists, vitamin and supplement manufacturers, naturopaths, and homeopaths. Healthy people do not consume hospital time and pharmaceuticals, and big pharma wants everyone to get sick.

It is a universal axiom that when a force rises up, a countervailing force will rise up against it. Witness any dictator or culture that tried to dominate the world. Regrettably the institutions that comprise allopathic medicine are trying to completely take over the entire medical and health fields, and the time has come for conscientious practitioners, who are seeking to provide alternative therapies, to find legal ways to practice their professions. A private medical, spiritual, psychotherapeutic, massage association based on the First and Fourteenth Amendments may be the way for many displaced practitioners to go. It is the way I have chosen to organize myself, and I made this decision after thousands of hours of research. You can begin your research by going to www.proadvocate.org or www.wellnessassociations.com. I do not have a financial interest in either organization.

Appendices

Appendix I

Some of the Liver's Functions

1. Synthesizes proteins such as prothrombin, fibrinogen (both clotting factors), and albumi (the major blood protein)
2. Converts forms of amino acids when needed for proteins
3. Converts toxic ammonia to less-toxic urea, which can then be excreted
4. Uses amino acids and proteins for energy production or converts them to fats and carbohydrates for storage as glycogen and lipids
5. Can rapidly break down large amounts of carbohydrate (glycogenolysis) and release them as glucose into the bloodstream
6. Can create glucose from lactic acid
7. Can break down and release stored fat for extraordinary needs
8. Synthesizes cholesterol from fatty acids and vice versa
9. Aids in the production and excretion of bilirubin
10. Detoxifies drugs and alcohol
11. Excretes toxins into bile
12. Alters the molecular structures of hormones to deactivate them
13. Stores all fat-soluble vitamins: A, B12, D, E, and K
14. Stores iron and copper. Too much can damage liver cells
15. Activates vitamin D
16. Synthesizes bile salts to emulsify fats

Appendix II

Supplement Considerations

I have been using nutrition supplements since my cancer diagnosis in 1982, and of course I dispensed them to my clients during my sixteen years of clinical practice. Suffice it to say that they work, and they are absolutely essential to any healing-cleansing program, because they provide the body with nutrient concentrations that it cannot get any other way.

Total body detoxification requires energy and specific organ support that can be obtained only from high-octane foods (whole-food supplements) or concentrated chemicals. Cold-processed, organically grown, whole-food supplements are the most bioavailable, because the cold processing keeps all their nutrient composition and enzymes intact.

Few companies bother to grow and process whole-food supplements because of the high expense of cultivation and concentration. In this appendix, I discuss two companies, A Major Difference, Inc. (AMD) and Genesis PURE (GP), which offer whole-food, cold-processed supplements to laypeople. The designations *whole food* and *cold-processed* indicate the highest nutrient bioavailability of any processing method. Most of the high-quality food supplement distributors sell to licensed practitioners only, but if you know what you are looking for and know how to read a label, you can find some excellent supplements on your health-food grocer's shelves.

I also discuss a third company, Life Extension, because of the quality of its research and because it offers practitioner-grade chemical formulations to laypeople and practitioners alike.

As I mentioned in the first chapter, Standard Process, the oldest whole-food supplement company in the United States, offers the most comprehensive line of whole-food detoxification-support products. You can contact the company through its website (www.standardprocess.com) to locate a practitioner near you.

Supplement Classifications

Supplement ingredients come in many different forms as listed on the next page, from the most expensive (and most bioavailable) to the least expensive (and least bioavailable). Bioavailability pertains to the ease with which they can be assimilated into the cells.

1. organically grown, whole-food, cold-processed juice concentrates
2. organically grown, whole-food, cold-processed, nutrient-dense foods
3. submicron, cold-processed micronutrients
4. chelated, heat-processed vitamin and mineral isolates from plants
5. vitamin and mineral isolates from plants
6. chemically derived formulations

Ingredients contained in the last three categories are usually expressed in milligrams (mg) per pill or capsule. These products are typically produced through heat-generating processes that kill off enzymes and precursors that aid in the assimilation of nutrients. Crushing, grinding, and pressing are considerably cheaper than processes that keep nutrients intact.

Submicron refers to the application of nanoscience to nutrition whereby cold-processed nutrition is broken down into nano-sized particles that are easily and completely assimilated into the cell. This method of nutrient processing will become more popular as companies develop new production methodologies.

Chelate means to grab or claw and refers to the attaching of a protein to a nutrient to force it into the cell. In my clinical experience, the assimilation rate of nonchelated, heat-processed products is less than 5 percent; chelation supposedly increases assimilation by a factor of four or more. Cold-processed whole-food and juice concentrates made from whole foods are generally believed to be 80 percent assimilated, depending on the individual's ability to process nutrition.

The Life Extension Foundation

For my money Life Extension is the best supplement marketer on the planet, and no other supplement marketer comes close. Founded in 1980 as a health-information company, it began marketing supplements in 1984 to retail and wholesale accounts. It offers hundreds of products for every nutrition need imaginable: sports nutrition, skin care, weight management, hormones, immune enhancement, concentrated antioxidants, inflammatory reactions, brain health, and so on, except for detoxification.

Life Extension Magazine, the foundation's monthly flagship marketing tool, carries the banner, *The ULTIMATE Source for New Health and Medical Findings from around the World,* and it delivers on that promise. It features well-written, well-researched, peer-reviewed articles on timely health topics accompanied by ads for the products mentioned in the articles. Self-serving? Yes. Designed to sell product? Yes. Biased? I don't think so. The articles are very well researched and well presented, and with several hundred products being offered, Life Extension can pick and choose from so many options and nutrient protocols that it can afford to tell the truth.

Besides it has fought and won many legal battles with the government, as the FDA has repeatedly challenged its First Amendment right to publish truthful information about food supplements. My wife and I read each issue from cover to cover. It's our main source of information and education on new developments and discoveries in the use of food supplements and nutraceuticals.

In chapter nineteen, I mentioned several of Life Extension's products that I incorporate into my personal program. I included them in this book because their products are useful adjuncts to my detoxification process. Because of my past battles with drug, alcohol, cigarette, and sugar addiction and my advancing age, I require high-potency support for brain function and blood-sugar management among other needs such as managing hormone levels, digestive-tract supports, and synthesizing vitamin D. Their formulas are mostly concentrated isolates, some of which are quite expensive.

Whether you are a layperson or a practitioner, I recommend that you get on the mailing list for the magazine (www.lef.org). You may have to buy something to get the magazine for free, but it is a great read. You will appreciate the education.

A Major Difference (AMD)

Rarely if ever does a company have an opportunity to test nutrition products in conjunction with a high-powered technology in a clinical setting over three years before offering them to the public. This fortuitous occurrence took place in Dr. Ted Winchester's office, when AMD first proposed that he develop seminars to show doctors how to integrate its technology into a clinical practice. Winchester had been combining laser and a weak ionizing footbath with nutrition supplements, but it wasn't until he inserted the IonCleanse into the mix that his program came together. Prior to adding the IonCleanse, Winchester would perform a neurological examination using applied kinesiology to identify neurological blocks and then test a number of supplements to determine the nutrition needed to clear those blocks. Since the IonCleanse by itself cleared the blocks, this enabled Winchester to conclude that all neurological blocks were caused by toxic buildup. This realization led to a second conclusion: the primary focus in the healing process is the removal and prevention of toxic buildup in the body.

Once Winchester came to these conclusions, the rest was easy: focus on food supplements that support and enhance detoxification. Over the ensuing months, he tested hundreds of products from many different manufacturers, and the most effective ones were selected to become the AMD product line (www.amajordifference.com).

AMD Product Listings

PaleoMeal Protein Powder: Whey protein from herds that graze on pesticide-free, chemical-free pastures. It is bovine growth-hormone-free, GMO-free, and contains no injected organisms. Phosphatidyl choline is added for brain and liver support. It also contains glutamine to promote optimal muscle growth and strength, glutathione for added antioxidant protection, folic acid to lower homocysteine levels and flaxseed powder.

IntraMAX: An all-in-one highly assimilated, trace mineral and multivitamin supplement containing a number of super foods with known healing and cleansing properties. This is an excellent detoxification support product.

Twice-Daily Essential Packets: A complete vitamin, mineral, and fatty-acid supplement in capsule form. Ideal for those who prefer to take their nutrition in capsules or pills.

PaleoCleanse Powder: A powerful liver-support and detoxification product containing high antioxidant levels, multivitamins, and minerals for detox enzyme support, botanical hepatics, and specific nutrients to support phase one and two metabolic pathways. (Phase one and two metabolic pathways refer to liver activities required to break down and neutralize toxins.) The proteins in this product are plant derived and hypoallergenic (does not cause allergic reactions).

PaleoFiber Powder: A combination of fibers derived from roots, fruits, vegetables, seeds, and tree extracts with beneficial bacteria and prebiotics added. Promotes faster transit through the colon and complete bowel movements.

PaleoGreens Powder: A lemon-lime-flavored green powder made from alkalizing grass juices, algae, prebiotics, enzymes, fruits, and vegetables. It is high in phytonutrients with no fillers or bulking agents added. *Phyto* means light-based, and organically grown plants and vegetables contain many phytonutrients that play significant roles in immune and endocrine function, cell performance, and body regeneration in general. An article in the July

2008 edition of *Life Extension Magazine* discussed a finding that some plant phytonutrients were found to act as sun blocks.

Detox Support Packets: Provides comprehensive support for liver-gallbladder detoxification. Daily intake provides over twenty antioxidants, liver-gallbladder support, herbs, and proteins to strengthen immune-system function. Add this product to increase the intensity of your detoxification efforts.

Argenta: A powerful antifungal, microbial, and viral formula made from colloidal silver. In large doses, silver can be quite toxic, but in electrically dissolved solutions it can be an effective defense against many different kinds of microorganisms.

Zeo-Tox: A powerful, submicronized formula for removing heavy metals.

EGCG Plus: A submicronized formulation of vitamins, antioxidants, and botanicals that are completely assimilated at the cell level.

SoluMIN Pure: Supplies submicronized regular and trace minerals in a pleasant-tasting liquid formulation.

GI Revive Powder: Contains therapeutic amounts of nutrients and herbs to (a) rejuvenate mucosal health, (b) promote proper intestinal permeability, (c) provide healing for ulceration and inflammation, and (d) promote regularity and healthy bowel function. Most Americans have leaky gut from stress, allopathic medications, alcohol consumption, and environmental pollution. GI Revive is an excellent addendum to any health-building program.

Unlike many powdered nutrient formulas, all the powders mentioned above contain no fillers and combine with each other to make a great-tasting shake.

Most of the ingredients in these products are organically grown and cold processed for higher nutrient bioavailability. Winchester gives these products the highest ranking for quality and efficacy, and he uses them in his daily shakes and clinical practice. "My first criterion for selecting a product for my practice is overall quality, which is tied to the reputation of the company," he said. "My second criterion, which is actually more important, is 'if it doesn't muscle test, I don't give it to the patient.' No further questions asked."

As I stated earlier, good supplements are expensive. AMD and Life Extension offer decent discounts for small-quantity purchases.

Discounted Health Consultation Services

AMD offers a more comprehensive discounted health-evaluation program than Life Extension, which involves hair analysis, blood tests, food supplement recommendations, and a phone or internet doctor consultation with Winchester. It is one of the most thorough evaluations I have ever seen, a copy of which is shown in appendix IV. Go to AMD's website and fill out the health questionnaire, submit it to AMD, and follow the instructions on submitting your blood, stool, and hair samples. Your hair analysis will reveal heavy-metal toxicities and how well you are assimilating minerals.

Ionization Therapy Rental-Lease Program

AMD has recently initiated a short-term rental program for its IonCleanse device. This program, called the Pay-Per-Cleanse, will enable a family to do a three-month detoxification program at home for less than $10 per session. I highly recommend this program for anyone wishing to do a three- to four-month annual cleanse but who may not have the capital to purchase a footbath outright.

Genesis PURE

I was recently introduced to a few of the Genesis PURE products and am pleased to report that they are the best I've ever consumed.

Dr. Lindsey Duncan, the founder of Genesis PURE, is a nationally recognized master herbalist and formulator, and this accounts for the incredible quality and effectiveness of his products. He has been in private practice for over ten years. He founded and operated a successful nutrition-distribution business that he sold at a handsome profit, and he has put together some potent formulations that sell at the lowest prices I've seen for products of this quality. Obviously I've made many of his products a part of my daily nutrition intake. His products are now available through most health-food store chains. The products I now use and recommend are:

Nutrition Pure: An easily assimilated vitamin, mineral, and multiple-nutrient drink with over two hundred bioavailable nutrients from vegetable sources in liquid form with noni-juice added. It is an excellent, all-purpose, starter-food supplement that will quickly nutrify a depleted body. I recommend two capfuls per day during intense detoxification periods.

Liquid Cleanse Pure: An internal cleansing program unto itself. It simultaneously provides cleansing support for the liver, lungs, kidneys, skin, lymph, colon, and blood.

Cell Water Pure: Effectively transports nutrients, enzymes, and proteins into the cells; removes waste products; and helps maintain communication between cells. Its high oxygen content helps to neutralize petrochemical-residue buildup on cells and organs. As I stated earlier, this petrochemical-residue buildup impedes the utilization of hormones at the cell receptor site—a serious problem for seniors who need to utilize hormones efficiently in order to slow aging and for pregnant women who need to keep hormone disruptor levels low to avoid birth defects.

Acai Secret: The acai (pronounced *ah-sigh-ee*) berry, grown in the Brazilian rain forest, is rich in anthocyanins (a class of phytonutrients), essential fatty acids, proteins, and a number of other vitamins and minerals. It has positive effects on energy and stamina levels, builds healthy libido, offers support for digestion and liver functions, and elevates mental clarity and mood. As a digestive aid, it acts like bitters, an herbal formulation that increases hydrochloric acid production, which is essential for protein digestion. It is highly recommended for endurance athletes.

Noni Secret: The bark of the noni tree absorbs over 160 minerals and nutrients from volcanic ash. Taken in juice form, these nutrients ameliorate inflammatory processes and support healthy serotonin levels (significant for older people with sleeping disorders), immune function, digestion, detoxification, and energy levels.

GoYin: A blend of twenty superfruits and herbs designed to bring the body back into balance. It supports healthy energy flow, increases vigor, provides antioxidant power, and reduces tension, depression, and fatigue.

Goji Secret: The polysaccharides in the goji berry contain high levels of essential cell nutrients necessary for intercellular communication and immune function. Among other benefits, goji berry supports healthy liver, eye, endocrine, blood-pressure, immune, and cardiovascular functions. It also helps with mood and libido.

Mangosteen Secret: Contains the highest amounts of polyphenolic compounds, which are powerful antioxidants that give this fruit one of the highest ORAC (oxygen radical absorption capacity) ratings of any substance on the planet. It promotes cardiovascular health and slows cell aging. It provides nutritional support to combat infections, inflammation, fever, fatigue, heart, and circulatory concerns.

When I first added these products to my daily regimen, I immediately experienced two phenomena. The first was that my total food intake decreased, indicating that the nutrition in these foods was indeed getting into the cells with great efficiency. The second was that my urine developed a powerful odor, indicating that these foods were creating a powerful detoxification in my body. I can't think of a better testimonial.

Substantial research on all of these juices attests to their healing properties and justifies the product claims listed above. Produced from berries and fruits grown in optimum soils around the world, these foods are probably the most nutrient-rich substances on the planet. Ancient cultures have consumed them for centuries. They deserve their reputation, and Genesis PURE uses cold-processing technology to convert the berries and fruits into juices with all nutrients intact.

Other Detoxification Protocols: Homotoxicology

Homotoxicology is a branch of natural medicine that has its origins in homeopathy. Developed by Dr. Hans Heinrich Reckeweg during his more than forty years of clinical practice, homotoxicology is a discipline currently practiced by thousands of medical doctors, naturopaths, and homeopaths throughout the world. I have not studied this healing art directly, but I have consulted several homeopaths over the years and personally know several highly competent practitioners.

Homotoxicology is based on many of the principles outlined in this book, beginning with the principle that all disease emanates from toxic buildup somewhere in the body. Reckeweg used his knowledge of homeopathy to design complex formulas from multiple homeopathic remedies to treat different symptoms at the same time. He was the first homeopathic doctor to do so.

His remedies consisted of liquid drops made from herbs, minerals, plants, and flowers according to homeopathic practice and were tailored to treat specific symptoms, including their emotional components. Based on these complex formulations, it's obvious to me that Reckeweg knew what twenty-first-century doctors are finding out now: that emotional traumas park themselves in particular parts of the body, depending on the nature of the trauma and the emotion attached to it. I will write more about this in my next book.

Homeopathy is a healing art developed in the late nineteenth century by Dr. Samuel Hahnemann. It is based on the law of similars, which states that an extremely dilute form of a substance can heal a physical problem that is caused by the concentrated form of that same substance.

Hahnemann discovered that a dilute form of quinine—the concentrated form of which caused malaria—would relieve malaria. He went on to perform hundreds of "provings," where dilutions expressed in the part-per-billion range were created to heal many different ailments. In today's language, an individual suffering from heavy-metal poisoning would be cured by consuming dilutions of the metals in question. That there are thousands of homeopaths in active practice 150 years after Hahnemann founded the homeopathic discipline testifies to the effectiveness of his discovery.

Not only did Reckeweg recognize the emotional component of the symptom, but also he included allergy testing, lifestyle coaching, diet and nutrition support, and environmental cleanup in a total approach to healing. The man understood the origins of disease.

Many homotoxicologists use ionizing footbaths in their practices since the device provides powerful support to any detoxification effort. As I have attended several homotoxicology seminars and know the education and dedication of these practitioners, I highly recommend seeking out their service if one is in your locality.

For more information on homotoxicology, I suggest visiting www.gunainc.com, www.seroyal.com, and www.heel.com, three of the best companies specializing in homotoxicology products. These companies actively promote practitioner seminars throughout the world.

Appendix III

Glossary of Terms

Adrenal fatigue: This is the most common affliction of modern society. Virtually everyone over forty has adrenal fatigue to a greater or lesser degree. The adrenals are the prime regulators of energy production, and when they have been weakened by stress and bad diet, no real recovery will occur until they are regenerated.

Alpha lipoic acid (ALA): Supplemental ALA has been used in Europe for over three decades to treat peripheral nerve degeneration and to help control blood-sugar levels in people with diabetes. It also helps detoxify the liver of metal pollutants, block cataract formation, protect nerve tissues against oxidative stress, and reduce blood-cholesterol levels. This supplement plays a crucial role in the generation of cellular energy, is a significant immunologic stimulant that increases circulation, and has been approved in Japan to treat congestive heart failure.

Beta-blockers: These drugs are prescribed for hypertension, congestive heart failure, coronary heart disease, atrial fibrillation, and angina.

Blood-thinning medications: These medications, which can be highly toxic, are intended to prevent life-threatening blood clots and strokes.

Calcium-channel blockers: These drugs are prescribed for hypertension, arrhythmia, and angina.

Chelation therapy: The administration of chelating agents to remove heavy metals from the body.

Colon: The colon, approximately five feet in length, is part of the large intestine that comes after the small intestine in the digestive tract. The colon is mainly responsible for storing waste, absorbing water from indigestible food matter, maintaining water balance, and absorbing some vitamins, such as vitamin K and vitamin B12.

Colonic irrigation (also known as colon hydrotherapy): A procedure that helps remove impacted feces and other waste products from the colon and identify worms or other parasites in the intestine.

Detoxification: Detoxification is the removal of toxic substances from the body.

Digestive tract (also known as the alimentary canal): The digestive tract is a system of organs uniquely constructed to extract nutrients from food, turning it into energy, and to excrete the resulting waste. The major functions of this tract are ingestion, digestion, absorption, and defecation. Digestion breaks down food mechanically and chemically to make it available for the body. Digestion begins in the mouth where food is chewed and mixed with saliva. The stomach continues to break food down mechanically through churning and chemically through the action of enzymes. Absorption occurs both in the stomach and intestines, and excretion of waste takes place in the colon.

Electrolytes: Electrolytes are important because they are used by your cells (especially nerve, heart, and muscle cells) to maintain the cells' electrical conductivity and to carry electrical impulses (nerve impulses and muscle contractions) to other cells. Your kidneys help balance the electrolyte concentrations in your blood to maintain normal blood pH.

Emotional detoxification: This is the release of toxic emotions, which often occurs as you detoxify the body. As toxins are stirred up and released, you may experience short-term symptoms of mental-emotional detoxification such as depression, sadness, fear, and anger, among others. Conversely, conscious release of toxic thoughts and emotions can also aid physical detoxification of the body.

Enema: The introduction of liquids into the rectum and colon via the anus. An enema washes out and eliminates waste products from normal body functions, but colonics would be required if the intestinal walls are covered with a toxic lining.

Enzymes: Enzymes are protein catalysts that increase the rate of virtually every chemical reaction in the body. Digestive enzymes help break down food so that you absorb the maximum level of nutrients. Digestive enzymes also help break down old mucoid plaque that coats the bowel wall and work with psyllium seeds (fibrous binding agents) to bring this material out during enemas. Digestive enzymes may increase the electromagnetic frequency in and around cells to fight off free-radical damage—a cause of premature aging and disease.

Essential fatty acids (EFAs): EFAs are beneficial fats that the body cannot synthesize from other dietary fats or nutrients and therefore must be ingested.

Flavonoids: Especially potent antioxidants and metal chelators. More than four thousand chemically unique flavonoids are known.

Healing: Physical healing is the process by which cells in the body regenerate and repair. Physical healing incorporates both the removal and replacement of necrotic tissue. Mental-emotional and spiritual healing involve recognizing and assuming the power you have as God-creator to change anything about yourself. *God-creator* means that within parameters defined by your consciousness you use the energy of the universe to create your life.

Heavy-metal poisoning: The most common heavy metals are mercury from vaccinations and dental amalgams; cadmium from cigarette smoke; and lead, arsenic, nickel, aluminum, and beryllium from industrial products. Keep in mind that all metals, including calcium, can be toxic if they are not properly assimilated.

Hydration: Proper hydration is important for the health and functioning of cells and organs in the body. Drinking the correct amount of water will help curb your appetite and can increase the strength of your metabolism. It aids digestion and the absorption of nutrients, can help prevent internal infections, and can lower blood pressure. Proper hydration can also stop decay and infections in the mouth.

Immune-suppressing medications: Typically these are taken after an organ transplant to prevent the immune system from destroying the new organ. Unless your doctor specifically approves, I do not recommend any detoxification procedure or herb that lowers the medication level in the blood. I suggest that periodic colonics, lymph massages, daily exercise, and dietary modification will go a long way toward extending healthy vitality.

Intestinal flora: The human intestines contains trillions of bacteria. Mostly made up of friendly bacteria, intestinal flora contributes to digestion, the metabolism of vitamins, and also plays an important role in the formation of the immune system. The intestines contain a balance of this friendly bacteria and pathogenic bacteria. Changes in this balance can increase the risk of food allergies or chronic inflammatory intestinal diseases.

Leaky bowel syndrome: Fecal matter can leak back into the blood through a weakened bowel wall. Causes include a prolapsed colon from overeating and lack of exercise, a low-fiber diet, excess carbohydrate consumption, constipation, and stress.

Melatonin: A hormone produced in the pineal gland, melatonin is one of the few antioxidants that can penetrate the mitochondria, the cells' power plant, and protect them from free-radical damage. Laboratory studies with nonhuman subjects have shown that supplemental melatonin can inhibit cancer growth and protect against degenerative diseases.

Metabolic syndrome: *Taber's Medical Dictionary* defines this condition as the presence of four interrelated atherosclerotic factors: insulin resistance, hyperlipidemia, hypertension, and obesity. The main event here is insulin resistance, which occurs when cells lose their ability to take in insulin—an essential step in the utilization of blood sugar from carbohydrate metabolism. This condition evolves from the overconsumption of carbohydrates, especially carbohydrates from refined flours and sugars. As the cells become insulin resistant, this condition can extend to complex carbohydrates as well.

Microorganisms: These include but are not limited to tapeworms, pinworms, flukes, and many forms of undesirable bacteria too numerous to mention here. Again, poor diet, stress, and emotional factors create an environment for these critters to flourish.

PH level: pH is a scale that measures how acidic or alkaline a substance is. The ideal pH level of your blood is between 7.3 and 7.4 and cannot vary much from this level if life is to be sustained.

Probiotics: Probiotics are dietary supplements containing friendly bacteria.

Toxins: These are agents capable of causing our bodies harm.

Vitamin A and the carotenoids: These prevent night blindness and other eye problems. They also enhance immunity and help heal gastrointestinal ulcers and are needed for maintenance and repair of epithelial tissue. They are important in the formation of bones and teeth; they aid in fat storage and protect against colds, flu, and some infections. The body cannot utilize protein without vitamin A, which is also a well-known wrinkle eliminator. Carotenoids are a class of compounds that are converted to vitamin A by the liver. Thus far over six hundred carotenoids have been identified.

Vitamins and minerals: For the most part, vitamins are obtained from food, but a few are obtained by other means.

Yeast overgrowth: Products to treat vaginal yeast are frequently advertised on television, but yeast can also accumulate throughout the body. Consumption of birth-control pills, prescription drugs, and too many refined carbohydrates are the primary physical causes, but emotions play a role as well.

Appendix IV

Patient Symptom Survey

Toxicity Assessment Form

Name: Date:

Lifestyle Toxic Exposure

Please mark yes or no with an *X* next to the following eight questions related to your lifestyle and habits that may contribute to overall toxicity:

1. Do you drink alcoholic beverages? Yes_____ No_____
   How many per day? _____________
2 Do you smoke or use tobacco? Yes_____ No_____
   How many or how much per day? ______________
3. Do you drink coffee, caffeinated beverages, or energy drinks?
   Yes_____ No_____
   How many per day __________
4. Do you drink tap water? Yes_____ No_____
5. Do you use plastic in the microwave or for cooking?
   Yes_____ No_____
6. Do you use cosmetics, soaps, lotions, shampoos, or deodorants with ingredients that you can't pronounce? Yes_____ No_____
7. Do you eat commercially grown (nonorganic) food?
   Yes_____ No_____
8. Do you use a cell phone or computer? Yes_____ No_____
   How many hours per day? _________________

The following are questions that assess how you have been feeling during the last sixty days. These questions are designed to evaluate specific organ systems that may be compromised due to toxicity and lifestyle.

For each question circle the number that describes your symptoms.
0 = No or Rarely
1 = Occasionally (less than once per week)
3 = Often (two to three times per week)
5 = Frequently (four or more times per week)

Hypochlorhydria (Low Stomach Acid):

1. Excessive belching or burping within one hour of eating
   0 1 3 5
2. Gas immediately following food
   0 1 3 5
3. Bad breath
   0 1 3 5
4. Constipation
   0 1 3 5
5. Feeling extremely full after meals (food feels like it sits in the stomach)
   0 1 3 5
6. Gas, bloating, and discomfort from raw vegetables and fruit
   0 1 3 5
7. Undigested food found in the stool
   0 1 3 5
8. Small meals make you feel full
   0 1 3 5

Gastrointestinal Inflammation:

1. Strong emotions aggravate your stomach or make it hurt
   0 1 3 5
2. Feeling hungry an hour or two after a good-sized meal
   0 1 3 5
3. Heartburn from spicy foods, fried foods, chocolate, peppers, alcohol, coffee, or citrus fruits
   0 1 3 5
4. Temporary relief after having food, antacids, milk, or carbonated beverages
   0 1 3 5
5. Digestive problems subside with rest and relaxation
   0 1 3 5
6. Heartburn when lying down or bending forward
   0 1 3 5

Small Intestines and Pancreas:

1. Difficulty losing weight
   0 1 3 5
2. Gas and bloating
   0 1 3 5

3. Bowel movements after eating (within one hour)
   0 1 3 5
4. Diarrhea (frequent loose stools)
   0 1 3 5
5. Indigestion, gas, fullness two to four hours after meals
   0 1 3 5
6. Undigested food in the stool
   0 1 3 5
7. Foul smelling stool
   0 1 3 5

Liver and Gallbladder:

1. Greasy or high-fat foods cause gas or bloating
   0 1 3 5
2. Massaging under right ribcage causes pain or tenderness
   0 1 3 5
3. Midback, right side of neck, right shoulder pain (possibly worse at night)
   0 1 3 5
4. Unexplained itchy skin (possible worse at night)
   0 1 3 5
5. Dry or flaky skin
   0 1 3 5
6. Bruise easily
   0 1 3 5
7. History of gallbladder problems (stones)
   0 1 3 5
8. Pain behind eyes or throbbing temples (associated with overeating or alcohol use)
   0 1 3 5
9. Aching muscles not due to exercise
   0 1 3 5

Colon:

1. Stool is small, hard, and dry
   0 1 3 5
2. No urge to have bowl movements
   0 1 3 5
3. Generally constipated
   0 1 3 5

4. Pass mucus in stools
   0 1 3 5
5. Alternate between constipation and diarrhea
   0 1 3 5
6. Rectal pain, itching, or cramping
   0 1 3 5

Central Nervous System:

1. Have dizziness or balance problems
   0 1 3 5
2. Hands tremble for no apparent reason
   0 1 3 5
3. Often bump into things, trip, stumble, or feel clumsy
   0 1 3 5
4. Speaking and forming words does not feel automatic
   0 1 3 5
5. Responding to verbal commands is confusing or takes longer than it should
   0 1 3 5
6. Have a low tolerance under stress or ordinary daily activities
   0 1 3 5

Adrenal Function:

1. Need coffee to get going in the morning
   0 1 3 5
2. Have dizziness from standing suddenly
   0 1 3 5
3. Have afternoon fatigue
   0 1 3 5
4. Crave salty foods
   0 1 3 5
5. Catch colds or infections easily
   0 1 3 5
6. Have difficulty staying asleep
   0 1 3 5
7. Fatigue or get exhausted easily
   0 1 3 5
8. Have many sore spots in muscles
   0 1 3 5

Unstable Blood Sugar (Hypoglycemia):

1. Crave sweets during the day
   0 1 3 5
2. Drink two or more cups of coffee or soft drinks
   0 1 3 5
3. Fatigue relieved by food
   0 1 3 5
4. Feel agitated, anxious, or nervous if you miss a meal or go too long without eating
   0 1 3 5
5. Wake up at night between 1:00 and 3:00 a.m. after eating a large evening meal
   0 1 3 5
6. Low energy, sleepy, or crave sweets or caffeine two hours after lunch
   0 1 3 5
7. Poor memory, forgetful
   0 1 3 5

Note: *Symptoms of frequent urination, unusual thirst, slow wound healing, numbness or tingling in your feet, and unusual hunger maybe be signs of diabetes.*

Toxicity Assessment Questionnaire Nutritional Key

Preventive Nutrition

IntraMax liquid multiple½ oz. twice/day with meals

OR

Twice Daily Essentials Packets 1 packet twice/day with meals
And
Three A Day Antioxidant 3 capsules/day with meals
And
Probiotic Synergy 2 capsules/day (empty stomach)

Meal Replacement Nutrition

1. **PaleoCleanse Shake**
   2 scoops PaleoCleanse
   1 tablespoon PaleoFiber
   1 tablespoon PaloeGreens
   1 teaspoon GI Revive
   (Blend with water and frozen organic berries)

2. **PaleoMeal Shake (Strawberry/Vanilla)**
   1 scoop PaleoMeal
   1 tablespoon PaleoFiber
   1 tablespoon PaleoGreens
   1 teaspoon GI Revive
   (Blend with water and frozen organic berries)

3. **Dairy Sensitive Shake**
   2 scoops Pure Pea Protein
   1 tablespoon PaleoFiber
   1 tablespoon PaleoGreens
   1 teaspoon GI Revive
   (Blend with water and frozen organic berries)

Note: *All of the flowing nutritional recommendations should include intraMAX liquid multiple or Twice Daily Essentials packets.*

Hypochlorhydria (Low stomach acid)

Betaine Plus1-4 tablets/meal
Start with 1 per meal the first day. The second day 2 per meal, third day, 3 per meal and the fourth day 4 per meal. If a burning sensation occurs in stomach reduce the dose by 1 capsule.

GI Revive 1-2 teaspoons/day mixed with water

OR

Pure Pea Protein 1 scoop
GI Revive 1 teaspoon
PaleoFiber 1 tablespoon (blend with water and frozen berries)
Betaine Plus 1-4 tablets/meal

Gastrointestinal Inflammation

GI Revive 1-3 teaspoons/day mixed with water
Probiotic Synergy 1-2 capsules 3 times/day (empty stomach)

Omega Synergy 1-3 capsules/day

Note: *If GI Inflammation and Liver/Gallbladder score is moderate to high include Liver/Gallbladder support nutrition to GI inflammation nutrition.*

Shake for Gastrointestinal Inflammation (1-2 times/day)
2 scoops PaleoCleanse
1 teaspoon GI Revive
1 tablespoon PaleoGreens
1 tablespoon PaleoFiber
1 Omega Synergy capsule
(Blend with water & frozen organic berries)

Note: *If gastrointestinal inflammation occurs with a moderate or high adrenal score include:*
Adrenotone Plus 1 capsule/day before 3:00 p.m. with meals
Adrenal Complex 1 capsule/day before 3:00 p.m. with meals

Note: *Reduce or eliminate spicy foods, fried foods, chocolate, coffee, and alcohol.*

Small Intestine and Pancreas

Digestzymes 1-2 capsules with meals
Probiotic Synergy 1-2 capsules 2 times/day
PaleoGreens 1-2 tablespoons/day
GI Revive 1-3 teaspoons/day mixed with water

OR

Small Intestine/Pancreas Shake (1-2 Times/day)
2 scoops PaleoCleanse
1 teaspoon GI Revive
1 tablespoon PaleoGreens
1 tablespoon PaleoFiber

Note: *Meal replacement shakes five the digestive tract a rest and promote healing because they are easier to digest and eliminate possible food allergies.*

Note: *Reduce or eliminate spicy foods, fried foods, chocolate, coffee, and alcohol.*

Liver/Gallbladder (1-2 times/day)

Dextox Support Packets 1-2 times/day
PaleoGreens 1-2 tablespoons/day mixed with water
PaleoFiber 1-2 tablespoons/day mixed with water
Probiotic Synergy 1-3 capsules/day

Liver/GallbladderShake (1-2 times/day)
2 scoops PaleoCleanse
1 tablespoon PaleoGreens
1 tablespoon PaleoFiber
1 teaspoon GI Revive

Note: *Reduce or eliminate alcohol, caffeine, drugs (recreational, pharmaceutical), partially hydrogenated oil.*

Colon

Probiotic Synergy 1-3 capsules 3 times/day
PaleoFiber 1-2 tablespoons 2 times/day
Digestzymes 1-2 capsules with meals

OR

Colon Shake
2 scoops PaleoCleanse
1 tablespoon PaleoFiber
1 teaspoon GI Revive
1 tablespoon PaleoGreens
(Blend with water and frozen organic berries)

Note: *If hypochlorhydria score was moderate or high add Betaine Plus.*

Note: *To function efficiently the colon requires fiber, plenty of water, and appropriate intestinal flora.*

Central Nervous System
Twice Daily Essentials 1 packet 2 times/day after meals

Detox Support Packets 1 packet 2 times/day after meals

Note: *The central nervous system is very sensitive to toxins a series of Ion cleanse footbaths are highly recommended.*

Note: *Neurotransmitter production is very dependent on proper intestinal tract function. If you have a moderate or high score in hypochlorhydria GI inflammation, small intestine/pancreas, liver or colon apply necessary protocols.*

Adrenal Function
Adrenotone Plus 1 capsule 2 times/day Before 3:00 p.m.
Adrenal Complex 1 capsule 2 times/day Before 3:00 p.m.

Note: *Adrenal fatigue has an intimate connection with unstable blood sugar (hypoglycemia). The Zone Diet by Barry Sears or the Atkins Diet is recommended to treat blood sugar instability.*

Unstable Blood Sugar (Hypoglycemia)
Twice Daily Essentials 1 packet 2 times/day after meals
Glucoset 1-2 capsules 3 times/day after meals
Adrenotone Plus 1 capsule 2 times/day before 3:00 p.m.
Adrenal Complex 1 capsule 2 times/day before 3:00 p.m.
PaleoFiber 1 tablespoon mixed with water after meals

Note: *Zone Diet or Atkins Diet recommended.*

Appendix V

Nutrition Evaluation Report

WINCHESTER CHIROPRACTIC & WELLNESS CENTER
Dr. Ted Winchester, D.C.
6940 S. Holly Circle Suite 108, Centennial, CO 80112
Email: dani@winchesterhealth.com
Phone: (303) 221-0195 Fax: (303) 221-0196

NUTRITION EVALUATION: 01/24/2011

PATIENT INFORMATION

Neill Moroney
6940 S. Holly Circle #108
Centennial CO 80112
Sex: M
Age: 29
Blood Type:

DATA USED FOR ANALYSIS

PSS	01/11/2011
Urinalysis	01/11/2011
Blood	01/07/2011
Stool	01/17/2011
Hair	01/12/2011
Vitals	01/24/2011

VITALS

Height: 6'0"
Weight: 174
Blood Pressure: 139 / 80
O2 Level: 98%
Heart Rate: 59

PRESENTING SYMPTOMS

Desires Nutritional and Metabolic Analysis • General Good Health • Base of fingernails are purple • Fingernails have ridges or white spots • Hair loss • Often annoyed by people • Upset by criticism • Frequent foot cramps • 6 or more bowel movements per week • Belching and burping after eating • Drinks alcohol • Had 4 alcoholic drinks in one day less than 3 months ago • Regularly exercises • Takes vitamins

PRIMARY FINDINGS SUGGESTIVE OF

- Hypocholesterolemia
- Hypoglycemia
- Dehydration effects
- Noted Blood Values
- High Hair Mercury
- Possible cardio effect
- Gout
- Increased Thyroid Function
- Very High Hair Uranium
- Noted Hair Values

The purpose for this nutrition and lifestyle program is to create an optimum environment in which your body can heal and repair itself. This is achieved by eliminating foods and toxins, which adversely affect the body, and by providing nutrients that the body may be lacking.

INTERPRETING ALL TEST RESULTS

Your test results are color coded for ease of analysis:
Yellow = values are outside the healthy range but still within the clinical range
Red = values are outside the clinical range
Blue = values extremely higher or lower than the clinical range limits.

INTERPRETING BLOOD LAB RESULTS

On the blood test results page found later in the report, you'll notice two columns on the right side of the page labeled "Healthy Range" and "Clinical Range". The clinical range is used by the medical community. Any values outside this range are indicative of a disease process. The healthy range is more narrow than the clinical range. Test values outside of the healthy range indicate results which are not as good as they should be. The tighter guidelines of the healthy range allows us to see signs of any developing diseases/conditions.

INTERPRETING HAIR LAB RESULTS

The hair analysis screening is looking for essential, nonessential and potentially toxic elements. These elements are irreversibly incorporated into growing hair. The amount of each element found in the hair is proportional to levels in other body tissues. This makes the hair analysis a suitable indirect screening for physiological excess, deficiency or maldistribution of elements in the body. All screening tests have limitations which must be taken into consideration. Scalp hair is vulnerable to external contamination by water, hair treatments and other products. The data provided by a hair analysis should be considered in conjunction with symptoms, diet analysis, occupation and lifestyle, water source, physical examination and the results of other laboratory tests. However, accepting these limitations, hair analysis can provide useful insights into the toxic load and biochemical condition of the body.

For each elevated toxic element in the hair, the most common sources of exposure are listed in the report. Due to pollution, our industrial culture and other environmental factors, it is impossible to completely eliminate your exposure to some toxic elements. However by knowing the sources of toxins elevated in your body, you can work to reduce your exposure, thus lessening the total toxic burden on your body.

DIAGNOSTIC FINDINGS

CORONARY RISK ASSESSMENT

- **Total Cholesterol:** 147
- **LDL Cholesterol:** 77
- **HDL Cholesterol:** 61
- **VLDL Cholesterol:** 9

Coronary Risk Assessment: 2.41 Probably Protected
The coronary risk is determined by taking the total cholesterol and dividing it by the HDL. To reduce your risk of cardiovascular problems a value below 4 is recommended. The Total Cholesterol is determined by adding the HDL, LDL, and VLDL together. Recent studies have shown a correlation between a high HDL and longevity. Think of HDL as the healthy cholesterol and generally the higher the better. LDL is the bad cholesterol, as it tends to plug the arteries. The VLDL is the very worst cholesterol and is more like sludge. Lower is better for the LDL and VLDL in determining coronary risk and overall health.

HYPOCHOLESTEROLEMIA

The Cholesterol and Triglycerides are a little low and the LDL is a little high. The LDL being high with the Cholesterol and Triglycerides being low is a little unusual. Basically too much of the cholesterol that is in the blood is the bad cholesterol. This needs to be modified. Total Cholesterol is very important in the immune system, production of hormones, energy, cell and nerve structures. Make sure you get enough of the good fats in your diet, preferably more plant fats, such as avocados, almonds, flax-seed oil, pumpkin seeds and olive oil. No hydrogenated fats or oils are allowed.

Nutrients Recommended:
Opti-EPA 500

POSSIBLE CARDIO EFFECT

The Homocystine is a little high which does contribute to an increased coronary risk. Low thyroid is commonly associated with this finding.

The Creatine Kinase (CK) is very high and the C-Reactive Protein (CRP) is a little high. This elevated CK is commonly associated with breakdown of muscle, either cardiac or skeletal. This could be the result of strenuous exercise in which case the nutrient recommendation can be reduced. It could also be a sign of a more serious condition developing or heart involvement. This slightly elevated C-Reactive Protein indicates mild nonspecific tissue injury and inflammation. It doesn't tell where, just that there is a problem and this value is good to monitor response to treatment. NOTE: Recent studies have shown that the CRP is one of the best markers for predicting the chances of a heart attack or stroke. A CRP close to zero is desired.

This finding is supported by:
Low Blood Phosphorus • High Blood A/G Ratio • High Blood Creatine Kinase • High Blood CRP C-Reactive Protein • High Blood Hemoglobin • High Blood Homocysteine

Nutrients Recommended:
Carnitine 250 • Citrus Q 10 • Inflavonoid (Turmeric) • Sublingual B12FA

HYPOGLYCEMIA

The glucose is a little low which is associated with hypoglycemic symptoms. Follow the hypoglycemic diet defined later in this report. The main thing is good snack every 2 hours that includes some protein.

This finding is supported by:
Low Hair Chromium

GOUT

The Uric Acid is a little high which is seen in many conditions and diseases including a tendency toward gout. This could also be due to notable physical exertion.

DEHYDRATION EFFECTS

High Chloride.

High Albumin.

The Serum Iron and RBC are a little high and the Hemoglobin and Hematocrit are high. Dehydration is the first consideration, There are several factors and reasons that could contribute to this including smoking, exercise, high altitude and vascular disease. Ferritin should be tested if not already done, which would rule out hemochromatosis.

INCREASED THYROID FUNCTION

The T3 Uptake is high. This is usually seen in hyperthyroid function. Increased thyroid function may be associated with weight loss, weakness and/or leading to decreased activity.

This finding is supported by:
Low Blood Globulin • Low Blood Total Cholesterol • Low Hair Manganese

Nutrients Recommended:
Iodoral

NOTED BLOOD VALUES

The platelets are a little low. This is probably associated with chronic infection. This may also be due to drugs or vaccines.

The Globulin is a little low. This can indicate a mildly reduced immune system with a tendency for infections. A diet with sufficient high quality protein is recommended.

The GGT is a little low and this may be caused by medications, usually medications that are used to lower triglycerides.

The Basophils are a little high and probably indicate a mild inflammatory reaction.

The Carbon Dioxide (CO2) is low. This is metabolic alkalosis, which can be due to many things and many drugs including steroids, antacids or as simple as low protein levels and poor diet. Be aware that the CO2 tests run through LabCorp of America are in reality Bicarbonate testings. The significance is that the results are opposite of CO2. When Bicarb is low one would be too alkaline. When the Bicarb is high then one would be too acidic.

The Calcium/Albumin Ratio is low and the A/G Ratio is high. The C/A Ratio is seen with insufficient calcium and the high A/G Ratio is seen with excess protein.

The Triglyceride/HDL Cholesterol Ratio is optimal. Recent studies have shown that the ratio of triglycerides to HDL was the strongest predictor of a heart attack. In adults, the triglyceride/HDL ratio should be below 2.

The MCV is a little high which indicates a B12/folate deficiency and/or cell dehydration. The MCV (Mean Corpuscular Volume) is the size (volume) of the average red cell.

The Glomerular Filtration Rate Estimated (eGFR) is optimal. The eGFR is a calculated estimate of the actual glomerular filtration rate and is based on your serum Creatinine concentration. The calculation uses formulas that may also include your age, gender, height, and weight. In some formulas, race may also be used in the calculation.
The kidneys filter blood and help control blood pressure. They remove waste and water and produce urine. eGFR is one of the best tests to indicate how healthy your kidneys are. It is important to know your eGFR because one may not be able to feel kidney damage.
Over 59-preferred
35 to 58-early kidney damage
16 to 34-moderate kidney damage
1 to 15 severe kidney damage
* Please note that if your test result is less than 15, dialysis or transplant may be needed soon.

The Vitamin D and Phosphorus are a little low. Most doctors and research scientists recommend a value of at least 32.00 to be at the minimally accepted level of Vitamin D in the blood. This nutrient is converted by the skin while in the presence of sunlight. The Phosphorus is a little low. This can be seen in many conditions but the most common is a vitamin D deficiency, although this is not always the case. Along with the Vit D, eat potassium rich foods such as broccoli, sweet potatoes, avocados and bananas.

The Serum Iron is a little high and the Ferritin is optimal. This is mild iron overload or possibly inflammation. Reduce iron intake.

Nutrients Recommended:
Calcium MCHC • Sublingual B12FA • Vitamin D

VERY HIGH HAIR URANIUM

The uranium level in the hair is very high. Hair is a good indicator of uranium exposure. Blood and urine have been noted as NOT being representative of the body burden since the blood is rapidly cleared of uranium. Most forms of uranium are poorly absorbed by the body with the exception of the lungs, which absorb airborne uranium readily. Uranium forms many complexes with proteins, bone and can substitute for calcium. It is deposited throughout the body and chronic fatigue is often reported in assoication with high hair levels. Published data correlates uranium exposure, nephrotoxicity and all forms of cancer. Kidney and bone are the primary sites of uranium accumulation. Uranium has been noted to be higher in female hair than males living in the same home.

Uranium is considered to be a toxic element, although its toxic effects are not well known. It is a moderately common element with three isotopes. U238, the most common isotope, represents over 99% of the naturally occurring element. It is the only isotope of concern in this analysis. It is reasonably stable with a low level of radioactivity and a half life of 4.5 billion years. **Uranium is used in glass manufacturing, ceramics, colored glass, high phosphate fertilizers and in some chemicals. Drinking water is a significant source of U238 in many regions. Radon can be a by-product of U238 decomposition.**

Nutrients Recommended:
Chlorella Clean • Iodoral

HIGH HAIR MERCURY

The mercury level in the hair is high. Mercury (Hg) is a toxic element for humans and animals. Hair mercury level is an accurate indicator of mercury body burden. A considerable variance in the sensitivity of different individuals to mercury has been observed, with some exhibiting symptoms at 3 to 5 ppm. Even very low levels of mercury have been found to suppress biological selenium activity. After dental amalgams are used, elevated hair mercury may be observed for six months to over a year. Hair mercury has been found to correlate with acute myocardial infarction where on average a 1 ppm mercury was found to correlate with a 9 percent increase in acute myocardial infarction risk.

Mercury displaces selenium (which is a major anti-oxidant), zinc (protein, DNA and energy metabolism) and copper. Supplementation of magnesium, zinc, calcium, selenium, and manganese has been shown to be beneficial in relieving mercury loads.

Symptoms of acute contamination: metallic taste, thirst, discoloration and edema of oral mucosa, burning mouth pain, salivation, abdominal pain, vomiting, bloody diarrhea, severe gastroenteritis, colitis, nephrosis, anuria, uremia, shock.

Symptoms of chronic contamination: gingivitis; weakness; ataxia; intention tremors; chronic fatigue (caused by inhibition of thyroid conversion of T4 to T3); depression; poor memory and cognitive function; learning disabilities; behavioral disorders; emotional instability; speech impairment, irritability; peripheral numbness, tingling or neuropathy; sleep disturbance;

decreased senses of touch, hearing or vision; hypersensitivity and allergies; persistent infections including chronic yeast overgrowth; compromised immune function; cardiovascular disease. It disrupts intracellular transport in neurons and can decrease the production of neurotransmitters. Eventually this can lead to autoimmune diseases such as SLE (systemic lupus erythematosis), myelinopathies such as MS and myasthenia gravis, rheumatoid arthritis, MCS (multiple chemical sensitivity), and chronic candidiasis. An inverse relationship has been observed between hair mercury levels and intelligence scores in elementary school children.
Other sources of mercury are: large fish, pesticide residues, mercurial fungicides on seed grains, dental fillings, coal burning, calomel (mercurous chloride), interior paints, pharmaceuticals, the manufacture of paper, pulp and plastic products, and water.

Nutrients Recommended:
Chlorella Clean • Powdered Vitamin C with Ribose • Vital Trace Minerals

NOTED HAIR VALUES

The iron level in the hair is low. This does not necessarily correlate with low serum iron. Dietary sources include organ meats, poultry, fish, and dried beans and vegetables.

The manganese level in the hair is low. This trace element is a cofactor for a number of important enzymes and functions with vitamin K in the formation of prothrombin. The functions of manganese include: glucose utilization, lipid synthesis and lipid metabolism, cholesterol metabolism, pancreatic function and development, prevention of sterility, normal skeletal growth and development, important for protein and nucleic acid metabolism, activating enzyme functions and in thyroid hormone synthesis.
KNOWN DEFICIENCY SYMPTOMS: fatigue; lack of physical endurance; slow growth of fingernails and hair; impaired metabolism of bone and cartilage; dermatitis; weight loss; reduced fertility; increased allergic sensitivities; inflammation; ataxia; fainting; hearing loss; weak tendons and ligaments and possible cause of diabetes. Manganese activates several enzyme systems and supports the utilization of vitamin C, E, choline, and other B-vitamins. Inadequate choline utiliization reduces the acetylcholine synthesis, causing conditions such as myasthenia gravis (loss of muscle strength).
Seizures are occasionally reported to be assoicated with severe manganese deficiency.

The vanadium level in the hair is low. Vanadium is found in the body of mammals, and there is evidence that it is essential for chicks, rats, and goats. Chickens require vanadium for the growth and development of wings and feathers. In rats, inadequate vanadium intake results in stunted growth. Vanadium-deficient goats show irreversible bone deformities in their front legs. Vanadium catalyzes the oxidation of catecholamines (norepinephrine: adrenergic vasoconstriction, epinephrine,dopamine: vasoconstriction), may inhibit cholesterol synthesis and lower phospholipid levels in blood, may have anti-hyperglycemic function, a weight-reducing function, some anabolic effects, reduces caries formation, and influences sodium/potassium transport. Vanadium supplementation reduced fasting blood glucose levels after only a few days. Vanadium activated transport and conversion of fructose independent of insulin.
Source: liver, pancreas, kidneys, thyroid, and testes are rich in vanadium. This element is found especially in fiber-rich foods. The highest concentration is found in vegetable oils. Dill seeds, parsley and black pepper are especially rich in vanadium. Vanadium is poorly absorbed by the gastrointestinal tract.

The lithium level in the hair is low. Only very small amounts of Lithium are needed. Hair levels of lithium do not necessarily indicate a deficiency according to most recent studies.

The sulfur level in the hair is high. This does not necessarily correlate with high serum sulfur. It may the result of using certain shampoos.

The aluminum level in the hair is a little high. Any aluminum is too much. Aluminum toxicity is associated with Alzheimer's and Parkinson's disease, behavioral/learning disorders such as ADD, ADHD and autism. Aluminum has neurotoxic effects at high levels, but low levels of accumulation may not elicit immediate symptoms. Early symptoms of aluminum burden may include fatigue, headache, and other symptoms. Aluminum is a heavy metal that displaces your other good minerals, such as magnesium, calcium, zinc and phosphorus. One of the things that you should do to help your overall long-term health is to reduce your aluminum intake. The most common sources of aluminum to avoid are: antiperspirants, aluminum cookware, antacids, some baking sodas, baking powder, some breath mints, pickles, some skin lotion, some cosmetics, aluminum foil, canned goods, emulsifiers in some processed cheese, table salt - anti-caking compound, bleaching agent used in white flour, buffered aspirin, some toothpaste, dental amalgams, cigarette filters, and drinking water (tap water). Do not eat or drink anything that comes in a can. Read your labels before you purchase. Aluminum has also been found in a granola bar.

Aluminum rods are commonly used in hot water tanks in area of acidic water. These rods will dissolve neutralizing the water, thus protecting the hot water tank. A rod of magnesium is an option for the same purpose.

Note: Fluoride and fluoridation increases the absorption of aluminum.

Chlorella and magnesium with malic acid have been reported to be quite effective in lowering aluminum.

The arsenic level in the hair is a little high. Chronic arsenic exposure is known to cause: Bone marrow depression; leukopenia; normochromic anemia; exfoliation and pigmentation of skin; neurological symptoms; polyneuritis; altered hematopoiesis; liver degeneration; kidney degeneration; skin cancer; cancers of the respiratory tract; agitation; learning impairment; and confusion. Delayed toxicity symptoms include abdominal pain, nausea, vomiting, hematuria, and jaundice. Ingestion of relatively large amounts of soluble arsenic compounds, especially on an empty stomach, affect the myocardium, causing death within a few hours. Ingesting smaller amounts of arsenic can cause epigastric pain, vomiting and diarrhea, followed by inflammation of the conjunctiva and respiratory mucous membranes, epitaxis, transient jaundice, cardiomyopathy, erythematous or visceral rashes, and sweating. Other symptoms: malaise; muscle weakness; eczema; dermatitis; increased salivation; strong "garlic breath", alopecia totalis, vomiting, diarrhea and skin cancer. Hematological, renal, or pancreatic dysfunction may be observed. Symptoms of neuropathy are experienced typically appear as with tingling and paresthesia in the extremities. Proteinuria and methemoglobinemia are frequently observed, causing renal failure and death.

Arsenic can be absorbed by the human body through the respiratory and gastrointestinal tracts and through the skin. Arsenic is found in tobacco smoke and is a suspected causative factor in lung cancer. Metal smelting and the production of glass, ceramics, insecticides, fungicides and herbicides mobilize environmental arsenic. Drinking water may also be a source of arsenic, and the use of arsenic-containing paints is a known source of arsenic poisoning. Elevated hair levels are seen long before acute clinical signs of arsenic toxicity are obvious.

Therapeutic consideration for chronic overexposure: antioxidant therapy, especially ascorbic acid or calcium ascorbate, vitamin E (all tocopherols), increased intake of sulfur-containing amino acids, vitamin B6. Note: arsenic suppresses iodine and selenium.

Research: the relationship between cognitive functions and hair mineral concentrations of lead, arsenic, cadmium, and aluminum was examined for a random selection of 69 children. The data obtained showed a significant correlation between reading and writing skill and elevated arsenic levels, as well as interaction between arsenic and lead. Children with reduced visual-motor skills, had clearly elevated aluminum and lead levels.

The titanium level in the hair is a little high. Titanium generally has low toxicity. Titanium (Ti) has wide industrial uses, and elevated Ti may be the result of industrial exposure. Titanium is used in metal alloying and is used as titanium dioxide to coat welding rods. Titanium dioxide pigment is present in **paints, inks, dyes, shoe whiteners, plastics, some cosmetics, toothpaste, conditioners, shampoos, paper fillers and ceramic glazes. Elevated hair titanium also may be an artifact (false high) of hair treatments such as dyeing or "highlighting". Surgical or dental implants may be a source of titanium in the hair.**

Nutrients Recommended:
Calcium MCHC • Chlorella Clean • Lithinase (Lithium) • MagMalic • Manganese • Multiple • Vital Trace Minerals

To help get these heavy metals out of your system, which is very important, Chlorella is recommended. Magnesium and selenium, are both very important in getting these toxic metals through the kidneys. Chlorella and cilantro have the unique ability to actually get these heavy metals out of brain, liver, heart, and lung tissue. Adding fresh cilantro to the diet is also recommended. Cilantro is an herb that can be found in most supermarkets. Chop it up and add it to salads, sauces, etc. Since we are constantly being exposed to heavy metals in our society, it is recommend that even after you are feeling better that you continue with the chlorella.

LIFESTYLE / DIETARY RECOMMENDATIONS

DIET FOCUS

Food can be broken down into basically two categories:

1. Energy (calories from fat, carbohydrates and protein)
2. Nourishment (the nutrient density of the food; vitamin and mineral content).

When planning your meals, use this thought process:

1. Get at least 2 vegetables with each meal. Fruit should be limited only if you have glucose handling issues. However, always consume more vegetables than fruits.

2. Proteins: 25-35% of the meal needs to be of a protein source.
   - Focus on good quality protein and not the processed protein bars, drinks, and powders.
   - Most desirable proteins: meats (like chicken, fish, turkey and even red meat), eggs, beans, seeds, nuts, sprouts, quinoa, nut butters (ie. peanut butter, cashew butter, almond butter).
   - Eliminate these least desirable proteins: processed soy, processed dairy, pork, processed luncheon meats (those that contain "nitrates" or "nitrites").
   - Search Google "USDA SR 21" for a downloadable database to look up nutritional content of foods.

3. Carbohydrates: 40-60% of your meal needs to be carbohydrate.
   - Most desirable carbohydrates sources: whole grain breads, pastas (including egg noodles), and rice, whole vegetables, whole fruit.
   - Eliminate these least desirable carbohydrates: white sugar, white flour, fruit juice, high fructose corn syrup, chips, French fries, pop/soda

4. Fats: Your meal should contain anywhere from 15-25% fat.
   - Most desirable fat sources: nuts (cashews, almonds, pecans, walnuts, Brazil nuts (raw and unsalted are preferred), seeds (sunflower seeds, pumpkin seeds), avocados, coconut oil, fish, nut butters (peanut butter, almond butter, etc)
   - Desirable Cooking Oils: Grape Seed Oil, Olive Oil, Coconut Oil, Palm Oil
   - Eliminated these least desirable fat sources: anything with trans-fat (AKA: hydrogenated fat), interesterified fat or Olestra. Bacon, sausage, etc.
   - Strictly avoid hydrogenated/trans-fats: About 80% of trans fats in your diet come from processed foods, fast food, primarily snack foods and desserts.

5. Special instructions may be given based upon certain metabolic conditions such as cancer, diabetes, kidney disorders etc.

IDENTIFYING LOW NUTRIENT DENSE FOODS

Below is a list of foods and items that will help you identify low nutrient dense foods and cooking/storage processes that lower the nutrient density in foods. These are strongly recommended you avoid. READ YOUR INGREDIENT LABELS!! Later in your report, you will find exchanges for these items and helpful hints for implementing these lifestyle habits.

1. Artificial Sweeteners: "aspartame", "saccharin", "sucralose", "acesulfame potassium", "sorbitol", "maltitol", etc.
2. Flavor Enhancers and Preservatives: "MSG", "monosodium glutamate", "nitrate" or "nitrite" ingredients found in many dressings, sauces, Chinese foods, processed meats, pork products, bologna, some wieners, and many luncheon meat. HVP (hydrolyzed vegetable protein) and processed soy proteins can contain up to 40% MSG.
3. Artificial colors and dyes: look for terms such as "FD&C", "lake", "red", "yellow", etc. Read your supplement labels carefully.
4. Canned Foods and Drinks: choose fresh or frozen varieties. Limit canned food consumption to canned beans and tuna. Foods stored in glass are acceptable.
5. Microwave Cooking and Deep Frying lower the nutrient density more so than stove top cooking.
6. Artificial Fats: "hydrogenated" [a.k.a. "trans fat"] and "interesterified" fats are found in margarine, many pre-packaged foods, supplements, and dressings; avoid "Olestra" containing products.
7. Refined Carbohydrates: processed foods such as white sugar, white flour, corn syrup, "enriched" foods, etc.
8. Commercial Meats: Try to get the cleanest, freshest meat you can find. Look for meat that is labeled with terms such as "No Hormones", "No Antibiotics", "Free Range", "Organic", etc.
9. Shellfish and Bottom-feeders: crab, shrimp, lobster, oyster, catfish, etc.
10. Dairy Products: cottage cheese, yogurt, cheese, sour cream, etc. (anything with cow's milk). This does not include eggs.
11. Coffee (regular & chemically decaffed), Liquor (distilled), All sodas, Tea (black decaf & black regular). Organic herbal teas are acceptable.
12. Soy Products: isolated soy protein, texturized vegetable protein, soy supplements, soy protein powder, soy protein bars, tofu, etc. Limited fermented soy products (tempeh and miso) and whole soy beans are acceptable. Don't make soy your main protein source, limit to 3-4 servings per week.
13. Chlorine and Fluoride Sources: tap water, heavy chlorine exposure in swimming pools, fluoride toothpaste, fluoride supplements, fluoride mouthwash, etc.

HYPOGLYCEMIC RECOMMENDATIONS

1. Avoid all fruit juices.
2. Eat only one fruit and at least four fresh vegetables per day.
3. Eat a snack every hour and a half to two hours.
   - Eat by the clock. This is going to help take stress off your liver and maintain your glucose at a good level so it doesn't fluctuate so much.

- § The snack should be 4 to 5 bites of a complex carbohydrate, protein or foods that have good fats in them such as: whole grain bread with coconut oil or nut butter spread, sunflower seeds, pumpkin seeds, nuts, carrots with hummus or a few bites of chicken would be fine to eat.

4. Do this for at least the next two months or until your re-evaluation.

AEROBIC EXERCISE

Examples of aerobic exercise are jogging, cycling, elliptical trainer, fast-paced walking, etc. It is recommended that you build up to at least 40 minutes a day. If at first you do not have the energy to exercise this much, it is recommended that you start slowly by exercising 10 minutes two or three times a day until you can gradually build up to 40 minutes a day.

STRENGTH TRAINING

If you are not currently on a weight training program, a muscle building exercise (i.e. step exercise) 10 minutes a day is encouraged. If at first you do not have the energy or physical ability to perform this exercise, it is recommended that you start slowly by setting a goal to do this exercise 2 minutes two or three times a day until you can gradually build up to 10 minutes a day.

WATER CONSUMPTION

Drink 1 quart of clean, filtered water per 50lbs of body weight per day. Do not go over 3 quarts regardless of your weight. More water might be necessary depending on exercise, environment and perspiration. We recommend using a multiple filtration system for your drinking and cooking water. There are several types of these, which include reverse osmosis. Distilled water is not recommended. Since distilled water has little or no mineral content, it acts like a vacuum that can actually leach minerals from your system.

A word of caution - **anytime you make drastic changes in diet, vitamin intake, or exercise, realize that you may feel somewhat worse before you feel better.** It doesn't happen often, but as your body detoxifies, you may feel worse if it occurs too fast. If you do feel worse, don't panic, it will pass in a few days. If this problem does occur, take half of what is recommended for three days and slowly over two weeks progress to taking the complete program.

Everything that has been recommended is very important and many of these things work together. In order to get the most effective results, it is important that you follow the program exactly as outlined. Following the diet may not be easy, but if you do, you will get the best outcome. Likewise, if you don't take the vitamins, or only take part of them, you may not see the expected results. Many people with some very serious problems have been helped using this program. The purpose of this analysis is to benefit you. This is for your well being, so please do the program as recommended so that you will achieve the best results.

Attached is a list of vitamins that have been carefully selected for your specific problems. These vitamins are recommended because they are of the highest quality. Occasionally, you will hear rumors regarding vitamin toxicity. Rest assured that these issues have been researched and the risk of significant side effects is extremely low. Historical data and experience have shown these vitamins, along with the dietary changes, to be the best in helping you achieve the necessary improvements needed on your test results.

Please keep this report for future reference and bring it with you to your next evaluation.

If we can be of any further assistance to you or your family please do not hesitate to ask.

Yours In Health,

Dr. Ted Winchester, D.C.

Name: Neill Moroney **Lab: Quest** **Blood Test Results**

Legend: ☐ Warning ■ High Risk ☐ Critical ★ Optimal ☺ Improvement ☹ Worse Ø No Improvement

Test Description	Current Rating 01/07/2011		Prior	Delta	Healthy	Clinical	Units
Glucose	78.00	low			79.00 - 90.00	65.00 - 99.00	mg/dL
Hemoglobin A1C (Gly-Hgh)	5.30	★			4.61 - 5.40	4.50 - 6.00	%
Uric Acid	7.60	high			3.63 - 5.57	2.50 - 8.00	mg/dL
BUN (Blood Urea Nitrogen)	19.00	★			14.66 - 22.33	7.00 - 25.00	mg/dL
Creatinine	1.04	★			0.80 - 1.10	0.50 - 1.30	mg/dL
GFR EST (Glomerular Filtration Rate)	60.00	★			59.00 - 127.00	45.00 - 128.00	/min/1.73r
BUN / Creatinine Ratio	18.27	★			12.33 - 18.66	6.00 - 22.00	ratio
Sodium	140.00	★			138.66 - 142.33	135.00 - 146.00	meq/dL
Potassium	4.20	★			4.00 - 4.80	3.50 - 5.30	meq/dL
Chloride	107.00	high			102.00 - 106.00	98.00 - 110.00	meq/dL
Calcium	9.40	★			8.56 - 9.76	8.60 - 10.20	mg/dL
Magnesium	2.00	★			1.90 - 2.30	1.50 - 2.50	mg/dL
Calcium/Albumin Ratio	1.92	Low			2.10 - 2.50	2.03 - 2.71	ratio
Total Protein	7.10	★			6.77 - 7.53	6.20 - 8.30	gm/dL
Albumin	4.90	high			3.67 - 4.43	3.60 - 5.10	gm/dL
Globulin	2.20	low			2.86 - 3.53	2.10 - 3.90	gm/dL
A/G Ratio	2.20	High			1.30 - 1.60	1.00 - 2.10	ratio
LDH	147.00	★			120.00 - 160.00	100.00 - 250.00	mu/mL
Alkaline Phosphatase 25-150	73.00	★			55.00 - 90.00	33.00 - 130.00	mu/mL
Total Bilirubin	0.80	★			0.56 - 0.94	0.20 - 1.20	mg/dL
SGOT (AST)	23.00	★			18.00 - 26.00	10.00 - 40.00	mu/mL
SGPT (ALT)	21.00	★			18.00 - 26.00	9.00 - 60.00	mu/mL
GGT	19.00	low			20.00 - 75.00	3.00 - 95.00	u/l
Serum Iron	130.00	high			81.60 - 129.40	40.00 - 170.00	mcg/dL
Phosphorus	2.90	low			3.10 - 3.90	2.50 - 4.50	mg/dL
Ferritin	84.00	★			50.00 - 110.00	9.00 - 120.00	NG/ML
Total Cholesterol	147.00	low			150.00 - 180.00	125.00 - 200.00	mg/dL
Triglyceride	43.00	low			76.66 - 113.33	0.00 - 150.00	mg/dL
HDL Cholesterol	61.00	★			50.00 - 120.00	40.00 - 150.00	mg/dL
LDL Cholesterol	77.00	high			36.00 - 68.00	5.00 - 130.00	mg/dL
VLDL Cholesterol	8.60	★			8.00 - 20.00	5.00 - 35.00	mg/dL
Total Cholesterol / HDL Ratio	2.40	★			0.00 - 4.00	0.00 - 5.00	ratio
Triglyceride/HDL Ratio	0.70	★			0.00 - 2.00	0.00 - 4.00	
T4 Thyroxine	7.20	★			7.00 - 9.50	4.50 - 12.50	mcg/dL
T3 Uptake	35.00	High			28.30 - 31.70	22.00 - 35.00	%
T7 Free Thyroxine Index (FTI)	2.50	★			2.20 - 3.40	1.40 - 3.80	
TSH	1.16	★			0.75 - 2.00	0.45 - 4.50	U/mL
White Blood Count	5.10	★			5.00 - 9.00	4.00 - 11.00	k/cumm
Red Blood Count	5.03	high			4.00 - 5.00	3.70 - 5.40	m/cumm
Hemoglobin	15.80	High			13.00 - 15.00	11.70 - 15.50	gm/dL
Hematocrit	47.40	High			39.50 - 44.00	35.00 - 45.00	%
MCV	94.20	high			87.00 - 93.00	80.00 - 100.00	cu.m
MCH	31.50	★			30.00 - 32.50	27.00 - 33.00	pg
MCHC	33.40	★			33.00 - 34.00	32.00 - 36.00	%
RDW	13.90	★			13.50 - 15.50	12.10 - 18.20	
Platelets	185.00	low			223.00 - 306.00	140.00 - 400.00	k/cumm
Polys/Neutrophils (SEGS-PMNS)	56.30	★			55.00 - 70.00	38.00 - 80.00	%
Lymphocytes	35.10	★			26.00 - 38.00	15.00 - 49.00	%
Monocytes	6.00	★			0.00 - 7.00	0.00 - 13.00	%
Eosinophils	1.40	★			0.00 - 5.33	0.00 - 8.00	%
Basophils	1.20	high			0.00 - 0.00	0.00 - 2.00	%
Neutrophils/Polys (Absolute)	2,871.00	★			,500.00 - 5,500.00	,500.00 - 7,800.00	x10E/uL
Lymphs (Absolute)	1,790.00	★			,150.00 - 3,200.00	850.00 - 3,900.00	x10E/uL
Monocytes (Absolute)	306.00	★			300.00 - 800.00	200.00 - 950.00	x10E/uL

Test Description	Current Rating 01/07/2011		Prior	Delta	Healthy		Clinical		Units
Eosinophils (Absolute)	71.00	low			100.00 -	385.00	15.00 -	500.00	x10E/uL
Basophils (Absolute)	61.00	★			15.00 -	150.00	0.00 -	200.00	x10E/uL
ESR-Erythrocyte Sed Rate, Westergren	1.00	★			0.00 -	8.00	0.00 -	20.00	mm/HR
CRP C-Reactive Protein	0.10	high			0.00 -	0.01	0.00 -	1.00	mg/dL
Creatine Kinase	377.00	Very High			45.00 -	100.00	30.00 -	135.00	u/l
Carbon Dioxide (CO2)	21.00	Low			25.00 -	29.00	21.00 -	33.00	mmol/L
Homocysteine	9.90	high			7.40 -	9.00	5.40 -	10.40	umol/L
Vitamin D 25-Hydroxy	40.00	low			50.00 -	90.00	20.00 -	100.00	ng/mL

Name: Neill Moroney **Lab: Doctor's Data #1, (with Ranges)** **Hair Test Results**

Legend: ☐ Warning ☐ High Risk ☐ Critical ★ Optimal ☺ Improvement ☹ Worse Ø No Improvement

Test Description	Current Rating 01/12/2011		Prior	Delta	Healthy		Clinical		Units
Toxic Elements									
Aluminum	2.60	high			0-	2.20	2.21-	7.00	ug/g
Antimony	0.03	★			0-	0.06	0.07-	0.12	ug/g
Arsenic	0.04	high			0-	0.03	0.04-	0.06	ug/g
Barium	0.38	★			0-	1.00	1.01-	2.00	ug/g
Beryllium	0.01	★			0-	0.01	0.02-	0.02	ug/g
Bismuth	0.03	★			0-	1.00	1.01-	2.00	ug/g
Cadmium	0.01	★			0-	0.03	0.04-	0.05	ug/g
Lead	0.06	★			0-	0.40	0.41-	0.60	ug/g
Mercury	2.40	High			0-	0.50	0.51-	0.80	ug/g
Platinum	0.00	★			0-	0.00	0.01-	0.00	ug/g
Thallium	0.00	★			0-	0.00	0.01-	0.00	ug/g
Thorium	0.00	★			0-	0.00	0.01-	0.00	ug/g
Uranium	0.54	Very High			0-	0.03	0.04-	0.06	ug/g
Nickel	0.06	★			0-	0.25	0.26-	0.30	ug/g
Silver	0.03	★			0-	0.10	0.11-	0.15	ug/g
Tin	0.06	★			0-	0.29	0.30-	0.30	ug/g
Titanium	0.43	high			0-	0.40	0.41-	0.70	ug/g
Essential Elements									
Calcium	333.00	low			663.00-	753.00	300.00-	1200.00	ug/g
Magnesium	38.00	low			53.00-	62.00	35.00-	140.00	ug/g
Sodium	160.00	high			72.00-	126.00	18.00-	180.00	ug/g
Potassium	35.00	★			30.00-	53.00	8.00-	75.00	ug/g
Copper	33.00	high			18.00-	29.00	11.00-	37.00	ug/g
Zinc	180.00	high			150.00-	170.00	140.00-	220.00	ug/g
Manganese	0.07	Low			0.28-	0.40	0.08-	0.60	ug/g
Chromium	0.46	low			0.48-	0.57	0.40-	0.65	ug/g
Vanadium	0.02	Low			0.04-	0.05	0.02-	0.06	ug/g
Molybdenum	0.05	high			0.03-	0.04	0.02-	0.05	ug/g
Boron	0.55	low			0.65-	2.50	0.40-	3.00	ug/g
Iodine	1.30	★			0.76-	1.30	0.25-	1.80	ug/g
Lithium	0.01	Low			0.01-	0.02	0.01-	0.02	ug/g
Phosphorus	214.00	high			173.00-	197.00	150.00-	220.00	ug/g
Selenium	1.10	high			0.62-	1.03	0.55-	1.10	ug/g
Strontium	1.60	low			2.00-	2.90	0.50-	7.60	ug/g
Sulfur	50000.00	High			46000.00-	48000.00	44000.00-	50000.00	ug/g
Cobalt	0.02	★			0.02-	0.03	0.00-	0.04	ug/g
Iron	6.20	Low			9.00-	13.00	7.00-	16.00	ug/g
Germanium	0.03	★			0.03-	0.04	0.03-	0.04	ug/g
Rubidium	0.04	high			0.02-	0.03	0.01-	0.10	ug/g
Zirconium	0.18	★			0.07-	0.25	0.02-	0.42	ug/g

VITAMIN AND SUPPLEMENT RECOMMENDATIONS

PATIENT Neill Moroney
SEX: M AGE: 29 WEIGHT: 174

Supplement	Number Per Day
Calcium MCHC	2
Carnitine 250	1
Chlorella Clean	2
Citrus Q 10	2
Inflavonoid (Turmeric)	2
Iodoral	0.5
Lithinase (Lithium)	0.25
MagMalic	2
Manganese	0.5
Multiple	2
Opti-EPA 500	1
Powdered Vitamin C with Ribose	2
Sublingual B12FA	3
Vital Trace Minerals	2
Vitamin D	1

Endnotes

I–1 Robert Ader, ed., *Psychoneuroimmunology*, 1st ed. (Oxford, UK: Elsevier Publishing, 1981).

1–1 Life ExtensionFoundaftion, www.lef.org

1–2 Standard Process, Inc., www.standardprocess.com

1–3 Nutri-West, Inc., www.nutri-west.com

1–4 Apex Energetics, Inc., www.apexenergetics.com

1–5 A Major Difference, Inc. www.amajordifference.com

1–6 Association for Conscious Evolution, www.acei.com

3–1 Ted Winchester, DC, *Winchester Level One Instructional DVD* (Aurora, CO: A Major Difference, Inc., 2009), DVD.

3–2 Theo Colborn, Dianne Dumanoski, and John Peter Meyers, *Our Stolen Future: Are We Threatening Our Fertility, Intelligence, and Survival?* (New York: Plume, 1997).

4–1 *Bagavad Gita*, (4–2) *Upanishads*, and (4–3) *Yoga Sutras of Patanjali* are ancient Indian spiritual texts that come in many different translations and can be purchased from www.amazon.com and www.barnesandnoble.com.

4–4 Caroline Myss, *Why People Don't Heal and How They Can* (New York: Harmony Books, 1997).

4–5 "Addiction," dictionaryreference.com, Random House, Inc., 2013, http://dictionary.reference.com/browse/addiction?s=t.

5–1 Joseph Dispenza, *Evolve Your Brain* (Deerfield Beach, FL: Health Communications, Inc., 2007).

6–1 Phillip Smith, "Life Extension Interview with Dr. Bruce Ames," *Life Extension Magazine*, August 2011.

6–2 Joyce C. Mc Cann and Bruce N. Ames, "Vitamin K, an Example of Triage theory: is Micronutrient Inadequacy Linked to Diseases of Aging?," *The American Journal of Clinical Nutrition*, 90 (October) 2009: 889–907.

6–3 William Billica, "The Many Faces of Methylation Defects," June 2011, podcast, *Designs for Health,* http://itunes.apple.com/us/podcast/designs-for-health-teleconferences/id487864333.

6–4 Holistic Health International: www.holisticheal.com.

6–5 "Baby Blues: Epigenetics and Stress," *The Economist Magazine,* July 21, 2011: 75.

6–6 Stephen V. Joyal, "Guard Your Precious Proteins Against Premature Aging," *Life Extension Magazine*, April 2008: 37-43.

7–1 Bernard Jensen, *Tissue Cleansing through Bowel Management*, (Summertown, TN: Healthy Living Publications, 1981).

7–2 Jerry H. Gurwitz, et al., "Adverse Drug Effects Emergency Room Visits," *The Journal of the American Medical Association*, 289 (2003): 1107–1116.

7–3 David M. Angaran, "Drug Induced Dementia: Proceed with Caution," PowerPoint, *University of Florida College of Pharmacy*, March 27, 2003), www.alzonline.phhp.ufl.edu/pp_slides/03_27_03_angaran.ppt.

9–1 Anthony A. Goodman, *Understanding the Human Body: An Introduction to Anatomy and Physiology*, (Chantilly, VA : The Teaching Company, 2004).

9–2 Hulda Regehr Clark, *The Cure for all Diseases*, (Chula Vista, CA : New Century Press, 1995), www.curezone.com/cleanse/liver/huldas_recipe.asp .

9–3 Burt Berkson, *Alpha Lipoic Acid Breakthrough: The Superb Antioxidant That May Slow Aging, Repair Liver Damage, and Reduce the Risk of Cancer, Heart Disease, and Diabetes*, (New York: Three River Press, 1998).

10–1 "Kidney Dialysis Information Center," www.kidneydialysis.org.uk/kidneys.htm.

10–2 Mark Braun, "General and Systemic Histopathology, C601&C602," 1998, *The Trustees of Indiana University*, http://medsci.indiana.edu/c602web/602/c602web/renal/renal.htm.

10–3 Julius G. Goepp, "Protecting Against Glycation and High Blood Sugar with Benfotiamine," *Life Extension Magazine*, April 2008, 52–60.

10–4 Harry A. Elwardt, *Let's Stop the #1 Killer of Americans Today* (Bloomington, IN: AuthorHouse, Inc., 2006), 139.

10–5 Stephen V. Joyal, "Vitamin D Supports Healthy Blood Sugar," *Life Extension Magazine*, October 2009, 92.

10–6 Ibid.

11–1 Donald Lloyd-Jones, et al., "Heart Disease and Stroke Statistics—2009 Update. A Report From the American Heart Association and Stroke Statistics Subcommittee," *The American Heart Association*, December 15, 2008, http://circ.ahajournals.org/content/119/3/e21.full.

11–2 William Faloon, "How to Circumvent 17 Independent Heart Attack Risk Factors," *Life Extension Magazine*, May 2009, 54-77.

11–3 James Howenstein, "The Dangers of Blood Transfusions," *Nexus Magazine*, June/July 2009, 19-24.

11–4 Dharma Singh Khalsa, *Brain Longevity*, (New York: Warner Books, Inc., 1997).

11–5 Walter Last, "The Story of Dr. Ryke Hamer," *Mind Motivations*, Aug/

Sept 2003 http://www.mindmotivations.com/resources/articles/new-medicine.

11–6 www.neshealth.com.

11–7 Rupert Sheldrake, *Dogs That Know When Their Owners Are Coming Home*, (New York: Three Rivers Press, 1999).

12–1 Ronald Klatz and Carol Kahn, *Grow Young With HGH* (New York: Harper Collins, 1997), 195.

12–2 Phyllis A.Balch, *Prescription for Nutritional Healing* (New York: The Penguin Group, 2006), 62–67.

12–3 Ewan Cameron and Linus Pauling, *Cancer and Vitamin C: A Discussion of the Nature, Causes, Prevention, and Treatment of Cancer With Special Reference to the Value of Vitamin C, Updated and Expanded* (Philadelphia: Camino Books, Inc., 1979, 1993), xxi-xxii.

12–4 Jo Jordan, "Recommended Daily Allowances (RDA)," *Puristat, Inc.*, 2006-2013, http://www.puristat.com/standardamericandiet/rda.aspx.

12–5 Ewan Cameron and Linus Pauling, *Cancer and Vitamin C: A Discussion of the Nature, Causes, Prevention, and Treatment of Cancer With Special Reference to the Value of Vitamin C, Updated and Expanded* (Philadelphia: Camino Books, Inc., 1979, 1993), xi - xiv.

12–6 Ewan Cameron and Linus Pauling, "Survival Times of Terminal Lung Cancer Patients Treated With Ascorbate," *Proceedings of International Academy of Preventive Medicine* (1979).

12–7 Harold D. Chope and Lester Breslow, "Nutritional Status of the Aging," *American Journal of Public Health* 46 (1955): 61–67.

12–8 Ewan Cameron and Linus Pauling, *Cancer and Vitamin C: A Discussion of the Nature, Causes, Prevention, and Treatment of Cancer With Special Reference to the Value of Vitamin C, Updated and Expanded* (Philadelphia: Camino Books, Inc. 1979, 1993): xxi-xxii.

12–9 Ibid.

12–10 Ewan Cameron, *Hyaluronidase and Cancer* (New York: Pergamon Press, 1966).

12–11 Ewan Cameron and Allen Campbell, "The Orthomolecular Treatment of Cancer: Clinical Trial of High-Dose Ascorbic Acid Supplements in Advanced Human Cancer," *Chemico-Biological Interactions.* 9 (1974): 285–315.

12–12 Bryan Walsh, "America's Food Crisis and How to Fix It," *Time*, August 21, 2009, 31-37.

12–13 Michael T. Murray and Jade Beutler, *Understanding Fats & Oils* (Vancouver, British Columbia, Canada: Apple Publishing, 1996).

12–14 Stanley Leonard Robbins, Ramzi S. Cotran, and Vinay Kumar, *Robbins and Cotran Pathologic Basis of Disease*, 3rd ed. (Philadelphia: Saunders Elsevier, 2006).

12–15 National Research Council, *Diet and Health: Implications for Reducing*

Chronic Disease Risk (Washington, DC: National Academy Press, 1989).

12–16 Mark Borkman, et al., "The Relationship Between Insulin Sensitivity and the Fatty- Acid Composition of Skeletal-Muscle Phospholipids," *New England Journal of Medicine* 328 (1993): 238–244.

12–17 Ibid.

12–18 Edith J.M. Feskens, Carel H. Bowles, and Daan Kromhout, "Inverse Association Between Fish Intake and Risk of Glucose Intolerance in Normoglycemic Elderly Men and Women," *Diabetes Care* 14 (1991): 935–941.

12–19 Artemis P. Simopoulos, "Omega-3 Fatty Acids in Health and Disease and in Growth and Development," *American Journal of Clinical Nutrition* 54 (1991): 438–463.

12–20 Roy Laver Swank and Mary-Helen Pullen, *The Multiple Sclerosis Diet Book* (New York: Doubleday, 1991).

12–21 Global News, "Simple Cure for Multiple Sclerosis," *Nexus Magazine*, March/April 2010, 7.

13–1 Harry A. Elwardt, *Let's Stop the #1 Killer of Americans Today* (Bloomington, IN: AuthorHouse, Inc., 2006),123–140.

13–2 Ibid.

13–3 Justin Tobias, "Far Infrared Sauna Therapy," *Creighton University School of Medicine*, http://altmed.creighton.edu/sauna.

13–4 Theo Colborn, Dianne Dumanoski, and John Peter Meyers, *Our Stolen Future: Are We Threatening Our Fertility, Intelligence, and Survival?* (New York: Plume, 1997).

13–5 Mark Schauss, *Achieving Victory Over A Toxic World* (Bloomington, IN: AuthorHouse, 2008).

13–6 Jan Tuner and Lars Hode, *Laser Therapy Clinical Practice & Scientific Background* (Grangesberg, Sweden: Prima Books, 2002).

14–1 Diabetes Public Health Resource, "Lifetime Risk for Diabetes Mellitus in the United States," *Centers for Disease Control and Prevention*, March 16, 2011, http://www.cdc.gov/diabetes/news/docs/lifetime.htm, .

15–1 Bruce H. Lipton, *The Biology of Belief* (Santa Rosa, CA: Mountain of Love, 2005), xv.

15–2 Ibid., 126.

15–3 Ibid., 126.

15–4 Theo Colborn, Dianne Dumanoski, and John Peter Meyers, *Our Stolen Future: Are We Threatening Our Fertility, Intelligence, and Survival?* (New York: Plume, 1997).

15–5 Donella H. Meadows, Jorgen Randers, and Dennis Meadows, *Limits to Growth: The 30-Year Update,* (White River Junction, VT: Chelsea Green, 2004).

16–1 "What is in a Name?," *International College of Applied Kinesiology*, www.appliedkinesiology.com

16–2 "A Brief History of Electroshock Therapy (ECT)," *Electroboy*, htmwww.electroboy.com/electroshocktherapy.html

16–3 "Omega-3 Fatty Acids, Fish Oil, Alpa-Linolenic Acid: Evidence," *Mayo Clinic,* September 1, 2012, http://www.mayoclinic.com/health/fish-oil/NS_patient-fishoil/DSECTION=evidence .

16–4 "Omega-3 Fatty Acids: Overview," *University of Maryland Medical Center*, 2011, http://www.umm.edu/altmed/articles/omega-3-000316.htm.

16–5 Ted Winchester, *Dr. Winchester's Level One Seminar for All Alternative Healing Practitioners,* (Aurora, CO: A Major Difference, 2009), DVD.

17–1 *Water: The Great Mystery*, directed by Saida Medvedeva (Chehalis, WA: Intention Media, Inc., 2008), DVD.

17–2 Masaru Emoto, *The Hidden Messages in Water Seminar* (Hillsboro, OR: Beyond Words Publishing, 2004), DVD.

17–3 *Water: The Great Mystery*, directed by Saida Medvedeva (Chehalis, WA: Intention Media, Inc., 2008), DVD.

17–4 *What the Bleep Do We Know!?*, directed by William Arntz, Betsy Chase, and Mark Vincente (Hillsboro, OR:Beyond Words PublishingInc., 2005), DVD.

17–5 *Water: The Great Mystery*, directed by Saida Medvedeva (Chehalis, WA: Intention Media, Inc., 2008), DVD.

17–6 Ibid.

17–7 Ibid.

17–8 www.sciencenetlinks.com.

17–9 Norman de Lauder Mikesell. "Structured Water: It's Healing Effects on the Diseased State," 1985, http://www.naturesalternatives.com/lc/mikesell.html.

17–10 *Water: The Great Mystery*, directed by Saida Medvedeva (Chehalis, WA: Intention Media, Inc., 2008), DVD.

17–11 Ibid.

17–12 Brian Oram, "Ozone," *National Drinking Water Clearinghouse*, 1995, http://www.water-research.net/Waterlibrary/privatewell/TB12_ozone.pdf

18–1 Garry F. Gordon, "Gordon Research Institute," www.gordonresearch.com.

18–2 Harry A. Elwardt, *Let's Stop the #1 Killer of Americans Today* (Bloomington, IN: AuthorHouse, Inc., 2006).

18–3 William Faloon, "Cardiac Drugs That Cause Heart Attack," *Life Extension Magazine*, June 2003, http://www.lef.org/magazine/mag2003/jun2003_awsi_01.html.

18–4 Sharyl Attkisson, "Vaccines and Autism: a New Scientific Study," *CBS News*, May 31, 2011, http://www.cbsnews.com/8301-31727_162-20049118-10391695.html.

18–5 Robert S. Byrd, *Report to the Legislature on the Principal Findings from the Epidemiology of Autism in California: A Comprehensive Pilot Study* (Sacramento, CA: MIND Institute UC Davis, 2002).

18–6 "Vaccine Ingredients," *World Association for Vaccine Education*, 2008, http://www.novaccine.com/vaccine-ingredients/.

18–7 Donald G. McNeil Jr., "3 Rulings Find No Link to Vaccines and Autism," The New York Times, March 12, 2010, http://www.nytimes.com/2010/03/13/science/13vaccine.html.

18–8 "Symptoms of Chronic Mercury Poisoning," 1996, http://www.mercurypoisoned.com/symptoms.html.

18–9 www.ocida.org/oc_conference.

18–10 Mike Shields, "Anthony Elementary: An Amazing Turnaround, Leavenworth, Kansas," *Kansas Health Institute*, October 15, 2007, http://www.khi.org/news/2007/oct/15/anthony-elementary-an-amazing-turnaround/.

18–11 Stephen Laifer, "Keith Black Beating the Tumor Terrorists," *Life Extension Magazine*, May 2010, 87-90.

A–1 Eckhart Tolle, *A New Earth: Awakening to Your Life's Purpose* (New York: The Penguin Group, 2005).

A–2 Ryke Geerd Hamer, *Summary of the New Medicine* (Toronto: Amici di Dirk, 2000).

A–3 Theo Colborn, Dianne Dumanoski, and John Peter Meyers, *Our Stolen Future: Are We Threatening Our Fertility, Intelligence, and Survival?* (New York: Plume, 1997).

A–4 Doris J. Rapp, *Our Toxic World: A Wake Up Call*, (Buffalo, NY: Environmental Medical Research Foundation, 2004).

Index

A

B

C

D

E

F

G

H

I

J

K

L

M

N

O

P

R

S

T

V

W

Y

Z

Figures